Lesley Blanch, 1904–2007, was at heart a nomad. She spent the greater part of her long life travelling about those remote regions her books record so vividly but her lifelong passion was for Russia and the Middle East. A Londoner by birth, Blanch was features editor of British Vogue from 1937 to 1944 and was married to the Russian-French novelist-diplomat Romain Gary from 1945 to 1962. Life *en poste* took them to the Balkans, Turkey, North Africa, Mexico and North America. A Fellow of the Royal Society of Literature, Blanch was appointed MBE in 2001. Her books include *The Sabres of Paradise*, *Pierre Loti* (both Tauris Parke Paperbacks) and the bestselling *The Wilder Shores of Love*. At the time of her death she was writing the sequel to her acclaimed autobiography *Journey Into the Mind's Eye*. An inspiration to generations of writers, readers and travellers, Lesley Blanch was, in the words of Philip Mansel, "not a school, a trend, or a fashion, but a true original."

www.lesleyblanch.com

'*Pavilions of the Heart* is the story of the dwellings where great loves have been lived. Lesley Blanch's sumptuous prose matches the intensity of the emotions she evokes.'   Shusha Guppy

'From the Sahara to Saint Petersburg, the domesticity of passion has found the perfect historian in Lesley Blanch. This wonderful book bears out her remark "The placing of a desk, or a bed, or the choice of a chintz may prove more revealing than a documented study."'
                                                                    Philip Mansel

PRAISE FOR LESLEY BLANCH

'Lesley Blanch was one of the twentieth century's most exotic travel writers.'   Caroline Baum, *Spectator*

'Lesley Blanch's style and life were testaments of a vanished world, and no less of an achievement than the twelve unusual books which connoisseurs hold in uncommon affection.'
                                                        Alice Wooledge Salmon, *Guardian*

'A scholarly romantic in a school of her own, the depth of Lesley Blanch's research was such that other writers plundered her books shamelessly.'   Maureeen Cleave, *Daily Telegraph*

Tauris Parke Paperbacks is an imprint of I.B.Tauris. It is dedicated to publishing books in accessible paperback editions for the serious general reader within a wide range of categories, including biography, history, travel and the ancient world. The list includes select, critically acclaimed works of top quality writing by distinguished authors that continue to challenge, to inform and to inspire. These are books that possess those subtle but intrinsic elements that mark them out as something exceptional.

The Colophon of Tauris Parke Paperbacks is a representation of the ancient Egyptian ibis, sacred to the god Thoth, who was himself often depicted in the form of this most elegant of birds. Thoth was credited in antiquity as the scribe of the ancient Egyptian gods and as the inventor of writing and was associated with many aspects of wisdom and learning.

PAVILIONS OF THE HEART

The Four Walls of Love

Lesley Blanch

TPP

TAURIS PARKE
PAPERBACKS

Published in 2008 by Tauris Parke Paperbacks
an imprint of I.B.Tauris and Co Ltd
6 Salem Road, London W2 4BU
175 Fifth Avenue, New York NY 10010
www.ibtauris.com

First published in 1974 by Putnam
Copyright © 1974, Lesley Blanch

Cover image 'Life in the harem, Cairo' by John Frederick Lewis (1805–76)
© The Victoria and Albert Museum/The Bridgeman Art Library

The right of Lesley Blanch to be identified as the author of this work has
been asserted by the author in accordance with the Copyright, Designs and
Patent Act 1988.

All rights reserved. Except for brief quotations in a review, this book, or any
part thereof, may not be reproduced, stored in or introduced into a retrieval
system, or transmitted, in any form or by any means, electronic, mechanical,
photocopying, recording or otherwise, without the prior written permission
of the publisher.

ISBN: 978 1 84511 603 3

A full CIP record for this book is available from the British Library

Printed and bound in India by Replika Press Pvt. Ltd

To
N. after many years.

And thou – what needst with thy tribes' black tents
Who hast the red pavilion of my heart?

Arab Love Song
FRANCIS THOMPSON

Contents

Acknowledgements

I wish to record my gratitude to the late Professor Louis Massignon, the great Arabisant from whom I obtained many details of Aurélie Piccard's life in the Sahara among the Tedjani Confraternity. Then, I tender my thanks to another old friend, Monsieur Constantine de Grunwald, the distinguished Russian historian, always so generous of his time and knowledge, when we discussed the labyrinths of Russian history together.

L.B.

Introduction

OMMEMORATIVE PLAQUES often mark houses where distinguished persons have lived. But they do not necessarily indicate where they have *loved* – and indeed are, I believe, never placed solely with that purpose in mind. Yet the settings for high passions or profound love are surely worth recording, and, as surely, should reflect something of the emotions they once framed. It was with this idea that I set about tracing such settings, likely or unlikely, not only of romance, but of tragedy and drama too; settings where those who loved had met together for a while, a night, or a lifetime.

The span of time spent within the walls has little to do with the impression left; even the duration of an embrace, were it charged with enough intensity, might engender some ghostly echo, causing some vibration or tangible impression to linger about the scene for evermore. Thus a cave beside the Black Sea, which sheltered, briefly, the meetings of Pushkin and the Countess Woronzov – the impecunious, young, banished genius and the wife of the Viceroy – meetings which neither of them ever forgot, can be considered as much a Pavilion of the Heart as that house in St Petersburg, on the Moika Canal, where later the poet was to live, married to the uncomprehending and flirtatious beauty he loved so passionately. For her whims and vanities he had run deep into debt, accepted an insignificant post at Court, and at last, by her indiscretions, was goaded to a duel which killed him. The long hours of his dying were in the house on the Moika: in life and death it was the Pavilion of his heart, for he lived there, as he died there, for love of her. Likewise that smug Swiss villa at Triebschen, where Wagner and Cosima lived in an auto-intoxication of kisses and the score of *Siegfried*, is by the intensity of their emotions another Pavilion, while the dank Glasgow basement where Madeleine Smith dared to love, and later poison, the dandiprat L'Angelier could also be said to qualify, though disagreeably, by the force of yet another kind of emotion.

Within the various frames we linger, poring over each object that belonged to or surrounded the central figures. The placing of a desk, or a bed, or the choice of a chintz may prove more revealing than a documented study. How much the bedroom Tolstoy shared with his wife to the end tells us of their embittered life together. Or those two rosewood grand pianos which stand back to back in the fusty salon of the palace at Chapultepec, where the doomed Carlotta and Maximilian played duets – the tinkling trills serving to shut out that sinister rustle of the jungles that were closing round so implacably. Their drawing-room is eloquent of the tragic, yet ludicrous tenor of their life in Mexico, where every door and window at last gave on to death and madness, and only her love and his loyalty remained in the ruins of obstinate Hapsburg protocol.

In a sense, all my Pavilions are haunted houses. Whether Arab tents or Siberian *izbas*, an *enfilade* of apartments in some glittering palace, or the serene interior of a small manor, all framed degrees of loving which placed them apart, all housed lovers who are variously recalled. Most of these settings have now vanished, becoming legends themselves, reconstructed by hearsay, memoirs, old paintings, letters, or even the architects' blue-prints and the upholsterers' bills alone. A few remain intact, or have been restored beyond recognition: some are now inhabited by curators, but all, I think, by phantoms.

Legends can be as convincing as the most documented history, and legendary characters, particularly those long-dead lovers who are the stuff of legends, can obtain an obsessive hold. Sometimes such a pair cast a spell which vibrates on through the centuries, and although with time no stick or stone remains to tell of their setting, or the manner in which they lived, this impression of reality is such that, when we reach the scene of the legend (or only, glimpse it, even, from a photograph), the intensity which lingers there, or perhaps the chord it strikes in us, conjures up the whole life lived within.

One room, long vanished, like the house around it, should qualify particularly as a haunted Pavilion, for two people who haunted each other, as their story haunts us, lived out their tormented love behind its dun-brick façade. In the balcony room at 14 Chatham Place, Dante Gabriel Rossetti and his 'stunner', Miss Elizabeth Siddal of the fevered lips and goitred throat, once came together. She, the drooping broody dove who had been 'La Belle Dame Sans Merci', and he, the impassioned iconoclast, the poet-painter assuaging the flesh in Fanny Cornforth's more obliging arms. And below, the Thames, lapping on the mud and filth of the foreshore by Blackfriars Bridge, its stench rising, enveloping them, drifting into that strange room, ghostly in itself, crowded with relics of other ages, phantasmagoric scraps of musty Italian brocades, cracked Chinese porcelain and tarnished, shadowed gilt mirrors 'where one is afraid to look in', as the landlady put it. There the 'stunner' posed for him, long silent hours of love and misunderstanding, and chloral fumes, always ending in sorties by omnibus to small restaurants for mutton chops and cheap wine. All around them, darkening twilight, thickened by the damp river mists mingling with swirls of smoke and fog. London fog – that dense acrid fog of Victorian London which was as much a part of the city as the Thames itself, and which appalled Gustave Doré, its best illustrator. Strange ambience of gloom and doom for these two strange creatures come together in the river-room, strayed there from some bright-coloured medieval missal.

It may be wondered how and where to set about compassing these tell-tale dwellings. Down which centuries and across what continents shall I range? Where to begin or end? How to choose between Héloïse and Abelard or Victoria and Albert, Pocahontas' wigwam and Cleopatra's barge? Should this be rated as a Pavilion? And why not, for there, with the splendours of her person and her ambience, she quickened the pulse of two mighty Romans, and so passed into legend. Should the plurality of Great Catherine's appetites disqualify that violet-glass-walled alcove at Tzarskoe Selo? In principle, yes, for such plurality should have no more place in this book than the warrens of Top Kapou Serai, the Seraglio, which housed the countless ranks and complicated hierarchy of the Sultan's harem – a Pavilion of the *senses* rather than the heart.

Nevertheless I shall make an exception for the concentrated emotion generated by one room there, that of Sultan Murad III, perhaps the apotheosis of all romantic settings. Moreover, within its loveliness, which he created for his hours of dalliance, the mighty Padishah lived many years solely devoted to Safieh Baffo, his Italian Kadine, no concubine or odalisque ever threatening their unity; a very remarkable state of affairs there and then.

In general, I have concentrated on settings which reflect restricted relationships. Otherwise one might be tempted to embark on countless establishments where perhaps Eros ruled, but in terms of trade. In the establishments of the *grandes horizontales*, such as Cora Pearl or Marguerite Bellanger, creatures who embodied extravaganzas of luxury and rapacity, there was no place for the heart. Nor, I think, in those snug little villas round St John's Wood, where, in more modest terms, the Victorian man of fashion hid his kept woman, charming dwellings behind discreet walls, opening on to a little garden, where the path to the front door was usually covered by an ornamental iron-work roofing, protecting any comings or goings from the curious eye of neighbours peering from upstairs windows. Such houses were, in essence, business premises – a fascinating chapter, well-documented by memorialists of the period, but having no place here.

Not all houses or interiors appear, at first sight, to be unquestionably abodes of high passion. Yet some, however homely their idiom, are such. Those little low-ceilinged cottages of the vanishing English countryside, for example – hutch-sized, with sloping roofs or beetle-browed thatch over windows so small a head can hardly emerge. Lilac and honeysuckle and mignonette smother the handkerchief-sized garden which culminates in a lean-to privy. The walls of the kitchen are sprigged with a flowery, yellowing varnished paper which brings the garden inside and up the doll's house staircase to a bedroom totally possessed by a spreading feather bed where generations of lovers have floundered. These, too, are Pavilions, and have known great lovings.

As I came to form my choice I found it to be almost entirely nineteenth-century. Save for Tamerlane's Chinese Princess, Bibi Hanum, and the Portuguese nun, all the places and people I have dwelt on at length belong well into the last century. Perhaps because its romanticism is so exuberant, following on the logical strictures of the Age of Reason, and preceding our own, which might be described as the Age of Mechanized Chaos. Then, too, so much of the nineteenth century can still be traced; we are still linked, emotionally, with that other framework of architecture, objects, literature and art, as well as by the homely details of hearsay from our immediate ancestry.

Did I not hear from my mother, how my great-grandmother, having sewn black ribbons to her bonnet, had gone to see the Iron Duke's funeral procession from a house in the Strand, and there met a handsome dark Scotsman – my great-grandfather to be – who lodged there, and cajoled her to linger as the crowds dispersed? I often passed that way before bombs changed the city's face, and looking up, wondered at which window my forbears had stood, suddenly more aware of each other than the Juggernaut catafalque with its sable procession winding below. From which window, I wondered, did they turn away, later, and pulling the curtains, shut out the gathering dusk, to find themselves in the radiant ambience of sudden love? History – that historic moment – had passed my great-grandmother by. When questioned, she could never recall anything of the procession: but she recalled every detail of the room where she had met, and on sight loved, my great-grandfather. My mother, who had a penchant for the Iron Duke, would press for details of the procession, but it was always the same: 'I remember there was a Brussels carpet and dark green merino curtains edged with such a pretty fringe,' the old lady would say, dreamily . . . 'and the clock ticked so loudly, we hardly heard the tramp of feet, below . . . there was a big gilt looking-glass over the chimney piece and a marble bust of some Greek hero – not half so handsome as your grandfather was then . . . and I remember there was a little sofa covered in horsehair. . . . Not a very comfortable sofa,' she always added, at which point, my mother said, she invariably fell silent, no doubt recalling how little comfort had mattered to her, in love, in London, in 1852.

Her soft, tired old voice fades, my mother's, too, lost in the roar of today: yet for all our mechanized sophistication we are not wholly remote from nineteenth-century living. Such memories and voices are not yet quite stilled. Some links remain.

There are certain locales, notorious rather than celebrated, where sensationalism takes over, and the original emotions of the lovers involved are tarnished by popular curiosity. I am reminded of William Randolph Hearst, once Tzar of the American newspaper world, who, for all his power and millions, was unable to obtain the discretion he sought during the long years of devotion he shared with Marion Davies. Perhaps it was due to the country in which they lived – America – whose inhabitants are so often both prudish and prurient in their approach to the passions. In the Renaissance-styled pile, San Simeon, which Hearst conceived and achieved on the Californian coast, between San Francisco and Hollywood (though smacking of the latter, in spite of all its fabulous treasures), he ensconced his beloved in defiance of every American League of Decency, Daughters of the Revolution or any other moral bastion. On my only visit to San Simeon, long after their tenancy, I was too overcome by the wild jumble of treasures to have any other impressions. Yet this should certainly have qualified as a Pavilion of the heart, for here these two forgotten figures loved faithfully and long. They owned a New York penthouse, too, overlooking the Hudson River. Boat-trips round Manhattan Isle always slowed down as they came level with the building. It was topped by a wall of glass, screening the swimming pool, where, we may suppose, this ostracized couple frolicked in lonely luxury. The guide, booming out the city's landmarks through a megaphone, 'The Cloisters, The Empire State Building' and such, never failed to point out this penthouse as one of the sights, dubbing it a 'Love Nest'. By this phrase he managed to convey a subtle disapprobation, no doubt carefully calculated to assuage the scruples of provincial tourists, who nevertheless gaped avidly. 'Love Nest': it is a vulgar label, but expressive: and what else, in truth, are each of these more gracefully named Pavilions which are my subject? And yet, are there not variations, subtle distinctions and degrees of this over-all theme? To the true egoist, paradise *à deux* is a contradiction in terms, for concentrating on the dearest object of their affection – their darling self – they transform the place to which they have retreated into a temple of true love as surely as if it were a bower for two. Self-love is possessive and resents any other presence, any extraneous influence which might impinge on the total, all-enveloping devotion it lavishes on itself. Thus, for example, Ludwig II of Bavaria, however much he may have thought he adored and was adored by Wagner, was fundamentally besotted with himself, to the exclusion of all else. When he indulged in those frenzies of building, it was to frame his lonely days and nights of passionate self-absorbtion . . . Schloss Linderhof, the little sugar-plum palace, Neuschwanstein, its feudal turrets clinging to vertiginous peaks, a Moorish kiosk set in jungly glades, laid out in face of northern nature. The frowning Gothic of Falkenstein and the overboiling rococo of Herrenchiemsee, a pastiche of Versailles which was left unfinished at his death (and where, in all, he only passed twenty-three nights – alone) could, in a sense, all find a place here, being Pavilions he had devised to be united with his *doppel-gänger* self.

There are other, even more irregular categories of Pavilion – the ambulant or the floating; a carriage, such as Emma Bovary's *fiacre*, blinds drawn close, as it clops and sways along, and the coachman asks no questions, staring straight ahead. Boats; trains; those great trains which eat up the limitless distances while, in the rigid confines of their various compartments, lovers are strained together, some runaway romance, or a journey which will end in sad separation, or one of those sultry encounters which, to a whole generation of film-goers, caused the Shanghai Express to epitomize the source and symbol of all eroticism – gondolas, black-hooded alcoves, stealing dream-like through the canals of their dream-like city: punts moored snug under the willows of some English backwater. 'Sweet Thames! run softly. . . .' Narrow, flower-laden *shikaras* nosing among the water-lilies of the River Jhelum, in

Kashmir, sidling alongside, drawing close, allowing the occupant of one boat to enter another, while at a signal the awnings are let fall. . . . Caïques, Turkish caïques piled with cushions as the occupants drift down the Sweet Waters of Asia, a floating bed rather than a barque. Then there are summerhouses and gazebos, chalets, follies and kiosques, all offering romantic shelter. Bridges, even: I am remembering the Khaju Bridge at Ispahan. Its majestic span is entirely lined with alcoves, deep set, in the manner of boxes at the theatre, so that the occupants of each could be hidden from their neighbours either side. Only the river flowing below saw the *partis de plaisir* which were often held there. On the bridge the Shahs and their princely Court sometimes installed themselves for days and nights of *volupté*, their ardours cooled by the breezes blowing sweetly from the water. Here, with their painted women or boys, their jewelled *kaliouns*, or water pipes, their gold and turquoise vessels, their cushions and rugs and roses, their music and poetry, the hours slipped by from noonday heat to dusk, and the night. Sometimes, as a further refinement of pleasure, between the courses of a protracted feast, a basketful of kittens would be brought in, each guest choosing one from this furry bouquet, to fondle before the next course was announced, and the little creatures superseded by some pilaff scented with pomegranates.

So many kinds of Pavilion, each subtly reflecting the climate or century of its origin: but always deriving from the common denominator of the couch. A brass bedstead in the white-enamelled cabin of a *dahabiyeh*, or house-boat, on the Nile was, for Edwardian lovers, the sum total of romance, and today, seeing these *dahabiyehs* moored up, shabby and neglected in favour of hydrofoils and air-conditioned hotels, I find they still retain a strong, though melancholy aura of past romances. And as Pavilions, they would still be hard to beat. All the clichés of romance were found aboard; solitude, moonlight nights and the celebrated after-glow, that magical moment when the Nile shimmers to stillness, gold, then silver, and the sunset sky sinks to an incandescent emerald, pricked by the first stars.

'Ah! Egypt!' sighed an earlier generation of lovers, watching the whole drama of sunset from basket chairs on deck, as tourists still do, though less languorously, from a speedboat. On the banks of the great river, where Antony 'tumbled in the bed of Ptolemy', the vapours of evening steal over everything, the tombs of the kings and the palm-thatched hut of the *fellahin* alike, bringing that overwhelming sense of *volupté*, love and death which belongs essentially to Egypt. It is a force to which every dweller in the land responds, so that its air alone seems infused with a sensuous softness transforming every man and woman into the image of love.

The abiding Egypt is pastoral, its rhythm unhurried as the steps of the water buffalo behind the plough. Toiling, loving, bedding, breeding, dying, toiling, loving . . . so the circle renews itself in settings bare of comfort as interpreted by the West. But above, the stars rain down, glittering in the Nile, as if caught in a gently swaying net, showering down, like the moonlight, into the open courtyards or roof tops, where a straw mat and a rag of a rug are spread, another Pavilion, awaiting what the night may bring.

Ranging over the assorted Pavilions of my choice, and those others which come to mind, I am persuaded that domestic cares seldom intruded there. Excepting the harassed Countess Tolstoy, who, with eight children, a large household and estates to run, was also recopying the manuscript of *War and Peace* seven times (while the Count, wilfully seeking primitive conditions, was cobbling his own boots), all my characters seem to have been able to relegate to others the more monotonous, frittering daily round: and even the Countess, in the tormenting, tormented ambience of Yasniya Poliyana, or in the Moscow house, had a large staff which, in spite of the Count's teachings, fortunately retained serf-like attributes and that spirit of abnegation so necessary where domestic labour is concerned.

The course of history might have been changed, it is said, had Cleopatra's nose been another shape. . . . Now although the liaison of Napoleon and Marie Walewska did not change history as Polish patriots had hoped, much of the happiness they discovered together would, I think, have been diminished had they been obliged to fend for themselves. In the Prussian castles and Polish château where they found such perfect happiness, however softly loving the Countess proved herself, I doubt she would have been so single-minded, so wholly his, had she been snared by domestic preoccupations. They have an obsessive way of intruding, even at the most emotional moments.

'What are you thinking about?' asks the lover, seeing the loved one's head turn, suddenly restless, on the pillow. But the soup has been boiling itself away for the last hour, and well she knows it.

In varying degrees, service was once an integral part of living conditions, and certainly of conditions most propitious to the tender passions. No amount of clever gadgets replace human ministrations. *A bell, and someone to answer it!* Service, domèstics, slaves ... *Eheu fugaces!* No. While music may be the food of love, nothing is more truly sustaining to the emotions than the certainty that a hot meal will duly appear, prepared by some cypher figure lurking in the background. Those vast below-stairs premises of old houses, the spacious kitchens and sculleries, the stone-flagged larders and even the attic bedrooms, housed, we are now told, a wretched, martyred lot. Perhaps. But I see them divinely cast as lesser divinities – Cupid's messengers, servitors of Aphrodite, no less.

If there could be any one specific style of architecture or type of dwelling which would seem to offer most perfectly a frame for loving, I think the palm should go to the traditional Arab house, though the designation 'Arab', so loosely used, covers as wide a field in architecture as in peoples. Yet however differently expressed, all such houses have one linking theme – retreat, discretion, privacy – surely the first concomitant of a lover's life? From the brand-new, gold-plated palaces of the Saudi-Arabian sheiks, by way of the mountain fastnesses of the Berber princes in the Atlas mountains, to those most lovely palaces and old houses of Cairo and Damascus, there is always the pattern of withdrawal – the essence of intimate living. From the threshold, where the entrance way is blocked by a screen or L-shaped opening, which shuts off any glimpse of the inner courtyard, there is always this insistence on privacy. Such dwellings are designed to turn inwards and give little indication of the beauty and ease found within, having sometimes scarcely a window to break the severity of their façade.

But once inside, all is changed, all is designed to captivate. The noise and fret of the streets and the heat of the day are left outside. The spacious, many-roomed house is always built round, and gives on to, a central court, open to the dome of the sky, which, soaring above, seems to bring the outside world within; as it were, a skyscape rather than a landscape, so that there is no claustrophobic sense of constraint. Then there is always a fountain in these courts, its sound recalling cooling streams and waterfalls. Arab lands lie under blistering suns, in violent climatic conditions. This inward turning way protects the household from desert sandstorms and scorching winds, which never penetrate the central court, just as screened windows filter the glare, as well as protecting those behind them from indiscreet eyes.

How exquisitely civilized, how desirable, the quiet of these old houses with their selective luxuries of privacy and quiet seem to us today. How gladly many of us, worn down by the pressures of our age, would exchange so-called progress and freedom – rather comparative anyhow – for some less agitated way of life.

Those dim, sensuous, Arab interiors, where the fierce light falls through the *mouchrabiyehs* in spangled motes, seem designed, before all else, for dalliance in the terms of a painting by F. J. Lewis. This now rather neglected artist lived and worked much in Cairo and the Middle East during the first half of the nineteenth century. No one has ever captured better the romantic ambience of the Arab interior, such as we see in *The Harem*, reproduced here. Through his many paintings of Oriental houses we see the large lines and small details of life within. The world into which J. F. Lewis transports us is one where there is world enough and time for loving, something which, in the West, seemed threatened even in the poet Andrew Marvell's day, when he wrote:

> Had we but world enough, and time,
> This coyness, Lady, were no crime. . . .

Though in that instance, his lovers were threatened by 'Time's wingéd chariot' rather than our machine-made pace. But then it must be remembered that the East had, in Lewis's day, and indeed still retains, quite other notions of time to ours . . . 'That little ticking Sultan who rules your life,' as one old Arab said contemptuously of a watch.

The *mouchrabieyeh* shuts out all sound but the cooing of the doves and the soft flutter of their wings, as they circle round the plashing fountain. In such cool shadowed rooms, the torrid hours of noon simmer to immobility in overpowering wafts of jasmine and rose from the perfume booths along the Mouski. Those are hours when all movement is stilled, to the languid stirring of a fan, when to trace a drift of steam as it issues from the domed roof of the hammam across the courtyard is occupation enough for a whole drowsy afternoon.

The women of such houses, the wives, concubines, slaves and families of the Pachas or Beys knew no other life but that centred round their lord, obtaining or sharing his affections, or, greatly daring, embarking on intrigues and mischiefs to which their sensuality impelled them. Perhaps these *mouchrabiyehs* behind which a whole household lived, shut out not only the bustle of life beyond, but also cast a spell over those within, coming at last to shut out all else, all thoughts or desires but desire itself – desire for the loved one's presence. Is it not the lover's arms and the bed which best illustrate my title?

Those four lines left by an unknown sixteenth-century poet say this for every lover for evermore.

> O western wind, when wilt thou blow
> That the small rain down can rain?
> Christ, if my love were in my arms
> And I in my bed again!

1

Woronince
Russia

L ISZT WAS the embodiment of the Romantic Age: young, handsome
beyond measure, and a musician whose playing 'shook our inmost
souls', in the words of a contemporary. His whole aura breathed
romance, like his Hungarian background, which appeared wildly exotic
to Western Europe, at that time not given to travelling far afield. His
playing, the execution of his dazzling compositions, was transcendental:
and then there was some daemonic hint about both his appearance and
personality which proved perfectly irresistable to the aristocracy and
bourgeoisie alike, as to *la vie de bohème* and *la vie galante* of Paris.
Naturally he gravitated there, where he was at once acclaimed a genius
and pursued as the personification of every woman's hero. 'Beware of
women, my child, they will bring you trouble,' were his dying father's
words. They were prophetic.

It was the overboiling Paris of Balzac, Chopin, George Sand,
Paganini and Berlioz, all figures larger than life. What a crew! What a
collection of genius-show-offs, to whom every excess of behaviour or

emotion seemed natural. And when Liszt, the all-conquering virtuoso, fainted away at the keyboard he had stormed so superbly, the audience were as pale, trembling like aspen leaves, and it was all part of the magic, the frenzy, which he, as the archetypal Romantic, created round him. Chopin was a more languid figure, withdrawn, discreet and worldly, with no hint of the diabolic or the exotic, though all emotion: and both Paganini and Berlioz were downright plain, so that in the romantic field Liszt had no rivals. Yet there were always a few criticisms of his theatricality, his flowing locks, the Hungarian sabre and the green gloves, and that faint breath of the circus ring which, before it became Mephisto's sulphurous fumes (owing to his dashing reputation), was sometimes claimed to be his background, a légend to which his celebrated travelling coach, or caravan, all gilding and plush, with a bed, a library and a piano, lent substance.

Thus it was ironic that his life should have become entangled, so young, and his name forever associated, with a woman who enmeshed him in a web of domesticity. His liaison with the Countess d'Agoult was ill-starred, ultimately bringing great unhappiness to a number of people, the lovers themselves and their children first. For all its apparent intensity, the flight to Switzerland and the birth of three children (one of whom was to marry Wagner, and make for him, at Triebschen, a Pavilion of the heart, the intellect and the senses), I do not consider that the union of Liszt and Madame d'Agoult ever produced a setting qualifying for a place here: not even that villa on the lake-side at Como, which, at first sight, would seem to be the classic frame for love. Yet when after some years of dutiful domesticity, Liszt came together with the Princess Carolyne of Sayn-Wittgenstein, in her château of Woronince, remote in the steppes of Southern Russia, it was this extravagant and wild ambience which at once became for them the perfect setting for a love which was to continue through their long lives. Although, over the years, it gradually shifted to another, minor key, it remained their leitmotif. Moreover, it was the Princess, and the way of life at Woronince, which brought about Liszt's renunciation of the *perpetuum mobile* of concert tours, exhibitionism and adulation which had surrounded him as *'le Diable de l'harmonie'*. At Woronince the composer emerged.

But before that splendid flowering of time and place and loved one came about, there were those years spent trapezing about between the concert hall and the less flamboyant circles approved by Madame d'Agoult . . . years which perhaps served to sharpen Liszt's appreciation of all he was at last to find in the Princess's nature, and the manner of her life, at Woronince.

The Countess Marie d'Agoult was beautiful, aristocratic, cultivated, but *heavy*, and entirely without humour. She had German blood, and there was an earnest, governessy strain in her which must quite soon have begun to irk her tempestuous lover. They met at some *soirée musicale*, an amateur choir where she was singing and he conducting. This is how she described the impact he made on her at first sight.

The door opened and a wonderful apparition appeared before my eyes. I say apparition for there is no other word to describe the extraordinary sensation produced in me at the sight of the most extraordinary person I had ever seen. A tall, and extremely slender figure, a pale face with large eyes of sea green which radiated brightness like a blazing wave, a suffering, yet powerful countenance . . . a distracted and restless impression, like that of a phantom for which the bell is about to sound the hour of return to darkness. That is how I saw before me this young genius.

She was twenty-seven to his twenty-one, and like all the other *grandes dames* of the Faubourg, she was in transports over this intoxicating mixture of genius and beauty: that curious, upturned mouth, the voluptuous mouth of a marble fawn: and those eyes – 'angelic eyes, promising heaven'. . . . But exactly what kind of heaven was not postulated.

Soon they were in love – at a distance, exchanging letters largely composed of extracts from Dante, touching sublime love. Their emotions had been precipitated by watching together – chastely, at the bedside of her dying child. Next, overcome by passion, they fled to Switzerland, in open scandal. '*Le tout Paris*' talked of nothing else. 'She's gone! Eloped!' 'Eloped? With whom? How?' . . . 'Ma chère, with a grand piano!'

Thus the gossips, all agog for more. By this reckless move, Liszt abandoned his career in Paris at its glorious beginning, and the Countess gave up her name, her foyer and her children. But to be such a man's inspiration was worth it to the Countess, bored by an elderly husband, and unsatisfied by *le beau monde*: besides, such gestures were high style then. Every woman dreamed of being some man's Egeria. Alas! Instead of becoming Liszt's Egeria, she proved a dead bore. In Geneva, she set about organizing her lover. So many hours of music, so many of studying Dante together, and, one suspects, an equally precise distribution of time allotted to love. They were cut off from the *beau monde*, which continued to take a censorious view of such a very flagrant liaison: but among a more Bohemian set they were welcomed, and presently were invited to visit George Sand at Nohant, though this was not altogether a success. Liszt had preceded the Countess, who was detained by ill-health, and when at last she arrived, she could not conquer a suspicion that it had not been an entirely platonic sojourn prior to her arrival. George disregarded the conventions in quite a different manner to the Countess: and there was that flow of men always staying in the house, one after another . . . Balzac and Delacroix and more, besides her acknowledged lovers. . . . And then, those midnights of work, prolonged till dawn, in dressing gowns, smoking the same brand of cigars, writing, composing, painting . . . Franz's letters had been rather too enthusiastic. It was a sort of brotherhood from which she, Madame d'Agoult, was always debarred. Even now, as *maîtresse en titre*, she found herself being sent off to bed at eleven, while Franz and their hostess settled down side by side with cigars and strong brews of coffee, she with her manuscripts, he at the piano, to work all through the night.

Across the hall, Madame d'Agoult lay alone in the delicately elegant bedroom which had been that of George's grandmother, prepared specially for her, with its *lit polonais* and its charming *toile* curtains that George had made herself, when nervously refurbishing the place to receive this chic Parisienne, beside whom she admitted to feeling provincial. The curtains were not quite right – one was shorter than the other – and hung badly. It would not have mattered to George or Liszt, or any of their circle, but it was the sort of thing the Countess would notice immediately. How vulnerable, how artless and warm, George Sand is revealed by her anxiety over this detail.

Liszt and Madame d'Agoult remained together for seven years: a strained relationship soon developed, but his chivalry and her determination, and a joint belief in romance, kept them together when little else was left. George Sand described them as *les galériens de l'amour* – galley slaves of love – struggling to keep afloat. And when at last they parted, nothing whatever remained of the passions they believed they had inspired in each other. For Liszt, his real life of love and work was to begin: for her, everything was over. The rest of her life seemed a *postscriptum*. She had eloped with him, had three children by him, and he had dedicated a number of his compositions to her, yet nothing remained. In the manner of the age she now wrote a *roman à clef* under the pseudonym of Daniel Stern, in which their affair was recounted in detail: but it was not as well done as the two books in which George Sand and Alfred de Musset respectively unveiled the secrets of their own *alcôve*. Many years later, on learning of Madame d'Agoult's death, Liszt wrote of her to the Princess Carolyne with damning objectivity. 'She had above all, a taste, indeed a passion, for *le faux* – except in certain matters of ecstasy, of which she could never bear to be reminded later.' In short, their life together had been founded on a false premise, and so left no shell, no walls which could still echo their presence.

But now to the focal point of Liszt's emotional life – Woronince, that château lost in the immensity of the steppes, in Podolia, a district of South-west Russia. In 1842 Liszt had been giving a series of recitals in St Petersburg and Moscow, and his effect had been such that two distinguished musicians, Stassov and Serov, left the concert hall in a state bordering on dementia: they decided to return home and each write his impressions ot the performance, so that they could compare notes later, when less inflamed. In Kiev, five years later, in 1847, Liszt's virtuosity worked the same magic. The great landowners drove from afar to hear him, and were galvanized: among them, the Princess Carolyne of Sayn-Wittgenstein. She was Polish by birth, of the fabulously rich Ivanowsky family, and married, but separated from her Russian husband Prince Nicholas, who lived in St Petersburg and was an adjutant of the Tzar Nicholas I. The Princess was far from beautiful: but she had a sensual grace, fine dark eyes, and the long, well-shaped nose then admired, for features of an emphatic kind were considered to denote breeding: the pug-nosed look so sought after today, and even attained by lopping, was judged plebeian.

The Princess, who was twenty-eight when she met Liszt, he being then thirty-six, lived a solitary life on her vast estates; Woronince was only one of three, but there alone, several thousand serfs bowed to the ground before their young *Knyïeza* – princess. The château was typical of that legion of great country houses found across the whole of Eastern Europe, in Silesia, Poland, Hungary and Russia, and although all were classical in concept, a certain barbaric splendour was apparent, a quality which set them, like their inhabitants, apart from Western Europe. This emphasis on splendours and gilding and colour within (for their exteriors were coldly classic) was as if to keep at bay the bleak monotonous landscape without – rides cut through the forests, but leading nowhere, endless horizons of steppes, muffled under heavy snows for many months of the year.

Woronince was noble, with its lofty pillared portico, its encircling wings and outbuildings, stables and small church with the priest's house nearby. The interior must have been an impressive *enfilade* of spacious rooms, reception rooms, music rooms, summer dining-rooms, winter gardens where life-size marble statues emerged from jungles of tropic plants, libraries, billiard rooms, boudoirs, Oriental smoking-rooms and whole floors devoted to tutors and schoolrooms or less favoured guests. The pattern was similar in all these great houses. There were enormous gilded mirrors which enlarged the perspectives even further, fine marquetry floors, others of tessellated marbles, or quartz and lapis lazuli from the Siberian mines, to emphasize the note of extravagance. The rooms were painted in sombre colours, spinach green, dark blue or crimson, which set off the pale gold of the Karelian birchwood furniture, Empire or Biedermeier generally. Above all, there were the stoves – those tall porcelain stoves, some tiled in blue and white, some all white, which glowed and crackled by day and night, fed by logs brought in by relays of barefooted serfs who also tended the lamps and the hundreds of wax candles which were usually lit, to burn on, recklessly, all over the house, in occupied and unoccupied rooms alike.

Besides the classic family furniture of Woronince, there were, no doubt, the family portraits, earlier Wittgensteins (originally of German descent) who had fought at Borodino, or with Orlov, in the Crimea, or more lately, in the Caucasus, portrayed in Russian regimentals, militant figures; or courtiers in powdered wigs, wearing the orders and decorations of Great Catherine's reign. Beside them, the Princess's own forbears, and other Polish nobles, the earlier ones wearing their Oriental caftans, a style recalling the years of Turkish infiltration, with huge turban-like fur *kalpaks* above shaven pates, and the long, drooping mustachios of a mandarin – an exotic band, all staring down stonily on various mid-nineteenth-century innovations, the up-to-date furnishings inspired by the salons of Paris or Vienna, *faux-Gothique* pieces: overstuffed *vis-à-vis*, *confidantes* and the new-fangled *comfortables* (in fact, not nearly so comfortable as the divan, or ottoman), all upholstered in pale silks or dark velvets, heavily fringed and *capitonnés*, some *dos à dos* sprouting potted palms from the centre, tables drowned in heavy plush cloths, with clocks and ornaments under bell-glasses. Yet for all their typical mid-nineteenth-century elegance, I doubt they broke the fundamentally exotic flavour of Woronince. It was, as every interior always is, a reflection of its owner. With such a forceful personality, the Princess must have imposed herself throughout, a strain of exoticism, like her profound piety, being echoed everywhere, *prie-dieux* beside divans, low pearl and cedarwood inlaid coffee tables from Damascus or Cairo, with a *tchibouque* or two, to emphasize the Oriental mood, alongside some weighty treatise on scriptural interpretations.

Between the tropic plants and ivies which it was fashionable to train up against tall screens of bamboo or ornamental ironwork, there would have been many bird-cages full of unhappy little tropic prisoners, placed there to further the illusion of some torrid zone: and sometimes the châtelaine of such a house would make a play at watering this indoor garden, from a pretty, long-spouted *tôle* can. It made a change from embroidery or patience. Such must have been Princess Carolyne's setting: though I do not see her applying herself to any such pastimes. And after the advent of Liszt in her life, as in her house, there was never a question of any other preoccupation, and she too now set about becoming his Egeria.

In the fashion of both time and place, she was able to concentrate entirely on the object of her affections, because no material or economic problems intruded. Money was of no account. It was simply there whenever required, enormous sums relayed by deferential bankers. Orders were given and executed. A never-ending stream of servitors were everywhere, accepting hardships or benevolence with equal fatalism, crossing themselves and calling on their God on all occasions. They were all as much part of such establishments as the furniture, or the trees in the park, and no more regarded. In winter, they ambled about in *touloups*, shaggy fur coats that gave them the appearance of bears walking on their hind legs, as they swept away the snow which closed round the house. They were everywhere . . . sleeping anywhere, on the floors, on the stairs, on the stoves, or snoring across the threshold of their owner's bedroom in simple devotion, as ready to dance or die on orders.

At Woronince they formed a choir, chanting beautifully in the little chapel attached to the house, or singing to the guzla, or balalaika, ancient melodies of the land with which to entertain their *Knyïeza* during the long dark winter evenings. (Later, Liszt was to take some of these lovely airs and transcribe them, as *Les Glandes de Woronince*.) All around the château lay desolate marshes or forests, where wolves hunted in packs. Visitors were rare, neighbours far away. A Cossack courier rode up twice a month, bringing letters and journals in various languages, telling of life in the faraway capitals, London, Paris, Rome, Vienna. . . .

Although sequestered at Woronince the Princess was well aware of what went on in the rest of the world: she read all the newest books, studied the accounts of far-off concerts, or receptions and balls, and read all the 'fashionable intelligence'. Thus Liszt's inflammatory reputation was well known to her long before they met. Until then, her ardent nature had known few outlets, emotionally or intellectually, for she was something of a blue-stocking, plunging into the study of comparative religions and mysticisms. Otherwise, there were furious *gallopades* across the steppes, for she was an Amazon who could spend eight hours or more in the saddle. Then there were her equally protracted devotions, or the company of her little daughter and the inevitable English gover-ness, 'Scottie'. It cannot have been a really satisfactory way of life. But in the spring of 1847 the monotony of this existence was broken. The Princess left for Kiev (where she owned a town house in the Gothic style) expressly to attend Liszt's concert. After which everything was changed for both of them, for evermore.

It was a *coup de foudre*, and there was no going back. Madame d'Agoult, Liszt's three children by her, his professional commitments, his much-loved mother . . . all faded, all ceded to this new force which swept him far from them – and in the person of the Princess, *kept* him from them. She proved to be fiercely possessive, steely in her system of reorganizing his life, and ruthless in her manner of prising his children away from their mother, to be brought up in rigid solitude by her own old governess, a martinet, far from either the Countess or Liszt. For him, she had determined there was to be no looking back, no reminder of any other life or love. And Liszt acquiesced. Such was her spell. Only many years later was she to relinquish something of this hold, in Rome, when, marriage denied them by the Vatican, he had become transposed into the Abbé Liszt, soutane replacing the devilish Hungarian pelisse, and she was plunged into a theological maze, writing her *Causes inté-rieures de la faiblesse extérieure de l'Eglise* (in twenty-four volumes). But that lay far ahead. The moment of which I tell concerns their meeting and life together at Woronince.

Liszt did not return to Europe – the Europe he had known best was Paris and Vienna. At Kiev he must have felt himself on quite another continent. The Princess had recognized her fate on sight and invited him to join her at Woronince, and there, at once, they were lovers. In this woman, as in her domain and her whole way of life, he found an opulence, with the same wild, free Tzigane flavour he had sensed as a child between the Gypsy campments of the *puszta* and the big houses of the Hungarian nobility where his father had been steward and had taken him, the child prodigy, to play before the Esterhazys and their kind. Magyar, Tzigane, Slav . . . all came out of the East, stemming from some remote Asiatic past, and he recognized this and returned to it, atavistically, at Woronince.

The house, for all its luxury, was disordered: there were no time-tables to be kept, no conventions to be studied or near neighbours to condemn. We do not know what the governess and the resident priest, a Capucin (for the Princess was of Roman Catholic faith), thought of the *ménage*. As to the servants, the Princess had the aristocratic arrogance of her century and was no doubt as indifferent to their opinions as to their welfare. Sometimes the lovers remained invisible to the rest of the household for days and nights on end. The Princess, who suffered from insomnia, proved a most satisfactory audience. Rapt, she lay on fur rugs before a crackling stove, or stretched on the divans piled with the lively-coloured rugs of Bessarabìa or the Caucasus. Her taste always leaned towards extravagance: there were Turkish *tchibouques* to puff when she tired of her favourite strong cigars: mosque lamps in coloured glass and other Oriental trimmings emphasized the exoticism that was an integral part of her nature, rather than a theatrical gesture or pose, one so often found among women of the Romantic era. Later, in Weimar at the Villa Altenburg, the house where they were installed together, she favoured more sober, Germanic interiors. But at Woronince it was still a spectacular setting for these two people who were so, themselves.

In the château there were no domestic problems. Meals appeared and were removed without breaking the spell under which Liszt now lived and worked. There were again the strong coffees and cigars of Nohant, and local delicacies too, smoked meats and pickled soups, caviar, vodka and Tokay, to remind Liszt of his early life. We imagine these delicacies being called for at all hours, on a whim, and served magnificently on heavy silver dishes, with a fortunes' worth of china and crystal . . . and yet, retaining some delightfully picnic quality; midnight feasts, set up beside the piano or the divan.

Sometimes the lovers left the house to row on the lake, where in winter they would presently skate: or to canter along the overcast rides cut through the forest, ways that led nowhere but to further horizons of emptiness. Sometimes they agreed on a brief separation – he to compose, in his own suite, in another wing of the house, she to plunge into some abstruse theological treatise, later to be dissected together, since both were deeply religious (while the massive *prie-dieux* strewn about the château seemed in the nature of essential furnishings). During these periods of separation – the length of the house between them – they exchanged frequent letters which must have been at once reassuring and disturbing. Hers were entirely in keeping with that excessive strain found throughout Russian life; besides which, she had none of those reserves about recalling their transports – those moments of ecstasy of which Madame d'Agoult had so much disliked to be reminded. Quite the contrary. Here is one of the Princess's inter-château missives.

Je suis à tes piede chéris. Je les baise, je me roule sous tes semelles. Je les pose sur ma nuque. Je balaie de mes cheveux les endroits où tu dois te poser. Je me prosterne sur tes pas. Je t'aime.

After which it is not surprising to learn that Liszt stayed on at Woronince through the long snow-bound winter till the following spring, by which time they were planning to leave Russia together, and, when the Princess had obtained her divorce, to marry. Liszt's romantic exaltations matched those of his mistress. He called her his *amazone mystique*: she called him her radiant morning star. 'I believe in love through you, in you, with you,' he wrote. 'Without your love I want neither heaven nor earth. . . . Let us love, *ma seule, ma glorieuse bien aimée, en Dieu et en Notre Seigneur Jésus Christ*; and let no man separate those whom God has joined together for eternity.'

No man, or woman, ever did: but it was ironic, for these two devout believers, that the sacrament of marriage was ultimately denied them by theological intricacies.

At the great house, at Woronince, so full of careless splendour, Liszt the genius, the nomad – for so life had made him – was at home. The transitory, the impromptu, the careless rapture is always irresistible to the artist, and essentially as stimulating to work as to love. Yet however much lovers believe they crave permanence, a rest, the very thing that first brought them together is easily stifled by too solid a setting. Woronince may have appeared a permanent base, but it was not more so than a Gypsy caravan. That was part of its charm. At any moment the Prince might descend on them from St Petersburg to chase away the interloper who threatened to remove his wife – and her fortune. Or Madame d'Agoult might suddenly create problems regarding their three children, who had remained with her. Or some professional commitment would demand attention; in short, the problems of real life might refuse to be kept at bay any longer.

And so it turned out. When they left Woronince, Liszt was heading for Weimar, where the Grand Duke Frederick had persuaded him, some time earlier, to take charge of a grandiose musical scheme. There the lovers had decided they would set up in style – though a style far different from Woronince. It was to be a new life – still richly comfortable but organized to form a centre of musical life and culture, Monsieur and Madame Franz Liszt at home. Unexpectedly, the estranged husband refused to divorce his wife. It could have been arranged – they were already separated – but the Wittgenstein family were not going to stand by and see Princess Carolyne's vast fortune leave Russia with her. They made difficulties, and were supported by the Tzar, the iron-hard Nicholas I, never sympathetic to irregular situations or the passions. Moreover it was 1848, the moment of revolutionary ferment throughout Europe. None such poisonous idealism must penetrate Russia. Nicholas ordered his frontiers to be closed: no one should enter or leave the country. Liszt had already gone ahead and was now awaiting his mistress in Silesia, at the castle of Krzyzanowitz, which belonged to his friend Felix Lichnowsky, a young princeling whose uncle had been Beethoven's patron. But the Princess Carolyne was still in Russia, packing her trunks to leave Woronince for ever. On learning of the Tzar's repressive measures, she decided to make a dash for it. At the very moment that his Cossacks were approaching the frontier they were to bar, her berline rocked past the black and white striped boundary posts and she was free – free to join her lover; though not to marry him.

At Weimar, in a house discreetly removed from the centre of the little town, they lived together in perfect harmony, their devotion and his genius overcoming the scandal. Besides, he always kept a postal address at the Hôtel du Prince Héritier, a sop, or concession, to the conventions which had not been necessary when they were at Woronince.

Now life was in a different key, and in the Villa Altenburg an altogether other pattern crystallized. The villa was a large comfortable German country house, set high on a hill among sombre pine woods, through which the wind murmured and sighed ceaselessly. Liszt's rooms, painted blue, were soberly furnished, with something austere or professorial in their concentration on the Master's three pianos, one of which had belonged to Mozart, and another, it was said, to Beethoven, while Liszt's own specially designed *'monstre à trois claviers et seize registres'* had a complicated series of pedals to bewilder the most practised organist. There were, too, his vast library of scores and manuscripts, and his collection of orders, decorations and world-wide tributes. It was, in short, a shrine to a living god (although connected to the Princess's suite by a convenient and discreet corridor). At the Villa Altenburg Liszt wrote his twelve *Poèmes Symphoniques*, including the superb 'Faust' Symphony, and an enormous amount of other works, besides fostering so generously many less-established musicians, Wagner above all, whom Liszt came to hold in veneration. It was at Weimar, now realizing Liszt's dream of becoming a prodigious musical centre, that *Tannhäuser* and *Lohengrin* were first rapturously acclaimed. Those were years of fulfilment, of work and love, in the setting created for him by the Princess, and where, he was to write later, all had been illuminated by her love. Still, it was not Woronince – that had been the point of departure and, like so many Pavilions of the Heart, a point of no return.

2

Sestra
Sefronia's
Shrine

Bulgaria

SOMETIMES AN entire landscape, from foreground to horizon, takes on a colour or changes its fundamental nature by the presence of some building in its midst, while the basic architectural character of this building, whether manor, castle or cottage, deserted or inhabited, assumes, in turn, some alien mood imposed by the people and events of its history.

A snug farmhouse, seemingly the frame for generations of serene living, broods among its green pastures, casting a gloom over the surrounding countryside. Approaching, we are aware of some indefinable sense of dread. Suddenly the day seems overcast; a chill wind rustles in the tree tops, and we do not linger. Conversely, some darkling shuttered tower holds an air of secret joy which defies the sombre forests or moorland of its setting and we draw near, intrigued by the promise of some romantic revelation.

I am remembering a small convent in Bulgaria, one of many such forgotten *metohas*, to give them their local name, which has haunted me ever since I chanced on it while wandering about that most lovely countryside where the Rhodope mountains rise above the Rose Valley and the hills are veined with waterfalls, and blue- or white-walled villages are set in groves of walnut trees, and the scent of roses, jam-sweet, pervades everything. Not at first sight a tragic or terrible scene: yet, coming over a wooded hill and looking down on the complex of buildings which made up the *metoha*, refectory, chapel, cells, kitchens and outbuildings gathered round a central courtyard, I was suddenly aware of some gentle melancholy, as if a cloud had gathered, obscuring the radiant day. I did not then attribute this sense of sadness to the *metoha*, for I dote on these Balkan convents or monasteries and the traditional hospitality they provide for passing strangers such as myself, who may lodge among the inmates in sober, though to me not severe, surroundings, lulled by the calm routine of life within. There the small low-vaulted churches are sombre yet welcoming caverns, where the sticky dark frescoes of brooding saints or sly-eyed, long-nosed Byzantine martyrs, and Biblical events, like the domestic lives of rich medieval donors, are all rendered in terms at once naïve and dramatic. Before Bulgaria was liberated from Turkish oppression (by the aid of their Russian co-religionists, in 1878) the country endured terrible sufferings. Driven underground, the Church sheltered many partisans. Besides its own stubborn determination to preserve the Orthodox religion, and to steel the people against pressures to abjure Christianity (which, by so doing, gained them material favours from the local Turkish overlords), some priests took up arms, fighting beside the revolutionaries. Monasteries housed partisans as well as priests, and convents too became involved.

As I approached the *metoha*, I saw that the steep hillside where it was set straggled over with graves of former inmates, or of the village, which lay some miles away; this deepened my sense of melancholy. The *metoha* lay behind high walls, and its massive doors, with their overhanging, fluted *porte cochère* so typical of Bulgarian (and Turkish) architecture, lost something of their impressive character by the proximity of a rather higgledy-piggledy shed containing a number of white wood coffins, a reserve ample enough, it seemed, to provide for a village holocaust. The coffin maker, planing and hammering as if the devil were after him, was, I later learned, a celebrated old soak, inheriting this propensity like his trade, and the rickety shed, from his father and grandfather before him. The sound of hammering had always been as much part of the *metoha* as the chapel bell or his successive bouts of lachrymose repentance. Within the high-walled courtyard, fortress-like, as are most of the ecclesiastical buildings here, there were tall trees, cypres, and an ancient plane tree, from which hung an enormous bell, like some fabulous fruit. Vines threaded overhead and twined along the wide *saïvant*, a roofed wooden gallery, or verandah, running round three sides of the house. This is a typically Bulgarian feature of most country dwellings. It protects the inmates from snow in winter and the burning summer suns, and is the centre of all domestic life. Here the spinning and weaving, the preparation of vegetables and all the tranquil daily tasks are performed. Here I joined a group of nuns darning sheets, and settled down to await my presentation to the Igumenka or Abbess.

Sitting there, I reflected with a positively voluptuous contentment that for a while, at least, I should be with, if not of, this enclosed world of quietness. Such worlds, all disciplines and denials, offer the fascination of the unknown to those who, like myself, are both undisciplined and self-indulgent. I have not shared the toil, the midnight prayers or the denials. I have only passed through as a visitor or, as sometimes in those monasteries open to pilgrims, as guest of the Igumen, among the bands of pious peasants. I used to watch them lumbering about in their shaggy sheepskins, preparing their food in the great cauldrons provided by the monastery, chawing raw onions, crossing themselves and belching with equal gusto, prostrating themselves before the shimmering ikons like so many crouching bears, their interminable incantations growled out, to further the illusion. Memories of such monasteries, Batchkovo, Rilla, or the Transfiguration at Tirnova are among the most treasured of my wanderings.

The cell allotted me was called Sestra Sefronia's cell, I learned from the old nun who conducted me there. Its small cross-barred window gave on to an interior court where a tall cyprus stood beside a well, shadowing court and cell alike. But birds flittered in its dark depth, swooping to sip at the jars beside the well, and it was not gloomy there. Along one wall ran the usual wooden daïs or *mensofa*, which does duty for sleeping or sitting. It was spread with coarsely woven rugs and against the wall were the usual red rep bolsters, rock hard, but graced with white linen antimacassars. There was a lamp swaying and flickering before the ikon, and a tin jug of water, and, since I was a privileged guest, a small saucer of cherry jam. I found it perfect, as romantic as all my illusions, and fuel for all the fantasies I had woven round convent living.

Later I supped in the refectory, beside the autocratic old Igumenka – Maïka Igumenka, Mother Superior, who plied me with sharp questions concerning life in Paris. We were served bean soup, a vegetable and egg mess and yoghurt, all rather watery, except the latter, which being made from buffalo milk was of the consistency of Cornish cream, and quite as delicious. Our knives and forks clattered on the tin plates as the sisters served us and lovingly ministered to a half-wit child at the end of the table. When the great bell clanged from its leafy belfry I left the nuns to their devotions and returned to Sestra Sefronia's cell.

Someone had lit a kerosene lamp and it glowed cosily. Coarse linen sheets and a hairy blanket had been placed on the *mensofa*. Nuns, I supposed, had none of these amenities. I lay down on the unyielding boards wondering why it was that these forgotten convents of the Balkans cast such a spell over me, drew me back, time and time again, when I could have been resting my traveller's bones at some well-upholstered hotel.

I awakened during the night to see a sliver of light issuing from what I had taken to be a cupboard door. It was low and closed by a heavy lock: obviously, it communicated with another cell, but there was no sound from the other side. Was the occupant sleeping or praying? Suddenly I felt a violent longing to open the door – to discover what lay beyond, though this would have been unseemly.

I did not sleep well: the rest of the night mosquitoes zinged about, but it was the adjoining cell, not the insects, which disturbed me. There was no feeling of sinistry or the supernatural issuing from that closed door – only an overpowering sense of sadness, an awareness of some inexplicable tension or emotion. I wondered who Sestra Sefronia had been, and if it had been she, or some restless spirit, who had left this impression.

Next morning, in the dazzling morning sunlight, I found a line of nuns sitting along the *saïvant* busy stoning plums. Their black, wimpled heads reminded me of so many crows pecking at the fruit. This was destined, they told me, for a particular kind of plum brandy for which the region was famous, and which they made and sold to the Government tourist shops, thus bringing in a little extra for their needs. I had the impression their ways were frugal to the point of pinching. My Bulgarian, though elementary, is useful. I tried to question them about Sestra Sefronia, but got no further than something about a shrine. Returning to the cell later, I found the cupboard-like door ajar, and, from within, the sound of a broom. Peering in, I saw one of the oldest, most decrepit sisters sweeping what seemed to be an even smaller inner cell. There was no window, only a grating for air. It was quite empty, save for a fine silver-cased ikon set cornerwise, a lamp glowing before it, and beside, on a rough wooden shelf, a jar of flowers. Below, dangling from a large nail, hung a heavy old-fashioned pistol fastened to a twist of scarlet wool, and a wide leather cartridge belt patterned with brass studs and massively buckled. It was the kind of belt the peasants still wear when they go hunting, and seemed an odd sort of shrine to find in a convent; yet I knew I should get no further until, perhaps, Maïka Igumenka chose to enlighten me. But each night, the same sliver of light showed under the little door, and my cell was heavy with the same overpowering sense of melancholy.

The evening before my departure I was invited to join Maïka Igumenka in her parlous (plush armchairs, blue washed walls and sticky oleographs of Jerusalem) where she was receiving a visit of pro-tocolaire significance from the Igumen of a neighbouring monastery. I wasted no time in putting my questions. It seemed that the inner cell was indeed a shrine, but one consecrated to the memory of a partisan, a *bountovnitzi* rather than a saint of the Calendar. He had once been known as Brother Vikenti, said the Igumen, speaking French with a furry Slav accent.

The Igumen, whom the Igumenka addressed as Otez Eftemi, was a majestic bearded figure whose majesty was scarcely undermined by a large wart which sprouted grotesquely from the tip of his very long nose. I observed that he quelled Maïka Igumenka with a mere glance: all her autocratic manner gone, she sat meekly dispensing some home-brewed cordial while the Igumen, his feet in enormous coal-scuttle-like black boots, planted on a velvet footstool, launched into an account of the hero who was enshrined in *her* convent.

'Brother Vikenti is quite a national hero,' he began, 'but first our visitor must learn something of the persecutions endured by Bulgarian Christians.' He settled back, and I knew I was in for a historical lecture. He expanded on the people's furious resistance and how village after village rose, only to be crushed by the merciless Bashi Bazouks – had I heard of them? Turkish irregulars, once the scourge of the land? I had. Then had I heard of the even more terrible Yenichari (Bulgarian children born Christians, levied by the Turks to be brought up as Moslems)? These Yenichari became the worst, the most ruthless of oppressors, returning, sometimes to the village of their origin, quite indifferent to blood ties, slaughtering their proper families without compunction if they opposed Turkish rule. These levies were made three times a year and the Bulgarians fled to the mountains, or even killed their children to avoid surrendering them to the dread Yenichari. The Igumen expanded at length on the iniquities of Turkish rule. Though I firmly assured him I knew something of Bulgarian history, he was not to be put off, and recounted in detail the life and death of the great patriot insurrectionist Vassili Levsky, who has passed into the legends and literature of the nation. He had been sheltered in a convent, but captured at last tried to end his life by dashing out his brains against the walls of his prison. And when he knew all hope of escape was gone, he asked for a priest and went to his death on the gallows in a spirit of holiness.

'Our patriot heroes were all men of God at heart,' put in the Igumenka ignoring the Igumen's awful eye, for she had stolen his curtain line. Gradually I edged them back to the subject of another priest patriot, Brother Vikenti. He came from one of the rich merchant families of Jéravna, I learned, and had been destined for the Church, serving his noviciate at the monastery of Batchkovo. 'Did I know that monastery had been founded in the eleventh century by two Georgian brothers, prince-priests?' I did. The Igumen sighed gustily, and I perceived I had thwarted his passion to impart knowledge.

At Batchkovo, Brother Vikenti's piety and learning were acclaimed. Presently he was transferred to serve as secretary to the Archimandrite of Plovdiev. But sometimes he returned to humbler ways, in retreat at Batchkovo or serving the pilgrims at Rilla. When the Revolt came to a head, he laid aside his monk's robes and joined the partisans, fighting beside them, using a pistol and a dagger with the best.

One night – it must have been around the winter of 1877, the Igumen thought, and the Igumenka concurred – when the fighting raged across the country and the villagers barricaded themselves into their houses as the Bashi Bazouks set fire to the farms and massacred those who were believed to be in league with the *bountovnitzi*, there was a repeated knocking at the Convent gate. The portress, peering through the grille, saw a wild-looking figure begging for admittance. He wore the heavy sheepskin *shouba* and *kalpak*, or fur cap, of every peasant, and the portress hesitated to admit him, even though he told her he was a hunted man. She fetched the Igumenka, who, when the fugitive told her he was once known as Brother Vikenti of Batchkovo, ordered the gates to be unlocked. It was men such as he, who were defending her Church against the Moslem tyrants. She forbade the portress to speak of his arrival to anyone, and led him to the sacristy, where, behind the golden chasings of the iconostasis, he could be hidden until a safer place was found. This was not easy, for her own quarters were open to the main courtyard, while the nuns' cells all led off a main corridor, and were clearly impossible. At last she decided he would only be entirely safe in a small, inner cell – one once used for penitents. It was this cell from which the sliver of light had shone into Sestra Sefronia's cell; this cell in which I had seen the strange shrine.

'Now there is, as you may have observed,' said the Igumenka, 'only one way into the shrine – through Sestra Sefronia's cell. Our Maïka Igumenka had to make up her mind to trust Sefronia with the secret. But this she knew she could do, for Sefronia belonged to the Convent – she had known no other life, and her obedience was implicit. Besides she was still a child – not yet sixteen, the youngest of the inmates, all heavenly grace, an angel on earth; said Maïka Igumenka, crossing herself repeatedly. 'An angel who became a heroine, too,' added the Igumen, once again elbowing his hostess aside to take up the tale.

Sestra Sefronia had, it seemed, been brought up in the *metoha*. Her father had, in the Igumen's words, 'given her to God' at the age of four. 'He had been a most sinful man, but by this gift, he performed an act of contrition – praying that it would find favour in the eyes of Our Lord and win him eternal mercy.' The Igumen's voice took on an unctuous tone which exasperated me, and I suggested it might have been more eloquent of repentance had the sinner entered a monastery himself, instead of committing a helpless child to a life of sequestration.

Both the Igumen and the Igumenka looked shocked. 'Sestra Sefronia was a beautiful and happy child; she became the pet of this Convent and grew up here in holiness,' said the Igumenka. 'Her piety has never been forgotten – we pray for her still; we pray for her intercessions too. She lived here her whole life – and when she died, in God's own time, she was ninety-one, beloved and revered by all who knew her.'

'You mean to say she lived here, shut away, for over eighty years?' I heard my voice rising shrill in horror. 'Eighty-seven years – immured – *with no choice* – with no knowledge of the outside world – of what life might have offered? You mean to say her father tried to buy salvation at the price of his child's whole future? Do you call that noble? I call it wicked! She was a living sacrifice! No wonder that cell reeks of sadness.'

The Igumenka cast nervous glances at Otez Eftemi: my outburst had shattered the dignity of ecclesiastical protocol. The Igumen stroked his long nose and fingered his chaplet before replying. 'My daughter,' he said, speaking with studied calm, 'you are very hasty – too hasty. You do not know all the facts as we do. Sestra Sefronia – God's blessing rest on her – *did* come to know something of the world outside these walls, but she returned thankfully, living and dying here as a bride of Christ.'

'And as a *heroine* too,' added the Maïka Igumenka, determined that her Convent and its inmates should have their place in history.

Gradually, between the Igumen's dissertations on Bulgarian resistance and Maïka Igumenka's snatches of Convent legend, I learned why Sestra Sefronia was described as a heroine and patriot, and why Brother Vikenti had lain hidden in the inner cell for many weeks. He was carrying important papers and there was a price on his head. The Turks continued to search the countryside. The *metoha* was visited, the nuns questioned, and a perfunctory enquiry was made, for, though the monasteries were now known to play a part in the Resistance movement, the convents were not yet believed to be involved. After a severe warning as to what would befall convents that sympathized, the Turkish authorities withdrew.

It was late winter and snow still lay thick all round. Footmarks coming and going from the *metoha* stood out clearly, as did any figure crossing the white expanses. Turkish patrols were everywhere on the alert. It was not safe for Brother Vikenti to leave till the snows melted. He must continue to be hidden, not only from the Turks, but from the rest of the Convent, as well as from the priest, or Pope, as he is called in the Orthodox Church, who came daily to celebrate mass.

As the Igumen reminded me, by the rulings of Orthodoxy, no woman may perform this office. Only the portress, the Igumenka and Sefronia, the Convent's hostage to God, the symbol of a sinner's penitence, knew of his presence among them. But the Igumenka – she was two nominations back from that Maïka Igumenka who was now telling me the tale – knew Sefronia was a child, who had grown up as God's child, knowing nothing of evil, and unquestioning in her obedience and piety. She was preparing her noviciate, and spent most of her time in her cell, in solitary prayer and meditation, rather removed from the rest. Thus it was she who took the fugitive's food to him, night and morning, and always during the hours of service when the rest of the sisters were in the chapel. Then, too, it was easy for the Igumenka herself to communicate with him, to keep him posted with such news as she could obtain from the outside world, while under the guise of instructing Sefronia in the Scriptures.

I imagined the hunted man, the priest turned partisan, cooped up in the little dark inner cell, biding his time, for the sake of the papers he held – waiting, but chafing too at this inactivity. In those long winter weeks, did the priest take over from the partisan, I wondered? Was it Brother Vikenti who prayed and waited, or was it the young partisan fighter, who raged to be gone? To be, once more, part of that larger world he had discovered, in the freedom of the fight?

And Sefronia – this child of innocence – what did she feel, I wondered, coming suddenly upon adventure, stealth, danger – and a man? She who had known nothing but the quiet routine of the *metoha*; while the bearded old Popes, skinny or paunchy, who came to serve mass, must have been all she knew of man.

Did the fugitive talk to her – did she question him as to life beyond the convent walls, I wondered? My imagination seized on the dramatic possibilities of the situation, but this was, of course, due to my incurable romanticism, and not a subject I could broach in the Igumenka's parlour.

The two old holy hypocrites, for as such I now saw them, resumed their tale. Spring came, melting the icicles under the eaves and turning the snows to torrents surging to join the streams – torrents of spring, a time of release, time for the fugitive to leave. He might now have made his way across country: he might not. But he could not risk the papers he carried falling into the hands of the Turks, for they told of plans for a future rising, besides lists of certain partisans' organizations. There had been no certain way of getting them out of the Convent, until now. It was decided he should again put on priest's robes, and be driven out, boldly, in the old coffin maker's cart, heading openly for a monastery which lay near to the village where the papers could be delivered safely. To add to the appearance of verity, Sefronia the novice was to ride with them. She would be sent with a letter – Convent business, accounts, recipes for healing and such – to another *metoha* not far from the monastery to which Brother Vikenti was heading. There she would be received by the Sisters, and stay awhile, continuing her religious instruction there before returning. The coffin maker would return at once. It was a splendid ruse, said Maïka Igumenka, proud of her predecessor's guile. Sefronia was given the Convent letters, and a bundle of linen, wrapping an ikon, in which, slipped between the covers, the papers were concealed. She also carried a newly bound prayer book and a bottle of Convent-brewed raki – gifts to the Igumenka who would shelter her, and who, like the coffin maker, would know nothing of the real reason behind this journey. 'Our Igumenka thought of *everything*,' said Maïka Igumenka, and I agreed that such a cartload of piety was indeed unlikely to have aroused suspicion.

All went according to plan; Sefronia arrived at the convent, after delivering the letters to the monastery, and Brother Vikenti rejoined the fight once more. That was all that Sefronia could tell upon her return. She spoke little of the other convent, or of the Sisters, the villages and countryside she had seen for the first time. The outside world had frightened her, they thought: she seemed glad to be back, and spent all her time, now, preparing for her final vows with an added intensity.

'So you see,' said Otez Eftemi, 'you were hasty. Sestra Sefronia *did* come to know the outside world – and she had braved great dangers to – but she knew her place was here, as God had ordained.' Again that unctuous note crept into his voice.

'And Brother Vikenti – what became of him?' I asked, still curious as to the shrine. 'Ah! he died a hero's death,' said the Igumenka, and both the old holies crossed themselves with fervour. 'He is buried here. Yes, he came back once more,' they told me; and I had to wait, concealing my impatience, while Maïka Igumenka summoned a novice to bring a fresh brew of coffee, the gritty, sweet Turkish kind, but much adulterated with powdered nuts, for the *metoha* practised such economies.

'Yes, he came back once more – no one knew for what reason, for before he could reach the gates, the Bashi Bazouks rode up, and cut him to pieces – the portress saw it all. He was dressed as a priest, but they tore open his robes, and underneath he was wearing partisan clothing – arms, pistol, a knife and all. "There's your man of God for you," they said, and they strung up his body from the old tree where the bell hangs – you've noticed it, no doubt?

'And when they left,' added the Igumenka, 'it is said they pealed the bell like madmen, and rode off laughing . . . Satan's own!'

That night the nuns buried him in the graveyard on the hill. But it seemed while they were digging the grave, Sefronia had crept up, unobserved, and removed the cartridge belt and the pistol. No one knew until she died, when they were discovered under her straw pallet, where she had concealed them all those years. She left a request that they should be kept together with her ikon – the ikon in which the papers had been hidden – in the inner cell that had once sheltered him. She was venerated by all the convent, and her wishes were respected – 'So you see the cell has become a sort of shrine, one we honour, especially, in memory of a national hero,' said Otez Eftemi, rising to leave and blessing me, pompously, as he did so. I went back to Sestra Sefronia's cell with this sad tale to keep me company, knowing now, the reason why such sorrow hung forever on the air.

It was not till a few weeks later, in a village near Jéravna, while drinking tea with the local doctor, an old friend, that I heard a curious postscript to Sestra Sefronia's story. I had been recounting it to the doctor, for it haunted me. 'That's what they told you? Yes, I expect they would: perhaps they believe it all. But in fact things were a bit different. I remember seeing Sestra Sefronia when I was a child. My father was the best apothecary in the region, and sometimes the nuns would send for him to treat a sick person or replenish their stock of medicines. He'd drive over to the different *metohas* and take me with him. The Sisters used to give me spoonfuls of rose-leaf jam, I remember. . . . When I saw Sestra Sefronia she was very old, but she still retained a curious look of beauty, a sort of grace. She seemed to shine, as if lit from within. No . . . things weren't quite as the Igumenka told you. . . .'

He fiddled with the samovar, brewing more tea and refilling our glasses before he continued. 'I had it all from my father – and he had it from his sister, who had married a cousin of Brother Vikenti's – one of the rich merchants of Jéravna, one of the few there who didn't go along with the Turks: for, you know, Jéravna was a very rich community. They paid their taxes quietly, and the Turks mostly left them alone, and traded with them, to everybody's benefit. Well, anyhow, this is the story as I know it.

'Sestra Sefronia fell in love with the partisan Brother – I expect you guessed that? He's supposed to have been a devilish handsome creature – too handsome for the Church, anyhow. No one suspected anything, of course, and Sefronia was still almost a child – but she had no real vocation, being shut up like that by her father – yes, those sort of things used to go on: once it was quite an accepted thing, to give a child to God. Anyhow, during those weeks when Brother Vikenti lay hidden in the next cell, it seems that he – that they – well, there was something between them, and when fate, in the shape of the Igumenka, played into

their hands and sent them off together, that was that. Somehow, I don't
know just how, Brother Vikenti succeeded in making off with Sefronia
before she'd reached the Convent . . . I don't know how he squared the
driver . . .' (but I guessed a bottle of raki and money for more had
silenced his tongue, and brought him back to the Convent in an alcoholic
haze). 'They reached the house of Vikenti's sister in Jéravna at night,'
the doctor continued, 'being guided over the mountains by a Pomak who
had sold them a horse. They told her the truth; they asked to be together
for a week – one week – before they went their separate ways forever.
The Church – their vows? Eternal salvation or damnation? I don't think
they thought much about such things then. Vikenti was his sister's
favourite: she was a widow, independent, and as fearless as he. She took
them in. So, for a week, the lovers were together – in hiding and danger,
yes, here at Jéravna, as in the *metoha*: but on very different terms. For
the first time Sefronia knew what life could be, beyond the Convent walls.
Vikenti's sister lived in one of the finest of those old, traditional wooden
houses you admire so much. It's a museum now – I can show it to you,
tomorrow, if you like. It's a perfect specimen of Jéravna architecture,
and the carvings round the *saïvant* and in the main room are said to be
unique. . . . Well, once there, Vikenti got rid of his monk's robes, and
put on the black and brown, scarlet-sashed outfit all our men used to
wear, and his sister dressed Sefronia in clothes from her own cupboards.'

I imagined this young girl, seeing, touching, for the first time, the
sort of clothes that are a woman's birthright. I saw her dressed, for the
first time, in one of the lovely local costumes, bunchy scarlet, or black
and gold skirts, a gauzy muslin blouse, an apron embroidered over with
sparkling sequins, and beneath the hem of her underskirt, a good inch or
two of long, lace-edged pantaloons showing coquettishly. And on her
head – or, dreadful thought, could it have been shaved? – a twist of silk
kerchief edged with tinkling gold coins, and tucked over one ear, a rose:
the rose her lover stole into the garden to pick each morning in the half
light before dawn, before neighbours could catch sight of him, telling
her how the peasant girls of the Rose Valley always pinned one in their
hair as a sign they were willing to be courted and married. So now
Sefronia would pin the rose to her hair, to tell him what he already knew,
that she was his to court and love. But not to wed. For today, tonight,
and a few more hours of their week, they could still lie together in love,
on one of the broad *mensofas*, or cushioned divans, recalling that of her
cell. But how different – how softly spread, now. There would be bright

embroidered cushions and sheepskin rugs, and below the tall, conical chimney or *achmak*, a brass coffee pot sizzling in the embers, coffee heaped with sugar and dashed with rose water, a far cry from that of the *metoha*. And lying there in love and idleness, they could trace the elaborate curves and carvings of the ceiling above them – one of those sumptuous affairs inlaid with velvet – a tradition of the finest old houses.

Did they ever recall the Convent? Did the ikon set in its deep, niche-like iconostasis remind them of their state of mortal sin? Did they look back? There was no looking forward. Perhaps Ezra Pound's lovely lines would have expressed Vikenti's feelings, there and then.

> Sing we for love and idleness,
> Naught else is worth the having. . . .
> And I would rather have my sweet,
> Though rose-leaves die of grieving,
> Than do high deeds in Hungary
> To pass all mens' believing.

For Sefronia, cast suddenly into life in its richest sense, it is likely that she lived entirely in the moment. Such is perfect happiness: and that she must have known, at Jéravna, before each went their way, she to a life of prayer and remembrance in the *metoha*, he to his end at its gates.

Next day, the doctor took me over the old house at Jéravna. It is scrupulously preserved; 'one of our national monuments', said the guardian, showing me round the lovely rooms where a certain splendour, sober in its expression, owing most to proportion and the delicate fantasy of the carved decoration, never overshadows a basic sense of intimacy and well-being. The soft, pale nuance of the wood – for all is wood here, floors, walls, panelling and columns – is spiked by the brilliant crimsons, pinks and vermilions of the textiles, rugs, cushions and embroideries. Big rooms or small all follow the same traditional pattern; a niche-like iconostasis, a series of little open cupboard-niches, *férides*, set into the panelling, the conical *achmak*, and the low *mensofa*, usually placed under the window, with its carved rail, or balustrade, and columns at each corner. Only the two principal rooms – 'the great salon, or the Episcopal chamber' – set apart for the reception of guests of consequence, powerful merchants, or clergy, have the richly ornamented ceilings such as I had imagined above the lovers.

The guardian was swivelling a spotlight to show me details of the carving. He began shepherding me towards other parts of the house, justly proud of the treasures to be seen, but I lagged behind. Had it been this velvet-ceilinged, many-cushioned room, this 'Episcopal chamber' where I now stood, or that bleak little shrine cell which was, most truly, the Pavilion of Sestra Sefronia's heart?

3

Rue Fortunée

France

L'Etrangère – the stranger – was how Madame de Hanska, a Polish countess, signed her first letter of admiration to Balzac, and with it, enflamed his imagination and heart. For her he prepared that house in the Rue Fortunée which takes its place here as a Pavilion of the Heart – his heart, for I doubt it was ever hers – by those eighteen years of passionate longing and hopes deferred which lay between Balzac's first determination to make Madame de Hanska his wife, and that homecoming to the Rue Fortunée when she was, at last, his bride, but he, the bridegroom, a dying man, and the house a sepulchre of all his dreams.

Eve de Hanska's hold over Balzac appears quite incomprehensible, for he was accustomed to the most flattering advances from all manner of women who, it would seem, were more alluring. His genius and his subtle understanding of feminine psychology produced a ceaseless flow of letters and propositions from which to choose. Strangest and most romantic of all, that unknown Maria to whom he dedicated *Eugénie*

Grandet. She proposed that if he would love her for one year, she would disappear from his life afterwards. He did love her for a year; she bore him a child, and she did vanish, taking the child with her. Balzac never told her name. Madame de Hanska proved to be quite otherwise – possessive, demanding, capricious by turns, prudish, sensual, practical, and tantalizing. Yet from that first letter she had intrigued Balzac, and he had replied. Before the year was out, the correspondence flourishing, she had come to occupy his entire world. It was for his dream of marriage to her – for nothing less would do – that he sought so long and finally acquired No. 14 Rue Fortunée. Yet what should have been the apotheosis of all Pavilions, growing, taking form, during so many years of passionate longing, became a place of betrayal.

When, after a year of ardent correspondence, Balzac first met *l' Etrangère* (a small, dark, plump, elegant woman, twenty-seven to his thirty-three), it was at Neuchâtel, where she was discovered with an ailing husband, thirty years her senior, and a small daughter in tow. But three months later, at a second meeting, they were lovers, and with that brief bliss Balzac had to be content for some years, since his inamorata returned to Poland, leaving him to his hopes and dreams and debts – those ever-pressing debts which his prodigal way of life accumulated, and which his Titan labours by the pen could never diminish. But material problems, while exasperating him, did not strangle him, as they would have a lesser man: he continued to live on credit, or in that insubstantial glowing existence which his imagination created. A fortune would soon be made from various projects, nut trees, or silver mines in Sardinia . . . they came to nothing: *tant pis*: he continued sighting golden days ahead. Across the walls of his rooms he scrawled *Here will be a Rembrandt . . . a Raphael . . . here a Venetian mirror*. He was as hopeful, as unrealistic, in his approach to the Stranger during those eighteen years he continued in his *amour fou* – and in his letters the mystic and the sensual are blent into a passionate whole, and since he was French, *money*, making it, spending it, was a perpetual theme; accounts, descriptions of irresistible bargains or business deals, most of which alarmed and exasperated his more practical mistress, occupy an obsessional place in the correspondence. His Pantagruelesque longings for more of everything – money, glory, love – were sustained through long years of poverty and frustration.

During ten years of their liaison, the lovers were together barely ten weeks in all, snatched rendezvous in Vienna, Dresden or Italy, halfway houses between Paris or her fine château at Wierzchownia (now a collective farm).

Whenever he became too pressing, she always contrived to put him off by some suitable excuse. . . . On her husband's death in 1842 there seemed no more reason for him to be kept dangling, but a whole new crop of barriers appeared . . . problems with the inheritance, the estate, her daughter's forthcoming marriage, and, even, her good name, for it would not do to appear too eager to cast aside her widow's weeds. And still Balzac loved on, blindly devoted; he, the genius who in his writings saw women with such devastating clarity, was now like a gullible boy. He had invested *l'Etrangère*, long before he met her, with all the romantic attributes of his imagination, and so strong were his presumptions that he easily contrived to fit the factual woman into their fictional mould. And then, too, she was a countess, cousin of the Princesse de Ligne to boot. Balzac shared that odd reverence for titles found among so many brilliant figures of the Romantic Age in France. Titles seemed stabilizing, reassuring, to those who lived *la vie de Bohème*.

All of Balzac's own nature is to be found in his writings, his characters often his own mouthpiece. 'I know, to my shame,' says one, 'that for me love cannot be in poverty . . . *Vive l'amour* – in silk, surrounded by marvellous luxury . . .' That luxury he sought to create at the Rue Fortunée, buying recklessly, listing his acquisitions with pride. A Riesener commode – a treasure, a bargain, once belonging to Elisa Bonaparte – another commode, that of Marie de Médici, all inlays of rare woods and mother-of-pear. Porcelaine de Saxe, Chinese bronzes, marquetry, silk upholstery throughout, and architectural embellishments by Santé; though the odd little passageway connecting Eva's bedroom directly with the chapel of an adjacent church (something *unique* in Paris, he gloated) was to be left untouched. He admired her piety – now she could go from their bed to the chapel, all under the same roof. *Quel luxe*! . . . And then there was the water-closet! The marvellous, sybaritic water-closet which must be as sumptuous as all the rest; gilt consoles, Chinese porcelain, brackets for flower vases . . . a boudoir, no less.

Eight more years passed, during which time the lovers met infrequently, but still the enigmatic Madame de Hanska chose to keep her celebrated suitor dangling. . . . Did she ever love him? Was she impelled by boredom on her provincial estates – by vanity, at having snared the famous author? By a genuine interest in his genius and flattered to be considered his Egeria? We shall never know. Balzac refused to be discouraged, and continued the torrent of his writing. In 1849, at long last, he joined Madame de Hanska at Wierzchownia for a visit which prolonged itself for two years, partly due to his increasing ill-health, and partly to his overwhelming happiness at being received with such warmth by both his inamorata and her family, in the château where its pillared splendours and comforts both impressed the snob in him and comforted the lonely man. Yet there was still no positive plan for marriage until the following year, when the state of his health had deteriorated so alarmingly that perhaps Madame de Hanska thought it prudent to comply with his wishes. On 14 March 1850, Balzac was supported, staggering and choking, thirty miles across the snows, into the church of St Barbe de Berditcheff, where, at last, the Stranger became his wife. He continued alarmingly ill, and there could be no thought of returning to Paris to inhabit, at last, the Rue Fortunée, until the following May, when they set out, by slow painful stages, westwards across the steppes. Balzac's condition worsened at each wayside inn where they halted, the bridegroom racked, the bride bored. . . .

They reached Paris at the end of the month and drove straight to No. 14 Rue Fortunée. Balzac's mother had been warned of their arrival, and fulfilled all her son's minute instructions as to how the house should be massed with flowers, though she, his mother, was on no account to be there. (Was this Balzac's sense of the romantic occasion, or evidence of the grudge he had always held against his mother, dating from his neglected childhood?) It was dusk, and the curtains were undrawn; the travellers could see into the rooms where candles burned and flowers were everywhere. Yet no one answered the bell: no one came to open the door when they hammered on it. After eighteen years of longing, Balzac stood outside the barred door of his own Pavilion. At last a locksmith was fetched to break in. Seated in the hall, François, Balzac's faithful old manservant, was discovered, gibbering wildly, the excitement, the fulfilment, after so many years of hopes raised and dashed, which he had loyally shared with his master, had unhinged his mind. He was raving mad. 'What an omen! I shall never leave this house alive,' cried Balzac.

His premonitions came to pass. Three months later, he lay there dying horribly, neglected by his wife, cared for by some old woman fetched in to nurse him, for, as she said, 'it is not a pretty sight'. Balzac was literally decomposing, putrefying from the feet up; yet the brain, that marvellous brain which had created the world of the *Comédie*

Humaine, was still alert, knowing that his wife was no more beside him now than she had been all those years apart.

Perhaps, at last, he realized the truth of those words he had once written: *a man's last love strangles him.* Bitter words to write, and bitter to remember, on his death-bed. If we are to believe Octave Mirabeau's sensational revelations, which he claimed to have had direct from Jean Gigoux, the painter, who became Madame de Hanska's lover, she spent the last hours of Balzac's dying in bed with Gigoux in her own room. When the nurse knocked on the door, telling her the end was near, she did not stir, overcome by irresolution and fear, and Balzac died, as he had lived for so long, without *l'Etrangère* at his side. At the funeral she appeared veiled in crêpe ,'very dignified, very sad, very literary'. A few months later Gigoux was beside her in the house that Balzac had so lovingly prepared for her – that Pavilion which had contained all his dreams.

4

'Paradise
Merton'

England

W HEN LADY HAMILTON took Lord Nelson to her bosom, the
union of the overblown enchantress and the nation's hero,
hitherto a model of all the most cherished virtues, domestic
and heroic, the scandal rocked not only the Admiralty and the Foreign
Office, but most of the European courts, and was of the liveliest interest
to everyone who encountered them for the rest of their lives, remaining
to this day, a legend.

But it is not the splendours of the great Neapolitan palaces, where
they first met, nor some *rocaille* grotto in the gardens of La Favorita,
where they loved, nor yet the cabin on Nelson's flagship – also said to
have harboured their transports – that became their Pavilion: it is,
rather, a very modest house at Merton, some seven miles from London,
in the Wimbledon area, which takes its place here. The house has now
vanished and suburban-line trains dash to and fro over its site. It is
described as having been a comfortable *family* house, to the taste of a
family man. Such, at heart, Nelson, the great Admiral and legendary

lover was, and the pathetically short while he was able to occupy Merton with Lady Hamilton and little Horatia, his child by her, and a gathering of assorted relatives, was, to him, most truly the Pavilion of his loving, generous, gentle heart. To be among his own, 'people that do care for us', he wrote to Emma, for whom plurality had once been seen in other, less domestic terms – was his heart's desire. La Bruyère's words might have been his. *To be with those one loves is enough: to dream, to talk with them, or remain silent – one with them: thinking of them or thinking of nothing in particular, but beside them – then all is well.*

Let us see how, after the thunders of battle, the tempests of love and the uproar of scandal, Nelson at last reached the haven of Merton.

When he first encountered Lady Hamilton, he had been scouring the Mediterranean to trap Bonaparte's fleet; putting into Naples he had met, and been charmed by, the wife of the British Envoy to the Kingdom of Naples and the Two Sicilies. But her rapid ascendancy over the Admiral aroused political and diplomatic interest from the start, occupying pride of place in much private correspondence of the time, while the diplomatic bag of every foreign representative at the little Court came to be puffed out with the raciest details besides observations of the manner in which Lady Hamilton was involving the British Admiral in a lot of local Italian politics. But this imprudence had to be tolerated by the Foreign Office, since she probably did, as Nelson stoutly maintained, also provide much useful information for British interests, besides obtaining various concessions for the Mediterranean fleet, such as their watering in the Sicilian ports, thus stealing a march on the French. Lady Hamilton was *persona grata* at the Palace through her passionate friendship with the Queen, a sister of Marie Antoinette, and therefore violently opposed to the Republican régime in France, and Bonaparte in particular. She was a managing woman, who often overruled her degenerate, vulgar husband, King Ferdinand iv ('*Il Re Lazzaroni*', so dubbed for his frequentation of the hoi polloi). Thus she no doubt used Lady Hamilton to obtain the British Ambassador's ear whenever she deemed it necessary to her interests.

At the Royal Palace of Caserta a curious air of theatricality prevailed. For all its gilded splendours, its fountains and mirrored perspectives, its pompous protocol, it was faintly tawdry, all glitter, florid pronouncements and whispered asides. Then there was a marked *laissez-aller* in matters of *tenue*. It lacked style, said men of breeding, enjoying themselves, though carping, when writing home from their various embassies to relatives all agog in the more sober settings of other capitals. But then, Naples was never a city to be over-nice as to the ways of its inhabitants, high or low. It was into this highly coloured setting that Norfolk-bred Nelson was plunged.

Under the fuming menace of Vesuvius, fearful squalor went beside the extravagances of both nature and man. The great baroque palazzos swarmed with insect life: powdered-wigged footmen and gold-laced guests alike scratched themselves with abandon: lava dust sifted through the scented air, where wafts of tuberose and jasmine mingled with blasts of stinking fish and other unnamable odours simmering about the city. All the clamour of a big Mediterranean port vied with the perpetual uproar of the town; coaches and horses plunged about the cobbled streets, church bells clanged or tolled incessantly, as guitars and mandolines twanged, and by day or night the inexhaustible Neapolitan voices were uplifted, singing, yelling, bargaining, wheedling, quarrelling and loving with equal vigour. The *lazzaroni* bickered or snored away the torrid hours of noon sprawled about the shady side of the streets among the famished cats and dogs. Housewives shrieked across the lines of washing strung between the narrow alleys, children wailed, and street vendors, with their stalls or trays of food, yelled their wares, dubious-looking *frutti di mare*, polpi, chestnuts pounded to a cake, snails, grapes and richly sweet *pasticceria*. Shutters were banged close on some erotic prank, but did not shield it from the sharp eyes and ribald comments of the neighbours. All life seemed lived to the sound of some distant tarantella, its furious rhythms heating the already hot-blooded citizens to boiling-point. Homosexuality was prevalent and viewed rather in the Greek manner – as in no way reprehensible. Every prelate had his favourite: monasteries indulged their fancies freely. Convent life was anything but cloistered. Women of quality all had a lover or *cisebo*. There were no inhibitions in Naples. The stylish bordellos catered for every taste; a virgin of twelve could be had for a fair price, and in the slums the stews, like the mountebank theatres, provided entertainment of a less selective order at cut rates. In short, Naples was a city given over to pleasures.

Nelson must have found this cauldron of the senses a very far cry from the parsonage at Burnham Thorpe, which was his background. It was less strange, less far removed from the Ambassadress's early years: her chequered career, begun at fifteen, was said to have included an apprenticeship in the famous Regenerating Bed which an enterprising quack doctor set up in London. It was advertised as positively assuring virile joys to all those failing or nervous gentlemen who ventured into its curtained depths. With such as the buxom young Emma awaiting them there, no doubt such claims were not unfounded.

Emma Lyons – renowned as the perfect type of English beauty, and Romney's preferred model – was the daughter of a blacksmith in Cheshire. She was born around 1765, and first appears as Amy Lyons, or Hart, nursemaid in some country house, from where she was soon removed by Sir Harry Featherstonhaugh, to be set up as his mistress at Uppark, his Sussex estate. There, while being said to dance naked on the dinner table for the entertainment of his rakish friends, she was also given a chance to improve herself, that is, to acquire the rudiments of reading and writing, and to perfect those arts of pleasing with which she seems to have been born. When her lover tired of her and put her out, she was pregnant and desperate, and still had not achieved much skill in writing. Perhaps it was better so; her artless letter to one of Featherstonhaugh's circle, the Hon. Charles Greville, roused his chivalry.

> For Gods sake G. write the minet you get this & only tell me what I am to dow. Direct same whay. I am allmos mad. O for Gods sake tell me what is to become on me. O dear Grevell write to me. Write to me. G. adue, and believe (me) yours for ever Emily Hart. Dont tel my mother what distress I am in, & dow afford me some comfort.

He did. He took her on, paid for her child to be put out to nurse, and installed her in his London house with her mother, known as Mrs Cadogan, a widow who had been on poor relief, as his cook. Moreover, rather than displaying her charms naked on the dinner table, he launched her in a less flamboyant manner, among men of the world who appreciated her charming gaiety and good-natured simplicity as well as her beauty. Greville seems to have been aware of her potentials, culturally. Music masters, dancing masters, and professors instructed her with gratifying results. The many portraits which Romney painted have immortalized her: Emma in classic draperies, Emma in a bonnet, Emma as a Bacchante – Emma laughing or languishing, always lovely.

From afar the distinguished archaeologist and art collector Sir William Hamilton, Greville's uncle, had observed his nephew's acquisition and approved. When Greville, a cold fish, began to find Emma an encumbrance, for she was a reckless spender and had come to love him to distraction – fatal weakness in a mistress – he contrived to trade her over to his uncle as part of an arrangement to settle his debts. She was packed off to Naples (where Sir William was Ambassador), along with her mother, 'on a visit' said Greville, and she believed him, going gaily. When, on arrival, she learned the truth, she pined and sulked for weeks on end, until at last her good sense as well as her good nature prevailed, and she found life at the Embassy, and the Ambassador, to her liking.

At this time Sir William was a fine-looking man of fifty, rich, vigorous, unconventional and profoundly cultivated. He found Emma fitted well into his life, both as mistress and *objet d'art*, if not of *vertu*. On his journeys about Europe in search of treasures, he collected Etruscan, Greek and Roman remains, life-sized statues, urns, and such, so that huge crates were forever arriving at the Embassy, and were hardly unpacked before more appeared. Thus the Embassy, a nobly pillared and galleried palace, assumed a museum-like character, softened, however, by its luxury, its glittering chandeliers and mirrored panelling sparkling in the strong southern sunshine. Sir William delighted in conducting his guests on lecture tours; but they always ended up in ecstasies before Emma – his perfect, flesh and blood acquisition – *clou* of the whole collection.

Besotted he might be, but he retained his dry sense of humour. No doubt he enjoyed observing the varied reactions of his guests, noble or official personages, coming face to face with lusty, luscious Emma, who, quite *sans-gêne*, talked with them in a mixture of her native broad Lancashire and tutored Italian.

Emma soon queened it over the Embassy and the Neapolitan *ton*, becoming the intimate of King Ferdinand's consort, Maria Carolina: though she was not received at the Court of St James when she and Sir William visited London. Her past, and indeed her present, made her unacceptable there. But in 1791 Sir William married her, and thus she secured an unassailable, official status. Sir William was then fifty-six to her twenty-five. Here is Casanova on the marriage. 'Mr H. was a genius, and yet he ended by marrying a mere girl who was clever enough to make him in love with her. Such a misfortune often comes to clever men *in their old age* [the italics are mine]. Marriage is ever a folly,' concludes the fly-by-night Casanova.

Nevertheless Sir William continued delighted with his collector's piece. 'Poor Sir William is never so happy as when he is pointing out my beauty to them (the Embassy guests). He thinks I am grown much more ansome than I was. He does nothing but look at me and sigh,' writes Emma, retaining a disregard for her aitches, even on paper.

There was rather more reason to sigh, ten years later, when Nelson had appeared, transforming this harmonious union into a *ménage à trois*. Yet it was equally harmonious, and remained so till the end. Curiously, the Hamilton family motto was *Tria Juncta In Uno* (Three in One); it was in the person of Lord Nelson that it came to life, or rather, to be a way of life.

It was in 1798, after Nelson's victory at the Battle of the Nile, that he sailed once more into the Bay of Naples, to be given a rapturous welcome. The French fleet beaten, Napoleon's Egyptian designs thwarted, and the ogre Bonaparte on the run, said the Neapolitans, rather prematurely as it turned out. But at that monent it seemed so, and the British man-o'-war was hailed with rapture, every sailor a saviour, and the one-eyed, one-armed Admiral – there were no words enough for such a conqueror! Joy was unconfined. There were fireworks and flags, while boatloads of musicians rowed out fiddling and singing the Admiral's praises, and the King himself arrived in the State Galley, all gilding, with sequin-embroidered awnings. Lady Hamilton was quite beside herself. She dearly loved a drama, and was so overcome at the official reception that she swooned away, recovering in time, however, to be driven through the streets wearing a bandeau inscribed *Nelson and Victory*. At the state banquet Nelson was asked if this was not the happiest day of his life: but he still saw life in Burnham Thorpe terms. 'No' was the reply. 'The happiest was the day on which I married Lady Nelson.'

It was some months before a full report of the celebrations, and these gratifying words, reached England, by which time they no longer rang true, if indeed they had ever done so. Nelson's marriage, contracted in the West Indies in 1787, to a colourless widow, Frances Nisbet, had proved a failure from the start. But Nelson was not the son, grandson and brother of parsons for nothing. He had grown up in the sober Christian tenets of an English country parsonage. Marriages were made in Heaven. Until he encountered Lady Hamilton's wiles, the matter had rested there. He was ill-equipped to resist either the sultry ambience of Naples or the full battery of Lady Hamilton's charms, which were now directed solely at him. Since he was the hero of the hour, of course, excitable, greedy Emma must make him her slave. Nelson's innate good-ness and naïveté are revealed in a letter to his wife. 'I hope some day to have the pleasure of introducing you to Lady Hamilton,' he writes. 'She is one of the *very* best of women of this world. How few could have made the turn she has. She is an honour to her sex.' In short, proof that a reputation may be lost, and regained, all over again. Thus Nelson, naïve rather than gullible, at this point. A compatriot, Miss Knight, saw the Ambassadress less favourably. 'She is,' she wrote home, 'more stamped with the manners of her first situation than one would suppose, after having represented Majesty and lived in good company for fifteen years. . . .' Lord Nelson, she added, was a willing captive.

It was just this easy-going, lusty *joie de vivre*, this childish appetite for life in full measure, and second helpings too, which captivated Nelson and finally overcame his last scruples. But at first he was no more than a pampered, appreciative guest at the Embassy. It was a delightful life; everything seemed arranged for ease and pleasure . . . the balmy air, the tropic gardens, the beautiful luxurious *enfilades*, Sir William's wonderful collections, Sir William himself – for the men formed a friendship, then, which was to withstand every strain. Old Mrs Cadogan, too, pleased Nelson by her motherly solicitude and common sense. He found the Embassy both dazzling and intimate, and Emma a brilliant hostess. Guests without number invaded the place to salute the Admiral: champagne flowed at all hours, the food was delicious, and no doubt, after hard tack and rum, it was a rather overwhelming change.

All of it was heady stuff for Nelson; but Emma was the headiest brew of all. She hung on his words, spoiled and flattered him outrageously, and in all she said or did, seemed to wish only to please him. For him alone, it now seemed, she sang, played the guitar or danced, twining her gauze scarves aloft with unselfconscious exuberance, like the Bacchante that she was, at heart. For him alone, it seemed, though there might be a room full of spectators, she now struck those celebrated Attitudes, as Niobe, Daphne, or Agrippina carrying the ashes of Germanicus, rolling those melting, brimming blue eyes, and heaving that rather too sumptuous, too lightly veiled bosom in transports of emotion, as she gazed at her hero. When she sang, all her songs seemed directed solely at him, and pierced his heart. Emma had studied music with the best Italian professors, and had no false modesty where her talents were concerned. 'Mine is the finest soprano you ever heard,' she had written home, some years earlier. 'Sir William shuts his eyes and thinks of the Castrati singing. My shake or trill, or what you call it is so good in every note my master says he might think I was an angel.' (Nelson did think so, then, and for evermore.) 'Mind you,' Emma's letter continued, striking a pawky note, 'your Uncle Fred's daughter dont sing so well as I do. Tell her so.'

How refreshing she must have seemed to Sir William, after the splenetic nobility around him. No wonder he continued indulgent to her every whim, and apparently unconcerned or unaware of Nelson's growing passion. And in truth, perhaps it no longer mattered to him overmuch. He had his Etruscan vases – they were less demanding than Emma; he had never been one to abide by the conventions, so now he took an unconventional view of the situation; besides, he liked and admired Nelson: both were Tories, and they talked fishing together. It was easier to let things be.

Now there was no turning back. Nelson was, as Miss Knight had said, Emma's willing captive, lingering at her side when he should have sailed for England, intoxicated by the easy, luxurious life of love and flattery. Intrigue, too, for Siren Emma and the Queen used him for their political ends, and Nelson, whom the King had created Duke of Brönte, in Sicily, to mark his Nile victory, rapidly became a fervent Neapolitan Royalist, meddling and ill-advising the King to launch an attack on the French garrison's then occupying Rome. It was a fatal move, instantly and ignominiously crushed. King Ferdinand, rather a cowardly custard, and his quaking entourage packed up to flee before the threatened French invasion. Naples was in a screaming turmoil. Nelson embarked the Royal family, together with the Hamiltons, aboard his flagship, and sailed them to safety at Palermo, where, at once, his idyll with Emma was renewed in all its extravagance at the palace of La Favorita, and other settings so exotic that Naples appeared positively austere in retrospect. From here, from Emma's arms it might be said, he was contriving to direct the operations of his squadron and the blockade of Malta, still held by the French. But in June 1799, Sicilian dalliance gave place to a tragic interlude of bloodshed and misjudgement from which Nelson's name has never been cleared.

The Neapolitans had succeeded in ousting the occupying French, and while both the *lazzaroni* and the Royalists awaited their King's return, the kingdom became divided by a strong revolutionary party, Jacobins who wished to establish a republic along French lines. The King, his Queen and the Hamiltons all counted on Nelson to crush this dangerous development. By now, Nelson was so bemused that he saw it as his plain duty to do so, using the British Navy to enforce order. He felt himself to be acting at once for Britain, which had, in general terms, instructed him to support the King – in the sense of his being a strategically well-placed ally against Bonaparte – then, for his personal abhorrence of republic-anism, and lastly, in absolute compliance with the commands of Emma and, or, the Queen. What followed has never been entirely clarified. Betrayals and double-crossings, broken promises, savage reprisals and ruthless cruelties were interwoven.

The King's right-hand man, Cardinal Ruffo, had promised merciful terms to the rebels, who expected to be allowed to leave for France and, on that understanding, capitulated. This did not satisfy Nelson. It smacked of weakness. Any manifestation of Republicanism must be stamped out. The Republicans, believing in Ruffo's word, and unaware that Nelson had superseded him, gave themselves up. Most were hanged or shot on the King's orders. Their leader, Francesco Carraciolo, a Neapolitan naval officer whose influence was feared by the Queen, fell into Nelson's hands. He ordered him court-martialled, to be tried by Royalist officers but aboard a British ship, the *Foudroyant*. He was charged with being commander of the Republican fleet, guilty not only of rebellion but of attacking British and Royal Navy ships, and he was hung, forthwith, from the foreyard arm of the frigate *Minerva*. Nelson ordered his body to be cut down and thrown into the bay.

'The sentence was just but the procedure indecent,' was how one historian described it later. 'Such quick justice had great effect,' wrote Sir William Hamilton, complacently. But it was a year before English criticism reached Nelson. The whole affair had aroused a violent storm – Fox thundered that atrocities evidently did not belong exclusively to the French. 'Lady Hamilton's baneful influence over Lord Nelson was the cause of his indefensible conduct, she being the confidant of a dissolute and bloodthirsty Queen,' was how Lady Holland saw it. Malicious, and probably unfounded rumours circulated that Emma had watched the executions from Nelson's barge, and gloated.

In any case, Nelson continued spellbound, dawdling beside her in the Mediterranean waters while differences with his officers and Com-mander-in-Chief led to such bad relations with the Admiralty that he was at last given permission to return to London. This was something he had been soliciting ever since he learned that Sir William was about to be recalled. After thirty-six years as British Envoy his day was over, and it is clear that Nelson was determined not to be parted from his Dulcinea.

The now notorious trio set off overland, since the Admiral-in-Chief would not permit Nelson to sail with a line of battleships (and the Hamiltons) and plainly stated that Lady H. had commanded the Mediterranean station far too long. They went by leisurely stages, Prague, Dresden, a trip down the Rhine . . . roses, roses all the way, their evident enjoyment in each other's society recalling another celebrated trio, the Blessingtons and Count d'Orsay, on their peregrinations about Europe. Hero or no, Nelson met with a very cool reception from one British Minister. The large quantities of champagne which the party consumed was noted, as was Lady Hamilton's appearance: 'her taste in dress frightful,' reported the Minister's wife, 'and her waist absolutely between her shoulders. . . .' Lost beyond recognition, we must suppose. Emma had always been inclined to embonpoint.

On reaching London, the Hamiltons settled at 23 Piccadilly, between Clarges and Half Moon Street, but she was generally cold-shouldered. Nelson, although the people's hero, was also rather snubbed by the *ton*, for reports of the goings-on in Palermo had not been seen sympathetically by the King; but Nelson now insisted that Lady Hamilton must be included in every invitation or he would not accept. After first staying in a hotel with the bewildered Lady Nelson, he proposed sharing quarters once more with the Hamiltons. He had seen no reason why his wife should not go along with this, so little did he now care either for her feelings or the conventions: but this Lady Nelson would not tolerate, and they separated, never to meet again.

Soon afterwards, Nelson was ordered to join the Baltic fleet, sailing north where trouble was thought to be brewing owing to the aspirations of the Tzar Paul I and those of the Northern Confederation, which bogey, as it happened, was presently dissolved. Now Nelson's whole being was consumed by his passion for Emma, and the pride, anxiety and joy with which he awaited the birth of their child. Horatia Nelson Thompson, as she was known, was born in January 1801. But Nelson's daughter had to be hustled out of Sir William's house by night, in stealth. Emma had been brought to bed there surreptitiously, neither her husband nor the servants, it was believed, being any the wiser. She struggled up, tight laced and painted, the very next day, and herself took the baby, concealed in her muff, to the worthy woman who had been engaged as its foster-mother.

From that moment, all Nelson's thoughts and letters run on one theme – a house – his *own* house must be found, quickly, somewhere

where he could live beside Emma, and where their child could be brought up beside them in love and security. Horatia he saw as some God-given pledge crowning their marvellous love. His letters to Emma now exhort her to find a suitable place *without delay*, and above all, to retail every possible detail concerning their little pledge. A very silly subterfuge was now resorted to, by which the baby was supposed to be that of a Mrs Thompson . . . Thompson, the father, was a naval man and a protégé of Nelson's, who relayed Emma's news to him, 'somewhere at sea'.

It can have deceived no one. Emma, though dutiful towards the child, was less emotionally concerned: Nelson seems not to have known that she already had another daughter, fruit of her earliest years, now sixteen, and also kept at a discreet distance, passed off as a niece. From northern waters Nelson's letters now reach a crescendo of love and longing. He is flamingly jealous of the Prince of Wales, who takes an interest in Emma. Nelson cannot imagine any man coming within a mile of her without succumbing. 'I am ready to quit the world and its greatness to live with you a quiet domestic life,' he writes: which was, of course, the last thing Emma wanted. '*Ever, forever I am yours – only yours, even beyond this world,*' he writes, and signs it, with odd formality, *Nelson and Brönte.*

Emma had always enjoyed spending, and now, with Nelson's money jingling in her pocket, she set about finding the house her lover craved. Besides, she was anxious to establish herself beside him, publicly. Sir William was failing fast now. Some said he was in his dotage, that being the only excuse for his *laissez-aller*. She saw the advantages of creating a home (with Nelson paying), for all three of them – indeed, for four, or even five, counting her mother and little Horatia, to say nothing of the Nelson family, his brothers, their wives and children, to whom he was deeply attached, and his old father, now very frail, over whom Nelson worried. The Nelsons had all become very attached to Emma – they did not criticize what they described as 'the friendship'. They accepted her as part of the family, falling under her spell, dazzled by her charm and gaiety, and the high-coloured profusion of her ways. Of course they must all come to stay as soon as the right house was found, she said, and meant it. She knew how much Nelson's family ties counted, how happy and *anchored* he would be when they were all gathered round him.

When she found Merton Place her search was over, and letters flew between the lovers discussing every door knob. She seems to have made a good job of it, creating exactly the ambience Nelson longed for – *a home – a house of his own.* This he had never known, and being almost always at sea, he had never inhabited the house near Ipswich which he had acquired during the early days of his marriage.

Now he stipulated that *all* must be his, emphasizing that nothing of Hamilton largesse was to be there: not linen nor books nor pictures: not even their proffered cook. 'I only entreat that everything, even a book or a cook at Merton may be mine.' Perhaps, in spite of the intoxications of the Embassy, his dependence had irked.

Today nothing remains of Merton, but there are many descriptions of it, especially in Bartlett's *History of Wimbledon*, published in 1865. Although only seven miles from London, it was then in open country, with some rough shooting to be had. The original house had been standing a hundred years or so, and was a white-walled, unpretentious place, but with harmonious proportions. The entrance gave north, and a Palladian frontage had been added. South and east bow windows gave on to the garden, and wide verandahs, with rustic green trellis work, faced south. The house stood in big grounds, twenty-two acres of fine trees, with shrubberies, an orchard, a vegetable garden, greenhouse and paddock. There was, too, a dairy and an ice house, for further comfort. A little ornamental stream bordered the property – an offshoot of the river Wandle. It was spanned by graceful little bridges 'in the Italianate manner'. The household dubbed this streamlet 'the Nile', and Emma saw to it, with an eye to Sir William's penchant, that it was well-stocked with fish.

There were five suites of bedroom, dressing-room and water-closet – at that time a rarity, and it is to be supposed that Emma caused them to be installed. Two large drawing-rooms, a dining-room and breakfast-room and library all seemed particularly light and airy, 'with mirrors and glass doors in the continental style, which cast an abundance of light about the interior'. Emma had crammed the house with trophies of Nelson's glory – his flags, orders and decorations, coats of arms and much presentation plate commemorating various victories. The dinner service was Worcester, especially designed, for Emma worked fast: laurel and oak leaves encircled the crest of Viscount Nelson, Duke of Brönte. There were besides a number of portraits of Nelson and of herself too: one in particular displayed her as a pagan divinity – it was the fashion to be so rendered, and singularly appropriate to Emma's Bacchic nature. Some critics thought the display of portraits and trophies rather ostentatious, but it was entirely in keeping with Emma's flamboyance, spilling over, even here, in this rural retreat. And Nelson, who was not averse to the flattery with which she larded him, never questioned anything which she decreed.

'You are to be, recollect, Lady Paramount of all the territories and waters of Merton, and we are all to be your guests,' he wrote, when planning to settle the whole place on her, in the event of his death.

'Paradise Merton', Emma always called it, in her letters to him, and Paradise it seemed to him when at last he reached it in the autumn of 1805 for what he believed would be a life of retirement. Sir William had died in 1803, and now, Emma was all his. She awaited him at Merton with much of his family and the little Horatia, fetched from hiding to be among them all, petted and loved, as was her due. For nanny, she had Fatima, the Nubian serving girl Nelson had brought Emma from foreign parts. The little creature toddled and scampered about the gardens and was dandled by her doting father. In later life, Horatia, who married a clergyman and only died in 1881, had alas! but the vaguest memories of Merton, and none whatever of her father. Emma never admitted to being her mother; she was Horatia's guardian, she said and Horatia preferred it so. Poor Horatia was long to remain in doubt as to her relationship to Nelson, too.

Paradise Merton! Nelson basked in the realization of his dream. Emma, wonderful Emma, had brought it about! All round the big dinner table (where she presided) he saw the beaming faces of his brothers and sisters and their young families, some fetched specially from school by Emma, determined to create an atmosphere of perfect domestic felicity. Old friends were there too. . . . Here, then, was the home of his own, among his own people . . . : 'People that do care for us,' the lonely hero had once said, with unconscious pathos; and now, whenever his duties permitted, he was to be found at Merton.

Although the *beau monde* was kept at bay, certain visitors were inevitable; the Royal Dukes could not be gainsaid; besides, they flattered Emma. 'The passion hot as ever,' said visitors, feeding London gossip. Nevertheless Nelson craved, fundamentally, a home quite as much as an *alcôve*. He was not destined to enjoy home life for long. In October 1805, after barely six weeks of the retired life he had craved, the Admiralty called him back into service, and he tore himself away to take command of the *Victory*, sailing to death and glory at Trafalgar.

As might be expected, Emma displayed noisy grief, indulging in every exhibition of tragedy, receiving condolences from her bed, hung with crêpe, and subsequently fainting regularly at the mention of Trafalgar. Nelson, in a poignant codicil to his will written on board the *Victory*, a few hours before going into battle, had bequeathed Emma and Horatia to the nation's care. It was a charge that was not honoured, however, and recalls Charles ii's solicitude for Nell Gwyn. 'Don't let poor Nelly starve,' he had said, when dying. But then, hypocrisy has ever been a trait of England's ruling classes. They call it morality, to this day, and turn their backs on unions not to their liking.

For Emma, the road now wound downhill all the way. Her extravagances continued, neither checked nor backed by husband or lover. Merton was sold up, its contents dispersed, some things going to the Nelson family, but most to meet Emma's debts. Intemperance took hold; her looks gone, there followed the sad, inevitable sequence of writs, bailiffs, the dram shop, a year in the debtors' prison (where the Duke of Sussex came to dine, the food being sent in from outside, but with no knives and forks, so fingers had to do: 'Oh! you mustn't be particular here,' said Emma, still presiding with some of her old panache). At last, dragging Horatia along, she made her escape to Calais, which freed her from English duns, but the old ways continued. Drink, more drink, ill-health, lost looks, illusions of grandeur, dire poverty and, at last, merciful death.

Did she, dying in that mean little northern French town, remember her blazing heyday in Naples, all glitter and warmth and privilege? Or did she remember Merton, and its truer joys? There is little doubt which of the two were in Nelson's mind as he lay dying in the *Victory*. Merton – 'Paradise Merton' – that was the Pavilion holding Nelson's heart.

5

Kourdane
Algeria

S TENDHAL WAS snugly installed in a northern Italian consulate
when he wrote his celebrated dicta on love; but he was emphatic.
*'It is in the half-light of the Bedouin Arab tent that one must seek the
model of true love.'* Although he never budged from the strait-jacket of
polite European living himself, he seems to have been aware of that
curious climate of fervent sensuality and extreme discretion, spiced with
a wildness to match the surrounding deserts, which has proved so irresistible to generations of Western persons of romantic inclination,
particularly the English, both men and women. Like the pine tree of
Heine's poem, they dream, on their northern shore, of some faraway
palm – until, one day, sweet chance leads their steps abroad, and they
are enthralled for evermore. There must have been, over the centuries,
uncounted numbers of Crusaders, travellers and traders, besides the
raiding corsairs and even their captives, who, finding themselves in the
half-light of the black tents, took root there and never returned to the
West.

Such was the case of Aurélie Piccard, a little provincial French girl who was to become known as Lallah Yamina, *la Princesse des Sables*, a power in the Sahara and all across Algeria, a woman upon whom the French authorities, both civil and military, came to rely in their endeavours to achieve their 'pacific penetration' of the Sahara and to be accepted, in particular, by the Tedjanis, one of the most fanatic religious confraternities of North Africa. It was the Sahara which became the passion of Aurélie Piccard's life, so that Kourdane, the fabled domain which, under her hands, sprang from the desert, became the Pavilion which held her heart to the exclusion of every other thing, or person.

Her life of love and adventure begins in a small, glum provincial town, Montigny-le-Roi, in Northern France, where she was born in 1849. Her father served under General Bugeaud in the French conquest of Algeria, and at the end of his service he joined the local gendarmerie at Montigny, while eking out his meagre means giving riding lessons. On his retirement, the family moved to another grey little town, Arc-en-Barrois, where, with so many younger brothers and sisters to be fed, Aurélie went out to work at fifteen. She was neat-fingered and quick, and soon made herself indispensable to the milliner to whom she was apprenticed. At night she returned home to more work, washing and mending for the family; a pinched existence, and Aurélie dreamed of escape to glowing horizons – where, she could not define. The only colour in her life was when her father recounted his adventures in North Africa. She listened, rapt, to stories of the desert slashed by a line of charging Arab warriors; of Moorish palaces, of blazing stars and mysterious deserts – a world very far from her own.

To study the pattern of Aurélie Piccard's life is to believe in destiny; over and over again we find this recurring intervention of fate, bringing her undreamed-of chances. It has been said that character plus chance brings fortune. Aurélie's character was both audacious and tenacious, and she never missed a chance. Fate's first appearance was in the classic guise of the fairy godmother. Aurélie had quit the milliner's establishment to better herself as housekeeper in the château of Arc-en-Barrois, property of the Prince de Joinville, but leased to a députe of the Haute Marne, a Monsieur Steenackers. His wife took a fancy to the girl, and soon Aurélie found herself installed as *dame de compagnie*.

It was the open door she had craved. In these easy circumstances she set about improving herself. She read studiously and was able to ride the fine horses in the stables, for she was already a good horsewoman, having profited by her father's tuition. Above all, while learning to set off her natural good looks by an acquired polish, she was observing the general style of those around her, so that, one chance leading to another, when the decisive turning-point of her life came, she was ready.

It came in 1871 heralded by gunfire – the cannons of the Franco-Prussian war.

And now the scene changes from Northern France to Bordeaux, glowing among vineyarded hills, its mellow elegance set beside the wide waters of the Garonne. Here the provisional government settled, having removed from beleaguered Paris. Monsieur Steenackers, now Directeur Général des Postes, followed the provisional government, and he and his family were lodged in a hotel reserved for persons of consequence. Aurélie accompanied them, leaving behind her for ever the pinched existence of her family at Arc-en-Barrois. And if her new life did not, as yet, compass the glowing horizons of her dreams, it was no longer drab.

At this moment, almost the only means of communication with Paris was by carrier-pigeon, messages being sent regularly to and from the besieged capital by this means. In his official capacity as Directeur des Postes, Monsieur Steenackers received all such messages, but at whatever hour they arrived, the pigeons were first brought to Aurélie, who detached the tiny cylinders and took them to him. She was also allotted care of the birds, and so it happened that one day, as she stood among the swooping, muttering, pecking multitude, an impressive figure in Arab dress approached, staring intently. He was a romantic-looking creature, very dark-skinned, his face framed in a short black beard, his costume magnificent. A dark burnous was flung over another white one, and that over a white robe belted with a silk scarf, through which was thrust a jewel-handled dagger. His boots were of soft crimson leather spurred with gold, and pinned to his robe were a number of orders and decorations, some of which Aurélie recognized as French. As he approached her, wafts of some heady perfume accompanied him, so that he seemed to move in a special aura of exoticism.

This remarkable personage was surrounded by an entourage of guards, black slaves, courtiers and interpreters who waited obsequiously at his heels. Next day, and for several days following, he reappeared, always silent, always fixing Aurélie with a gaze at once romantic and incredulous, as if contemplating some celestial vision. And perhaps this

Roumia (or European), so fair-skinned and surrounded by the pigeons which are venerated by Moslems as sacred, did indeed seem such.

By now Aurélie had recognized her admirer as the Prince Si Ahmed Tedjani, a young Arab ruler from Southern Algeria who, with his half-brother Si Bachir, had been for some time of absorbing interest to all Bordeaux, object of the most flattering attentions in governmental circles, even being given a standing ovation when attending the opera from the Préfet's box. Public enthusiasm knew no bounds, for the brothers were representatives of such of the feudal Arab chiefs who now offered their allegiance and material support to the hard-pressed French. Not so long ago, the French had been their invaders, overcoming, at last, the great Arab leader, Abd-el-Kader, but that was the past. Abd-el-Kader was in honourable exile in Damascus, and the French were accepted by most of the Algerian leaders as a chivalrous ex-army worthy to guide (if not wholly subdue) them. Curiously, most Algerians, while still straining at the leash, found French domination – if domination was Allah's will, as it then seemed – infinitely preferable to the abhorred Turkish yoke, even though the Turks were their co-religionists. But the Kabyle revolts were still causing much bloodshed, and Algeria was far from calm.

Si Ahmed's background was as exotic as his appearance. He was the child of a Sudanese slave-girl and the Shareef of the Tedjanis, the mighty Prince Si Mohammed-Seghir, the Marabout and absolute ruler of the Tedjanis, a religious sect, one of many, throughout Northern Africa. The slave-girl, though *enceinte* by the Prince, had left his harem to follow another master, a not unusual procedure in that age of slave-traffic and quickly satiated masters. She vanished and nothing more would ever have been heard of her or her child had not Si Mohammed-Seghir died suddenly, leaving from among all his wives and concubines only one sickly baby son. (His fourteen daughters were of no account: 'I have three children – and two daughters,' a Moslem father of five will tell you.) The Tedjani nobles were uneasy that their dynasty rested with one frail boy, and when it was remembered the the slave-girl was said to have borne a son, they dispatched messengers in search of her. When at last she and her child were found, it was a robust little boy of seven who was brought back in triumph to the *zaouïa*, to be installed in state beside his half-brother, the weakling Si Bachir.

Between them the two Princes were co-heirs to the absolute power and glory accorded Shareefs. Such hereditary princes were of a special religious nobility, invested with spiritual as well as temporal power. They were Marabouts, seen as saints who, in however secular a manner they lived, were still holy, venerated figures, their *bordj*, or *ksour* dwelling being not only a fortress, but also the *zaouïa*, monastery and sanctuary, with mosques, theological college and alms-houses within the complex. The great doors were always open to pilgrims and the needy, who, by tradition, must be lodged and fed for three days: often, the blind or dying came there, and were never turned away. These confraternities might be likened to powerful Masonic lodges – but fanatic too. Since the Shareefs wielded enormous influence among the Arabs throughout North Africa, their goodwill was of paramount importance to the French or any rare person venturing into the unmapped interior.'

This, then, was the puissant figure whom Aurélie Piccard had captivated and was to subjugate entirely, first by her blonde charms, and, later, by her force of character. To begin with, the courtship hung fire, for they had no common language, and no doubt the presence of an interpreter was stultifying to one so passionately enamoured as the Prince. Aurélie met his advances with the downcast eyes and missish deportment then *de rigueur*. But her modest calm concealed a turmoil of hopes and fears. Here before her stood the means of realizing her wildest dreams. Demure and unattainable, she launched an occasional death-dealing glance from beneath her long lashes, and the Prince could think of nothing else. Accompanied by his suite (and a lagging brother, for Si Bachir already gauged and feared this Infidel's ascendancy), the Prince made a formal call on Madame Steenackers to ask Aurélie's price. He was prepared to pay anything for such a treasure – absolutely anything.

'But Aurélie is not a slave,' replied the astonished Madame Steenackers. 'She is not for sale.'

The Prince is said to have paled visibly, until the Député's wife explained that Aurélie could however be *married*.

'So be it,' replied the Prince, inclining ceremoniously. If such was the *Roumi* custom, he would marry Mademoiselle Piccard. At once. Now. Tonight! It was with difficulty he was edged away to his own apartments. In agitation the Steenackers sent for Aurélie's father. In agitation they awaited his arrival, for Aurélie had announced she would accept the Prince's proposal. By now the whole hotel was in a ferment. All Bordeaux talked of this extravagant romance.

Spurred on by love and, no doubt, a wish to dispense with the re-
straining presence of the interpreter, the Prince was making rapid progress with his French, though his exotic reputation and the splendid
jewels he wore, and now lavished on Aurélie, must have been as powerful an argument as any words to the girl from Arc-en-Barrois. In any
case, Aurélie's mind was made up. It was useless for anyone to counsel
prudence: she was going to seize this incredible chance; also, she had
begun to recognize a depth of sincerity in the Prince's protestations of
devotion and recognized, perhaps, how her own feelings for him were
growing. Above all, it was through him she would be able to reach that
Africa which her father's stories had evoked so tantalizingly.

It was decided that the marriage should take place in Algiers, under
French law, as her father stipulated, and when the Prince and his suite
sailed from Marseilles Aurélie and Monsieur Piccard were with them.
At that time Algiers was only a huddle of French barracks and military
headquarters grouped round the harbour where the new European town
was rising beside the cathedral. Behind, like some fantastic backcloth
for a pantomime – *Ali Baba and the Forty Thieves* – wound the steep cut-
throat alleys of the Kasbah, fastness of Arab and Moor, once stronghold
of Barbarossa's corsairs, and where, still, strangers seldom ventured.
Although there were no more impaled bodies on the city's walls, nor
decapitated heads spiked on the great gates, Algiers retained an air of
ill-concealed violence. All around lay savage scrub country, mountain
gorges and high plateaux, barely begun to be cultivated by the French.
Three hundred miles south, on the first expanses of the Sahara, lay Aïn
Mahdi, the Tedjani *zaouïa* destined to be Aurélie's home.

In Algiers preparations for a spectacular marriage were set in train.
The entire Piccard family, who had now followed Aurélie and her father,
and were treated by Si Ahmed as his own people, were installed in a
splendid Arab house he had acquired for them. Here Aurélie began to
learn some Arabic. Already she loved the graceful, unhurried life in this
beautiful old arcaded house with its fountained patios, its shimmering
blue and green tile work lining the cool dim rooms shaded from the
glare by their fretted *mouchrabiyehs*. The few but rich pieces of furniture,
low tables and coffers, were of cedarwood inlaid with mother-of-pearl;
the hanging lamps were of chased silver, and the divans were deep in
cushions and rugs. All round the walls, above the dado of tiles, numbers
of elaborate gilt-framed mirrors of varying sizes, of Italian or Spanish

origin, were hung at a curious, forward tilt which was a general practice in sophisticated Arabic interiors, where everything is scaled, or arranged for the horizontal, rather than vertical observer. Like the low-silled windows, making it possible for the lollers on the divans to see out easily, so the forward-slanted mirrors reflect downwards, and are thus enjoyed by those below. Musk and sandalwood perfumed the rooms, and countless slaves were always at hand, bringing trays of strange and spiced foods, or filling the coffers with more and more of the sumptuous trappings which were to adorn Aurélie as the Prince's bride.

But suddenly this agreeable life was shattered. The French Governor-General refused to sanction a Franco-Arab union. There was no provision for such in French law. He was obdurate and unsympathetic. Did this Arab dare . . . ? All the Piccards' pleadings fell on deaf ears. Aurélie wept and the Prince raged, threatening to raise a Tedjani insurrection. But officialdom remained adamant. Aurélie, too, remained firm. Marriage or nothing. The deadlock dragged on miserably, until at last she faced a humiliating return to Arc-en-Barrois where the pitying or spiteful looks of the neighbours were an unbearable prospect, especially after a foretaste of life as the Prince's wife. She pleaded with her family for more time. . . . Now the Piccards turned obstinate. Their daughter could not go round Algiers begging for the right to some native's favours! They would sail on the next boat, and all the jewels must be given back.

Aurélie wept; the Prince pleaded. While the arguments and protestations continued, Fate stepped in once more: this time, in no less a guise than Cardinal Lavigerie, the Archbishop of Algiers, who was just beginning his great missionary work in North Africa. He was at once visionary and practical; the story of the thwarted lovers interested him. He had noticed the downcast girl who came to pray in his church, and took pity on her situation. In these lovers he saw the embodiment of his ideals for Franco-Arab unity. Cardinal Lavigerie, it will be remembered, founded the Pères Blancs, and his hopes for a pacific penetration of the Sahara were later put into practice by such great figures as Maréchal Lyautey, the Père de Foucauld, and even, in a lesser degree, by Aurélie herself. The Cardinal sent for Si Ahmed, and sensing that this ardent young prince could be transformed into either a powerful ally or an implacable enemy, he promised on certain conditions to perform the marriage himself. Sour French officials warned Aurélie she would forfeit her birthright, and that she could no longer look to them if things went wrong. Shrugging, they turned away. But the Prince was overcome with gratitude and gave his word to the Archbishop. He would marry Aurélie in the Christian manner, as his only wife. From that moment he was always to prove himself loyal to France, always to aid Aurélie in her efforts to further French influences, and to promote peaceful relations.

The simple marriage ceremony was performed by the Cardinal in his chapel of Saint Eugène, but the Arab festivities were grandiose, and lasted a week at fever pitch. Night after night fireworks illuminated the sky, hour after hour the musicians made their seducing yet exacerbating music of *derbuka* and *rhaïta* (drum and flute) while the Ouled Naïl dancers postured and swayed in their ritual frenzies, their gold-coined, feathered head-dresses glittering in the torchlight, their breasts shuddering and their bellies undulating, their snake-like gestures inviting in the age-old pantomimes of desire. Arab notables had gathered from all over the country, from Morocco and Tunis too, to honour Si Ahmed and his strange *Roumia* bride, but the French colony banged their shutters close, and predicted disaster.

Then on a morning in late September a great cortège formed outside Si Ahmed's house. The Tedjanis were escorting their Shareef and his bride back to Aïn Mahdi. The camels were loaded up with all the baggage of tents and rugs, provisions and cooking utensils and painted coffers topped by Aurélie's European trunks and hat boxes. As the bride, she should have followed her lord and master in a *basour*, one of those close-curtained litters slung across a camel that lurch and heave at every slow step. These are the traditional mode of travel for Arab women. But with that strange instinct which always guided her in her dealings with the Arabs, Aurélie now took her stand. No *basour*, no veils, no traditions for her. She would begin as she meant to go on – of, yet apart from, this Arab world. It was an astute move, for it emphasized her rarity. The enraptured Prince could refuse her nothing. Mounted on a white Arab mare saddled in velvet with coral and silver trappings, Aurélie rode out to meet her future, unveiled, *beside*, and not following, her husband.

The journey took nearly a month, for at that time there were no roads and the caravan moved slowly under a devouring sun by day, and in an icy grip by night, towards glittering mirages and through blinding storms such as the dreaded *adjedj* like some terrible madness or rage of Nature, when the sky suddenly blackens and a fierce, suffocating wind lashes round, uprooting tents and terrifying horses and camels while the sands surge like tormented waves. After a matter of hours, or days, a sudden stillness falls, and the *adjedj* is no more. Then a sunrise or sunset of ineffable beauty suffuses everything, and the desert seems reborn.

With each mile, Aurélie fell deeper under the spell of this ardent, yet immobile land: such characteristics were found again in its inhabitants, lounging, sleeping, going silently about their business, yet, behind the langour, a reserve of force, an animal vitality seldom unleashed – the panther's spring. She noted it all.

At evening, when the tents were pitched and the camels were couched, snarling and grumbling, the loneliness of the wastes that closed round seemed lonelier for the eerie cry of the jackals, answered by the dogs slinking round the camp fires. How far, how very far, now, from Arc-en-Barrois; yet, how rapturously happy she was in this new life.

Aurélie's tent was an elaborate affair with all the hangings and cushions of those sultry interiors Delacroix loved to paint. Yet behind the luxury, the voluptuous mood, dangers lurked. Before the tents could be pitched, the ground had first to be prepared by being thrashed vigorously, to scare off lurking snakes or scorpions, as fires were lit to keep off the wild beasts that prowled near. (At that time there were still a few lions as far north as the Djebel Amour range.) But Aurélie was only aware of the beauty and romance of her new existence. On this journey, which might be considered her honeymoon with the Prince, she was in fact consummating her love for the desert. And when the huge stars glittered low, and the Prince lay beside her, furiously loving, there was a rival – the desert: it was the desert which already possessed Aurélie – the desert, rather than a man: but any means, or any man, bringing her closer to it must be made to serve her purpose. Thus Aurélie, a woman possessed, possessing.

It was now that she began to realize the full mystical significance of her husband's shareefan title, and the degree of veneration in which he was held. In Bordeaux he had appeared a princely figure of international importance. In Algiers, a grand seigneur accorded special prestige among so many other Arab nobles. But now she perceived another side. At each halt along the way, at the wells or by the *douars*, the black tent encampments of the nomads, they swarmed round to kiss the hem of his robes, to prostrate themselves or clutch at his stirrup, imploring the *baraka* or maraboutic blessing which he was divinely endowed to bestow. Si Ahmed was of the noblest shareefan blood which, in Islam, ranks higher than any other, for he traced his ancestry back to Idriss, son of Fatma Zorah, the Prophet's daughter. His was an unassailable position, and Aurélie knew she must, at all costs, maintain not only her hold on him but win the loyalty of his followers, the Tedjani, too. Were she to fail, banishment from this land she already loved without reserve would be inevitable.

At last, after passing El Aghouat and threading their way through a landscape of menacing aridity, they came in sight of Aïn Mahdi. Forbidding and splendid, the massive watch-towers and twelve-foot thick walls of the *zaouïa* rose out of the desert. Before the huge iron-studded doors a vast throng had gathered to welcome their Shareef, and now rode out, charging forward in clouds of dust, standing in their stirrups, firing their guns, hurling them high in the air, twirling them round their heads and performing all the spectacular feats of the Arab fantasia.

Along the battlements, like some frieze of doom, Aurélie made out a line of veiled women: they were shrilling their *zahrit*, that high, ululating cry which signifies joy, and can be, too, a war cry, inciting the men to battle. It is peculiar to women of the Arab world, from Mahgreb to the Yemen. The women on the battlements were Si Ahmed's wives and concubines. They had been waiting three years for their lord's return, and were now united in their intention to destroy the newcomer, by any means.

Such means were not lacking, for poisons and spells abounded. There were black magics and white, incantations to bring back a strayed lover, to render a rival sterile, to ensure the birth of a son, or the death of a rival's child . . . frightful potions, such as one quoted me long ago when in these regions. It was, if I remember rightly, designed to undermine a rival's *ménage*, and one can well believe it might, since it was composed of seven crushed beetles, the droppings of a crow, the pincers of seven scorpions, seven stones from an abandoned tomb, the urine of an aged Jewess, the moustaches of a cat, an ass's bone, mastic and oleander leaves, and a fragment of the shroud in which a corpse had lain overnight in his dwelling (a rarity in Moslem communities, where burial usually takes place within a few hours of death). This fearsome mixture had to be prepared on one specific day, and then thrown across the designated victim's threshold while pronouncing a ritual incantation. After which, I was assured, the *ménage* was invariably destroyed.

It was practices such as these which Aurélie now faced, as well as equally alarming manifestations of nature at its most malign. Enormous bats, scorpions, venomous snakes and deadly black spiders were all part of domestic life in the shareefan *ksour*, as in humbler dwellings. However sumptuous Si Ahmed's possessions had seemed, his costumes and jewels, his weapons, horses and *train de vie*, such as Aurélie had known in Algiers, Aïn Mahdi came as a rude awakening.

Besides having the frowning aspect of a fortress, there was that mixture of opulence and decay so typically Arab. It has been said that the desert Arabs possess *'le génie de la destruction'* – an atavistic hatred of permanence, of that which endures, so that the desert always creeps back unchecked to smother what is built, to seep through the cracks, rot woodwork and choke windows and doors. Only the tent survives.

So it was with Aïn Mahdi: decay to the point of destruction was everywhere. Bats flapped in the falling rafters where the lovely painted ceilings had crumbled; doors hung on rusted hinges; rats had chewed the magnificent rugs and teased the stuffing out of the cushions strewn over the dusty floors; while in the courtyards the mammoth cauldrons used to feed the household, the slaves, and ceaseless flow of pilgrims who passed through the *zaouïa* were blackened with rancid grease. Even the *Koubbah* or mausoleum of Si Ahmed's illustrious father was musty and neglected, and the green standards of the Prophet hung in tatters over his tomb. Only the fountains still lisped softly in the arcaded inner courts of the harem, softening its high-walled austerity. (*An Arab wife must see only the sky, and the walls of her house*, is a local saying.) Here Aurélie was conducted in state, and waited, behind its heavily barred doors and windows, to be greeted by her new family, her mother-in-law, the former Sudanese slave-girl, and her fourteen sisters-in-law, daughters of Si Ahmed's father by another wife.

At once, as if invested with some occult faculties, or guided by some strange prescience, this inexperienced girl took control. At once, she began to set both harem and *zaouïa* to rights. First, the Prince's wives and concubines were banished, pensioned off in honourable discharge, to live at El Aghouat, a discreet two days' journey distant. At once, her new family doted on her, the Sudanese mother-in-law and the fourteen sisters-in-law, like the slaves, marvelling as she opened the barred doors of the harem, coming and going as she pleased – and unveiled. The slaves – Dongolo negresses for the most part – scampered to do her bidding and the dignitaries of the *zaouïa* respected this *Roumia* on sight. Only her brother-in-law, Si Bachir, remained hostile, jealously observing her hold not only over Si Ahmed, but the entire complex of Aïn Mahdi. Curiously, when the harem left, Aurélie again showed that intuition or prescience which guided her in her new life. She could not know, at that moment, that she would remain childless, that again and again her hopes for an heir would be dashed. Yet, on her wish, a little boy, Si Ali, the Prince's child by one of the concubines, remained at Aïn Mahdi, to be loved and brought up as her own.

Barren women are soon repudiated or slighted by Arab custom. Yet Aurélie's supremacy was never to be challenged by the Tedjanis. It was Allah's will that Lallah Yamina, as they called her, should come to direct their lives, and it was Allah's will, too, she should be childless. She was a being apart, for both her adoring husband and his people.

At Aïn Mahdi, all Aurélie's French sense of thrift and good management was displayed. Soon, the withered gardens bloomed and household accounts tallied. The mystified slaves were initiated into the uses of a flat iron, and were to be seen laundering Aurélie's complicated underwear, the frilled petticoats, camisoles and drawers that were part of her trousseau, according to Arc-en-Barrois standards. She generally continued to wear European clothes, all buttons, basques and whalebone, for Si Ahmed now showed a marked preference for every manifestation of European living – including champagne, which was in defiance of Koranic vetoes. Though since he was so venerated, the Faithful held that on his lips alcohol became milk, and any signs of excess were attributed to mystic exaltation.

Aurélie had brought with her, along with the flat iron, a number of her accustomed comforts, bed-linen, knives and forks and such, and Si Ahmed no longer ate with his fingers, crouched on rugs, nor slept in the fashion of his people, wherever sleep overtook him, on a divan or the floor, rolled in his burnous or a sheepskin. Bedrooms – rooms set apart for sleeping – were not customary in Arab households. But now he savoured to the full the thrilling novelties his *Roumia* wife introduced. Aurélie had turned one of the tile-dadoed rooms into her bedroom, and installed a double bed of strictly European design. Here, as soon as buttoned into her long-sleeved nightgown, and lying between her smooth linen sheets, she was joined by the enraptured Si Ahmed. Her deliberate emphasis on European ways may have begun by a wish for familiar comforts, but she must soon have realized how much prestige these foreign habits gave her, and so continued them, long after she would have preferred to adapt herself to many local traditions.

Which perhaps explains why, later, she came to make numbers of journeys back to Algiers, there to load up trains of camels with such unlikely objects as grand pianos, crystal chandeliers, billiard tables and whole satin-covered suites of gilt furniture. They breathed splendour and strangeness to the Arab eye: though, like the garish clothes and enormous feathered hats she took to purchasing during her visits, they were much criticized by the French.

She never stayed long away, hurrying back to the desert as to a lovers' rendezvous. She had come to love the spreading Tedjani lands with that fiercely possessive instinct the French peasant shows towards the soil. All, all must come under her hand. Backed by the bemused Si Ahmed she summoned French engineers and agricultural experts. Tracts of waste land were irrigated, wells were sunk, new crops sown and new breeds of sheep imported. Forgotten trades were revived, markets established and commerce encouraged. The Tedjanis thrived. Hygiene and medicine saved many lives, while the mystical attributes with which the Arab invested their Shareef were now extended to his wife. Aurélie's touch, too, was believed to bless, heal and even render fruitful the barren. Together Si Ahmed and Aurélie dispensed their blessings from the *zaouïa*, which had been rescued from the tangled state in which a crooked agent had left it upon his dismissal. Once again Aurélie's sense of management, her tact and good sense triumphed: soon the *zaouïa* prospered, as the land around it flourished. And if, as her detractors were to say, later, she exploited local credulity, accepting, or demanding, valuable presents, tributes of gold and jewels, and even helping herself to the camels, cattle and possessions of the pilgrims in prayer at the *zaouïa*, at least she used these gains for the benefit of Tedjani people and Tedjani territories – *her* lands, *her* people.

Or did she also lay up treasure upon earth for her own use? Did the coffers crammed with gold pieces, precious stones and valuable objects which she flaunted before her astonished French relatives (to whom she was always unaccountably mean) originate in such exploitations? Did she see this accumulation as guarantees against her possible dethronement? Was she ensuring that were she ever to be renounced by Si Ahmed and the Tedjanis, at least she need never be parted from this land of sun, space and solitude which had become her whole life? Giving, giving to it with a lover's largesse was she also taking, taking from it with a lover's greed?

In her life as an integral part of the confraternity, Aurélie came to know much out-of-the-way Arab lore, legends and histories which were stored up by the old women in the harem, or told by the pilgrims or the *harratin* – negro workers on the land. In the early days of their marriage she and the Prince had ridden much about the vast territories together, and returning would often choose a track that led by a giant pistachio tree, where a little spring gushed in the desert. This spot was known as Kourdane, and here they would rest, grateful for the great tree's green shade. Dismissing their suite they would watch the sun sink below the desert's rim, while Si Ahmed recounted the legends and histories of his race, telling of heroes and lovers, of El Borak, the Prophet's miraculous winged horse, or the strange ways of the Moazabites, their neighbours across the black stone wastes of the Chebka in the five Holy Cities of the M'zab. There the curious custom of *Boumerkoude* – 'the child that sleeps in its mother's womb – prevailed. *Boumerkoude* was the absent husband's answer if, on returning from a prolonged absence trading (the Moazabites being famous traders), he found his wife had given birth to a child at a most unsuitable date. But it was always acknowledged as his own: he had sown the seed before leaving – two years, three years earlier, it made no difference – the child had simply not chosen to emerge. It had lain sleeping in its mother's womb. . . .' The dashing Chaamba tribesmen found this a most convenient doctrine when they rode into one or other of the Holy Cities, and were welcomed by the stay-at-home wives. Nevertheless, to the instinctively jealous Arab man elsewhere, *Boumerkoude* was heresy, and they despised the Moazabites accordingly.

These and many more strange tales Si Ahmed tells as he and Aurélie, this oddly matched couple, sit beneath the great pistachio tree of Kourdane. He, the majestic Shareef in his flowing robes, the *tespeyh* or string of prayer-beads clicking through his fingers as he spins his tales, and Aurélie hanging on his words, her stay-bones creaking in the heat, her china-doll complexion shaded, even under the tree, by a frivolous little parasol straight from Paris. Si Ahmed speaks in Arabic, for his wife has rapidly become proficient in the language of her new life. A fierce sun is declining fast, dipping behind the lilac haze of the western horizon, and now Si Ahmed is telling of the wonderful Tree of Paradise, which is tended by angels and has as many leaves as the sands of the desert, and on each leaf, a man's name is inscribed. In the middle of the month of Shaaban, at sunset, the Tree of Paradise quivers, and the leaves of all who are to die during the year fall to the ground. . . . A shadow falls across their bower, and Aurélie shivers. What if her husband were to die, and she be forced to leave Aïn Mahdi? Now Si Ahmed is recounting the ways of djinns and of their magics, of great consequence in this part of the world. Djinns are believed to be composed of a vapour: they fill the air around us and brush past us, though we are seldom aware of their touch. They must be humoured, for they can be vengeful, though also useful, when invoked to further some nefarious practice. They should always be offered small gifts, *ma' ruf*, a coin, or a dish of salt and ashes, which is their couscous. . . .

I remember a Targui, one of the blue-veiled men from the Hoggar, warning me that djinns are most likely to be about during the hottest part of the day, *el gaïla*, that hour when the noon day mirage shimmers across the desert and the sun seethes in a cruel white haze. Then the djinns and their female counterparts, the djinniyats, are abroad, seeking mischief. It was in Ouargla, at that very hour of *el gaïla*, that my Targui volunteered this information, speaking French in a curiously soft, sing-song way; and I remember how, abruptly, I was aware of a creeping sense of malevolence overcoming the brilliant day. But then some underlying vein of sinistry is always to be sensed in the desert, however beatific it may appear. Perhaps this is part of its spell.

Aurélie Piccard has never been truly assessed, I think, and remains an enigmatic, contradictory legend. She can only be interpreted according to the viewpoint of her interpreter, as I must present her, here. True or false – who now knows? As time passed, it seems that the romantic image of her beginnings, the charming young French girl, bride of the mighty Arab Prince, adored by the fanatic Tedjani confraternity and revered as holy by the peoples of the Sahara, gave place to a dominant, matriarchal figure, *la Princesse des Sables*. That inborn secretiveness and ambition which was hers from the beginning had crystallized, and in the process changed the image. She grew colder, tighter-lipped, more distant with those around her, and took to commanding the slaves' whip in hand, sometimes laying about her vigorously. 'I must be respected' was her only reply when reproved by her French family. While mar-velling at her achievements, they grew critical of her arrogance and avarice. Her mother was left to scrape along on a widow's pension, though no expenditure, no efforts were too great for Aïn Mahdi and the Tedjanis.

She is said to have been beautiful when young, in a sharp-featured French way. The only photograph I have been able to trace is not pre-possessing: it shows her in her late thirties, a full-blown woman, tight-lipped and tight-laced, tricked out in Oriental costume, beads, jewels, a fan, and bouffant Turkish trousers from which emerge solid white cotton stockings sagging slightly, encircled by ankle bracelets. But she gazes out complacently, very sure of herself. A forty-inch waist and cotton stockings do not trouble such a woman. Her slightly aquiline nose is haughty, her eyes seem to dart triumph. She is *la Princesse des Sables*, her powers extending even to the lunar landscape of the Hoggar. In everything she stands beside her husband, the mighty Shareef, guiding, controlling, *possessing*; living an inner life of love where no one else can follow.

This state of affairs was made easier for her by Si Ahmed's nature, for he was an indolent voluptuary: nevertheless he always upheld his religious responsibilities, as he kept to those promises he had made, so long ago, to Cardinal Lavigerie. There was never any question of his taking another wife, or of Aurélie's supremacy being challenged. Both were united in their care of the *zaouïa* and Tedjani affairs, as they were in giving support and hospitality to all those travellers, French administrators, military or civil, who came through Aïn Mahdi, some heading for the dangerous, unpacified regions of the central Sahara. This aid came to be acknowledged and sought repeatedly by the French authorities, and the administrative archives of Algiers at that time, both civil and military, are specific in their accounts of Tedjani cooperation and the Prince's support in various projects for the building of schools, and his gift of land to the Pères Blancs for a foundation of their order. Above all, the archives tell of the powers wielded by Aurélie, and in particular, her amicable relations with the intractable Tuareg chiefs. These blue-veiled warriors who, in 1881, were to annihilate the Flatters Mission in such terrible circumstances, always showed an especial regard for Aurélie, arriving from their remote fastnesses on their gigantic racing white camels, bringing lavish gifts and promises of goodwill, not always to be relied on, however. The Flatters massacre, it is believed, might have been avoided if the Mission (a military expedition to establish trading concessions) had not set off with such impetuous haste. Although they were accompanied by a Tedjani interpreter, they had neglected to obtain from Aurélie the letters of safe-conduct she was ready to address to a certain Targui chief upon whose protection they could have relied, against the treacheries which awaited them.

Thus the years of love, power and achievement passed for Aurélie, living her Saharan idyll and absorbed by her fierce ambitions; she scarcely noticed the decline of the Prince's affections; concubines came and went, but would things have been so very different had she married a European? Although Si Bachir fostered his brother's infidelities, Aurélie did not appear greatly disturbed. She had become used to Si Bachir's animosity, and shrugged off the menace of other women: she was secure in the knowledge that Si Ahmed's concubines could never come between herself and the land she loved so passionately. Other women might dally in the *alcôve*, but they could never usurp the key position she had won at the *zaouïa*. Nor could they ever weaken the hold she exercised over her husband; he was both contented and proud to leave all in her hands, and grateful for the material benefits of her administration.

Nevertheless it was about this time that she decided to establish herself outside the intrigues of Aïn Mahdi. In 1883, reckoning also on Si Ahmed's weakness for Western comforts and ostentation, she set about building a sumptuous new domain some seven miles distant, at Kourdane, where the great pistachio tree grew beside the little spring. It held so many memories of her early life with Si Ahmed, and was, for her, the heart and symbol of that desert she adored.

Kourdane, begun in 1883, grew rapidly, for Aurélie was impatient to see this Pavilion of her Heart take shape. She drew up the plans, was architect, mason, engineer and agricultural expert, overseeing every detail of local workmanship. An immense white-walled domed building rose from the sands, Arab in concept, though certain concessions to European living were found in the suites of guest-rooms and the kitchens. Balustraded terraces gave on to vistas of garden and orchard, where roses and jasmine scented the air, and fruit trees of a strain imported from France throve in this alien soil. There were great store-rooms, outhouses, a flour mill, and stabling for a hundred Arab thoroughbreds, besides quarters for fifty camels and donkeys. The house servants numbered sixty-six, and the grooms, gardeners and farm workers were without number. Kourdane was at once a prince's palace, rural retreat and an agricultural experiment. All the Saharan chiefs came there on visits of ceremony and curiosity; so did the French: Generals, Governor-Generals, députés, journalists, explorers, all found their way to Kourdane, to be received with princely hospitality, often finding their hostess in the gardens, seated beneath an enormous and elaborate tent, a ceremonial affair of red leather twenty metres in diameter, entirely lined with velvet, which had been presented to her by some of the Tuareg nobles.

One visitor describes being welcomed most graciously by Aurélie, who was wearing a *'toilette de réception'* of peacock-blue plush and hung with superb jewellery. She led them upstairs to meet her husband, an obese, panting personage, very amiable to his guests; and dressed, in contrast to his wife, very simply, in a shrimp-pink *gandourah*, his white muslin headscarves bound by the customary camel-hair cords.

He received them in a vast salon, its floor entirely covered by a gigantic Persian carpet of great value. The tall windows were lavishly draped in silk curtains. A sofa upholstered in black velvet, gold-embroidered with Arabic inscriptions, was the centre piece; above, a bronze and crystal chandelier 'such as one finds in churches' hung from the vaulted ceiling, while all around, the walls displayed a marvellous collection of arms, jewelled or damascened, of Arabic and Turkish origin. There was a great deal of pearl-inlaid furniture typical of Damascus, which, with gilt mirrors, are to be found in every Arab interior of consequence. But the proximity of a whole suite of carved French chairs, *style Henri II*, ranged stiffly round the walls, must have looked hideous and, like a large piano draped in embroidered silks, quite incongruous. But then, for all her force and vision, Aurélie was clearly lacking in taste. She had achieved splendour, which had been her goal from the start. The private apartments, which were never seen, were probably more inclined to the Arab style since they had no function to amaze.

The dining-room is described as being rather simpler, with tables and chairs, *à l'européen*, to suit European visitors and doubtless to intrigue Arab guests. A large portrait of the then French president was probably hung there for the same purpose. The prodigious banquet which was served started off with a French menu of eight courses, and was followed by an Arab feast of six courses: not one dish from either could be refused, according to Arab protocol: besides, the guests were solicitously watched by both host and hostess.

Soon Kourdane became not only a country house for Aurélie and her husband, where they reposed or received guests, but a continuation of the *zaouïa*, for wherever the Shareef lives automatically becomes holy, a lieu of pilgrimage where every newcomer must be lodged and fed. A family of nomads might plod five hundred kilometres of desert to receive the *baraka*, or blessing, of either Si Ahmed or Aurélie, be lodged at their expense, fed couscous in abundance and bring, as the customary offering, only a donkey-load of desert firewood. Or, in reverse, a group of pilgrims might offer a whole flock of sheep, which Aurélie would brand as hers, and in return she would give them a handful of seeds from her gardens, but which, coming from Kourdane, were deemed to have supernatural virtues.

There was only one shadow over this golden scene. Si Ali, the Shareef's heir, had turned out badly. He was irresolute, lazy and drank. Aurélie and her husband feared for the *zaouïa* and all their life's work when he should inherit the shareefan title, though such an eventuality seemed a long way off.

But in 1887 the Tree of Paradise shivered and Si Ahmed's leaf fell. While on a visit to the Tedjani *zaouïas* of Tunis, he died, unexpectedly, of blood poisoning. Poisoning, *tout court* some said, and Aurélie believed. His death was a profound shock to her, for they had been together through many marvellous years, and he was not yet fifty. Moreover, since he had died away from Aïn Mahdi, his body, by custom, must remain where he died, thus transferring all the shareefan glory and substance of Aïn Mahdi to follow his body. Aurélie battled with the authorities to have this changed, and being a European wife – the only wife, rather than one of a sheep-like harem – her efforts at last prevailed. Si Ahmed's body was brought back to Kourdane where, in the gardens he had loved, she built a simple and beautiful red marble *koubbah* as his monument: though the splendours of Kourdane and the well-being of the confraternity were a more fitting one – even though they had been, in fact, the work of his wife.

Now Aurélie had no more part to play in Tedjani affairs, and found, too, that her days at Kourdane were numbered, since Si Bachir, succeeding to his brother's title, was determined on her departure. She had imagined that Kourdane, her own creation, would remain hers. Not so. Aurélie had no more part to play in Tedjani affairs, and Si Bachir, the sickly, the malefic, determined on her banishment, not only from Aïn Mahdi but from Kourdane too. Aurélie now faced parting both from her life's work and the Pavilion of her heart. As withdrawn in grief as in joy, she retreated to Algiers. Even in this, the most bitter moment of her life, she was dry-eyed. Perhaps she remembered the Arab saying that all is Allah's will – that no tears must be shed at whatever Allah ordains, lest the tears form a river, dividing, forever, the mourner from that which he mourns. In Algiers, in a modest villa and bored by French bourgeois life, she brooded, bitter in the loss of all she held dear. To the French she had become *la veuve Tedjani*, of no more account now she had no more power. But was she of no more consequence?

Yet again, for the third time, we see Fate step in to change her fortune overnight. For some while, she had been tormented by hearing, from passing Tedjanis, of the disorder and decay to which Si Bachir's indifference and ineffectual rule had reduced both Aïn Mahdi and Kourdane the beloved. Gradually the Tedjanis, and even Si Bachir, began to realize that Aurélie's presence was vital to their prosperity: at the same moment, the French administration were becoming uneasy at a growing turbulence and lack of cooperation among the tribes of the southern territories. Such things had not been so marked during *la veuve Tedjani's* days of influence.

They hit on a most ingenious plan, and proposed that Aurélie should contract a marriage with Si Bachir, thus returning to Aïn Mahdi to be once more officially associated with the *zaouïa* and all its politics. In spite of their dislike of each other both Aurélie and Si Bachir consented to this arrangement, for it was to their mutual benefit. The marriage took place before the Caïd of El Aghouat, Aurélie now taking a particular pleasure in declining the civil marriage which, at last, after many years, the French authorities pressed on her.

Her return to Aïn Mahdi was triumphant, amid scenes of touching devotion from the Tedjanis. Having become, once more, wife of the ruling Shareef, she could resume her life's work. She and Si Bachir had agreed to go their separate ways, he to follow the old idling pattern, she to order and restore the Tedjani affairs. Kourdane, she decided, should be her headquarters, and with a lover's impatience she set out once more to cross the arid track that lay between her and her adored. The lover's rendezvous once more. But *Ouribet, Khouribet*! says the Arab proverb: *all that is of the desert returns to it.* So it was with Kourdane. Even in so short a while, the beautiful gardens were destroyed and the house become a tarnished mockery of its former glory. However, Aurélie was an undaunted energetic fifty. With a lover's devotion she set about restoring it, and soon it was as before; but now, all hers, doubly precious for the time of separation she had suffered.

For twelve more years Aurélie lived her Saharan love affair with Kourdane, and the marvellous desert from which it had grown. She sought no other company, though she still received in style: only now she no longer ate with her guests, joining them for coffee but taking her meals in her own rooms where, overlooking the desert's sweep, she was tête-à-tête with her love. She rarely tore herself away from Kourdane, even to order the affairs of Aïn Mahdi. Time was running out, and every day, every hour at Kourdane was precious to her. Every sunset and sunrise there, each flower or fruit it bore, like the rustle of the palms, the cooing of the doves, the song of the slaves or the starlight silvering the white walls and domes, or spangling through the leaves of the great pistachio tree, were part of this marvellous love affair she still lived to the full.

When Si Bachir died in 1911 Aurélie was sixty-two, and now, at last, knew that her life of love was ended, for Si Bachir's malice reached out from the grave. He had left her nothing – not even a life interest in Kourdane, which thus became Tedjani property, automatically inherited by the new heir, her stepson, the good-for-nothing Si Ali. He, too, was jealous of her powerful presence, and although generously disposed in material matters, demanded her departure from Kourdane. She was thunder-struck. When he suggested she should take with her anything she chose, her fury was uncontrolled. All was hers by right, she claimed: but all she wanted was Kourdane itself. She refused to leave. At last, implacably, Si Ali had her ejected by law. After her departure for Algiers it was found that she had razed the place. Rugs, silver, linen, furniture, bric-à-brac, the bronze chandeliers, the pearl furniture and the grand piano were all piled into wagons and trundled away. When asked to render the accounts of the *zaouïa* she refused, and for three years remained in obstinate silence, lodged in a small house into which were crammed the glories of Kourdane. Until a few years ago, there were people living in Algiers who remembered the little house and the extra-ordinary woman, and how, on the rare occasions when someone from the desert arrived, she would spread her superb carpets to overflow the tiny garden, send for dancers and musicians and prepare a feast, a *diffa*, to recall the splendours of Kourdane's hospitality.

Three years of this aimless existence dragged by, and once more, for the fourth and last time, Fate stepped in, to bring her once again to that glowing scene which was her destiny. And once again, as in the beginning, chance was heralded by gunfire.

In 1914 France was again in desperate straits, and when the Germans began fostering revolts in North Africa, the French remembered Lallah Yamina, *Princesse des Sables*. They sent for her and begged her to return to Aïn Mahdi, there to work for French interests among the tribes. Thus for six more years the sun shone on her: a sinking sun, but it warmed her through. Si Ali had become a reformed, if timid Shareef, and, all the old spites forgotten, welcomed her return to Aïn Mahdi. Thus, yet again, the *Princesse des Sables* reigned, to the benefit of the

Tedjanis, the furtherance of French interests, and the destruction of German influences. But with the armistice, Aurélie, at seventy-two, felt her Saharan life must finish. Her wartime efforts had exhausted her, the climate began to try her, and even Kourdane seemed too demanding. On her own initiative, she retreated – to Arc-en-Barrois: to go home, she said, though her home could never now be in that northern province. She had seized the chance to leave it and had never returned in all the years that had passed. She could not reconcile herself to Europe, either the people, their ways, or their petulant skies. Her money and possessions had long vanished. She was very poor nor was she made to feel welcome among her relatives. She fretted for Kourdane. She was over eighty now, but her love remained as strong as ever, Kourdane, the Sahara . . . it was all she craved, all that she had lost, had abandoned. . . .

In 1933, in a surge of the old temerity and resolve, she returned to Algeria. Unannounced, she arrived at Aïn Mahdi, having made the journey in a rackety tourist bus, she who had first made it at the head of that extravagant marriage cortège. She was an impoverished spectre, sitting there among the tourists, an old old woman, but still a woman in love. At Aïn Mahdi she asked to be allowed to return to Kourdane, and the Tedjanis agreed. Kourdane was of little account to the Confraternity, now.

Ouribet, Khouribet! Once more the Sahara had reclaimed its own. Kourdane stood, a lonely ruin, in the fertile wastes that had been her pride: lizards flicked across the parched fountains, emaciated sheep cropped weeds where once her roses had bloomed; the wells had dried up, the fields lay unploughed, sanded over, dotted by the black tents of the nomads. The desert had crept up, smothering all. *That which is Arab becomes ruin.* Aurélie wept the only tears anyone had ever seen her shed, and turned away. The Tedjanis took her to the Sœurs Blanches at El Aghouat. There, in a small room containing an iron bed, an old armchair and a statue of the Virgin Mary, she lay silently. Sometimes she whispered, in Arabic, seeming to relive those wonderful, audacious days of her Saharan beginnings. The Tedjanis and the Shareef's family came often to see her, all solicitude: the French priest visited her constantly, observing that a worn Bible at her bedside was inscribed with her name and the date of her childhood in Arc-en-Barrois. It had been beside her all these years, testimony to her unchanging faith. She was failing fast, now, and received the Sacraments, although the Sisters did not think the end was near. Next day she asked to be taken back to Kourdane. It was a long and terrible route, and the doctor forbade her being moved, but she would not be dissuaded.

'Kourdane – I can only die happy there,' they heard her whisper. The Tedjanis carried her across the desert she had loved to the ruined domain that was still the Pavilion of her heart. Twenty-four hours later she was dead. She had wished to be buried there, in a Moslem tomb, beside Si Ahmed, and all the fanaticism of the Tedjanis now rose round her coffin. They claimed she had been, at the end, converted to Islam, though this the French disputed hotly, citing her receiving of the Sacraments and her treasured Bible. It was well known she had never adopted her husband's religion, however much she had become one with the Confraternity. Therefore, said the French, she must have a Christian burial in the Catholic cemetery at Laghouat. Such arguments seem trivial in view of her expressed wish to lie at Kourdane. Yet the wrangling continued, Faith against Faith. Belatedly the French government accorded her the honours they had not bestowed during her lifetime, naming her Chevalier de la Légion d'Honneur and many more high-sounding titles. As 'the first French woman of the Sahara' they gave her, beside their usual *pompe funèbre*, a funeral with full military honours, her coffin draped with the *tricolore* and a salvo of guns to echo across the sands.

But the Arabs designated her a Maraboute, a Moslem saint, and buried her beside Si Ahmed, under the green vaults of the pistachio tree, surrounded by the desert she had loved more than any man. The Sahara had reclaimed its own.

6
Béja
Portugal

ONASTERIES, CONVENTS, cloisters and nuns' cells do not at first sight evoke terrestrial passions: yet many forbidden loves have flourished there, so that certain cells have certainly a place here. That of the Portuguese Nun at Béja has passed into legend, for there Soror Marianna Alcoforado lived her brief and burning loving with the French Chevalier, and her cell remains, as it were, consecrated to 'the midnight's kind admittance' and those five, now celebrated, perfervid letters she wrote her lover after he had left her forever in 1667. These letters amazed and mystified the Parisian *beau monde* (Madame de Sévigné and Saint-Simon among them), when they were discovered and published anonymously in 1669. Two centuries later, they were to inspire Elizabeth Barrett Browning's *Sonnets from the Portuguese*, as well as a great deal more speculation and admiration moving characters as dissimilar as Stendhal and Mr Gladstone, for they remain the perfect expression of love, anguish and pity flowering from an improbable setting.

Improbable? I wonder. It seems that by the very nature of contradiction such severe surroundings combined with the aura of stealth and eternal damnation prove particularly stimulating. The Marquis de Sade, snatching his sister-in-law from behind a convent grille; Louise de la Vallière, fleeing the Royal flesh and seeking perpetual penitence in her cell, but there still palpitating with a now unholy passion. Likewise, Héloïse in her convent and Abelard in his monastery; *Les Grandes Repenties* as the French call them, with relish. Something of this particular relish appears to actuate the steady flow of visitors who head out of Lisbon making for Béja and the Convent of Nossa Senhora da Conceição, where, having duly admired the radiant *azulejos*, the blue tiling so typical of Portuguese architecture, both domestic and ecclesiastical, they demand to be led to that cell where Soror Marianna once lay in love with the dashing Marquis de Chamilly.

The fatal cell, their presumed meeting place, is singularly unevocative, though at the window there remains an almost frivolous grille, fan-shaped, quite ineffectual as a guard, and evoking coquetries rather than restrictions. Within, dank stone walls and a bench are all that remain. Nor could it have ever contained much more: a narrow pallet bed, a wooden table and chair, a crucifix, perhaps some books of a pious nature, and a jugful of flowers. Nothing else.

But such austerity surely heightened their ardours. And to Chamilly, the adventure of it all must have been irresistibly stimulating. He was an experienced thirty to her virgin six and twenty: moreover, he was already accustomed to, if not satiated by, the luxuries and easy conquests of Paris. For him, it was, although spiced with danger, *le repos du guerrier*. For her, an overwhelming tide which swept her out of her depth, to drown alternately in waves of anguish or joy. And when he slid the bracelets – the only gift he dared to give her – to be concealed beneath the wide sleeves of her habit, she was unresisting, quite defenceless against her fate.

He had come riding into Béja beside her brother, Balthazar, a local gentleman, heading a regiment of French troops dispatched to Portugal by Louis xiv to oppose Spanish aggression. Between campaigns they had reached Béja, there to enjoy such distractions as the garrison town could provide: visits to the neighbouring gentry, the wine shops and the bordello. It was a small, dull, provincial hole, set in an austere, sun-baked landscape, with little of the architectural fantasy and stone carvings of twined ropes, bellying sails, pineapples and coral, which are typical of the exuberant Manueline style found elsewhere in Portugal, decorations which evoke the nation's voyages of exploration or conquest. But even in such austerity as the province and the white-walled Convent represented, a certain voluptuous tempo must have prevailed; the music of those sighing *saudade* or *fados* must have been borne on the night air, wafting throught the grilles to cast their spell.

Chamilly was presented to Soror Marianna by her brother, who went to visit her at the Convent. This was quite in order, since rulings were considerably relaxed for such as she; noble young ladies were often placed in religious institutions by their families, less as novices then pensionnaires, living there in piety and propriety, but without the more rigorous impositions, until they had taken their final vows. It was a convenient manner of settling unmarried or unwanted daughters, and much in fashion about Europe and Latin America too. Though there, among the guava fruits, the parakeets and monkeys, and the tropic exuberance of nature, man, in the shape of Spanish architects and prelates, had contrived an ecclesiastical architecture as lavish and intricate as the surrounding country. As to the religious observances, penances, impositions and abuses of sequestration, these reached refinements of cruelty and theatricality which could only have derived from a race which produced the *auto-da-fé* and the bullring.

In Portugal, a milder tempo prevailed in both man and land, and although the Convent imposed numbers of pious observances and long hours of religious instruction, fastings and confessions, by which it was held a novice would be led, eventually, to take the veil, it was a tempered severity. Soror Marianna had reached this intermediary stage of faith when Chamilly appeared in the Convent parlour beside her brother. This was before the reforms of Port Royal, and an indulgent abbess would often invite the local gentry, men as well as women, to visit her young charges. Thus Chamilly's appearance there, under the Mother Superior's eye, squinting benignly through the heavy grille, was of neither romantic implication or consequence. Or so it seemed.

But Soror Marianna had already caught sight of the handsome soldier from the Convent terrace, where, among a group of nuns, she had watched the troops riding into town. She had noted his careless swagger, his masculinity. '*Whoever loved that loved not at first sight?*' She saw him, and was lost. Did he glance up, then, and observe the pale, dark-eyed figure in the enveloping habit, and single her out from the rest? There are no known portraits of Soror Marianna, but she is said to have been beautiful. Probably she resembled that legion of young French nuns painted by Philippe de Champaigne, sallow or waxen complexioned creatures with melting dark eyes and a submissive countenance which promises infinite compliance. Their eyes roll gently heavenwards as if, in voluptuous ecstasy, they cast themselves, body and soul, upon their Maker.

Soror Marianna was to cast herself, with equal ecstasy, upon her undoing.

How her lover (for so the Chevalier de Chamilly became, after she had held him off for a year) obtained access to her we do not know. Some say it was easier, less likely to risk detection, to climb to the window of her cell, than to brave the corridor and stairway leading to the rooms in which her father had installed her, along with her little sister Peregrina, then a child of five. In placing both his daughters in the Convent Francisco da Costa Alcoforado planned to avoid the likelihood of their marrying, for this would have cost him their *dots*, thus reducing the patrimony reserved for his sons. He was not a rich man, and so the sisters were sacrificed to the interests of their brothers. And in a Latin society, this was considered perfectly reasonable.

'Vous ne trouviez jamais tant d'amour – et tout le reste n'est rien' (and all the rest is nothing) she was to write, when he had abandoned her, riding out of her life without warning, as he had ridden into it. Yet what else could he do, commanded by his king to the wars, and perhaps even recalled at the instigation of the Alcoforado family who had discovered the situation and were fearful of scandal? In 1667 he moved on, with his troops, and the secret of Soror Marianna. This he kept to the end of his life, and though conjecture raged round him after the publication of the letters, he never told her name, which was not discovered for many years.

Chamilly has been criticized for allowing the letters to fall into other hands: it seems certain that he himself had nothing to do with their publication. He was away at the wars for many months, returning too late to forbid publication and found it more discreet to keep aloof. Like many men before and after him, he had probably boasted of his conquest among his intimates and been cad enough to read some passages aloud. Somehow they fell into other hands and perhaps a friend, Monsieur Guilleragues, borrowed them to read at leisure and before returning them, sensing their quality, made a copy. Later it was Guilleragues who is supposed to have translated them from the Portuguese into French and, in 1669, launched them on that fashionable and intellectual Paris which was gathered around Mme de Sévigné, whose own letters to her daughter, though in other terms, expressed as overwhelming a passion. Speculation raged around the Portuguese nun's outpourings. Who had written them – who received them? Pamphleteers penned a series of replies; some people said they were fabricated, others that they were written by a man (and they certainly express the total devotion every man would like to inspire). Chamilly's sojourn in Portugal was recalled and although he was named, he still remained silent. No one knows what became of the original letters. The printed ones were read and reread over the centuries and may be said to have had a considerable effect on nineteenth-century Romantic literature.

As to Chamilly, he presently married comfortably, a plain, rich woman who also loved him deeply. In recognition of his military achievements he was created a Maréchal of France and prospered exceedingly. He seems to have given no more thought to the adventure of Béja.

For Soror Marianna, all life as she had come to know it, through him, was now at an end. She prayed for death, but she was to live on, for fifty years of repentance and abnegation – another of the *Grandes Repenties*. As Sister Portress of the Convent she was held in affection and esteem by the rest of the Sisters, who, it seems, were mostly unaware of the origins of her protracted penitences.

She is but one example of the extremes of romance and repentance sometimes found hidden behind those walls I count among my Pavilions.

7

Sultan
Murad's
Room

Turkey

T HE PLURALITY implicit in a harem, seraglio, *zenana* or *anderoun*
removes it, in general, from being ranked as a Pavilion of the heart.
It is, as I remarked earlier, rather a Pavilion of the senses, while
its furnishings reflect its Oriental setting and are generally little more
than bedding. The Khan of Kohkand, in his turquoise palace in the Fer-
ghana, beyond Bokhara, cannot have had much time for the pursuit of
true love, for it is said there were three thousand or more concubines
chattering, parakeet-shrill about the roof-top terraces which overlooked
the wastes of Central Asia. Here man's life was composed of hunting
sorties or battle. Like many other oriental overlords, the Khan probably
regarded his harem in the light of an oasis – somewhere he found refresh-
ment (though scarcely rest) after the violent tempo of these territories.

Yet, on occasions, polygamy gave place to some overwhelming single
love such as that of the Tartar Khan Sahin Ghirei, one of that exotic
band, the Krim (or Crimean) Khans, who descended from the Mongol
hordes. His love is said to have been a Polish noblewoman, Marie

Potocka, captured in a raid; though she is also said to have been a Georgian slave in his harem, one Deliareh Bekhé, before becoming his adored and only wife. She was in any case a Christian, who displayed the most inflexible religious scruples which quite blighted the bliss she might have shared with her Moslem adorer. When she died, pining away as if in condemnation of her apostasy – or marrying outside her Faith – he was inconsolable, building a noble octagonal marble mausoleum to commemorate his love. And here, beside her tomb, unmoved by the blandishments of any other woman, he mourned the years away, monogamous in grief as in joy.

But his love is better remembered by a fountain – that celebrated Fountain of Tears which he also erected in her memory. It is still to be seen, set among the overgrown cypress trees and now rather neglected rose gardens where once they wandered together. The melancholy of this romantic scene inspired one of Pushkin's loveliest poems, *The Fountain of Baktchiserai.*

Deathless loves have a way of producing splendid memorials.

After such elegaic sorrows it is positively tonic turning to the recusant sensuality which prevailed, generally, in the Vieux Sérail or Seraglio, Top Kapou Serai to the Turks, fortress and domain of the Ottoman Sultans from the sixteenth century until the fall of their dynasty in 1918. The Seraglio (an Italianate derivation of the eastern sérail, or palace) has always been surrounded by legends of terror and debauch, which, sometimes exaggerated, were based on truth. Thus it might be wondered why I should choose it for one of my subjects.

Because of one room, that of Sultan Murad III.

Among all the beautiful, sinister or dramatic settings within the complex of the Seraglio, the divans, kiosks, places for strange doings, inner courts and corridors such as that one where 'the Djinns hold Consultation', or that 'Golden Road' down which each new odalisque was ceremonially led to the Imperial couch, it is still Sultan Murad's room which remains the heart of the honeycomb. It has been said to be the loveliest room in all the world, and is the perfect setting for lovers' meetings, romantic beyond measure. Even in its present deserted state it retains some overwhelming quality of emotion, as if the shades of Sultan Murad and his Italian Kadine still lingered there, 'emparadised in one another's arms'. It is the archetype of all my Pavilions, and I shall describe it and tell of the lovers it housed later. First, something about the Seraglio as a whole, since through many centuries, to the world outside, its name alone epitomized some fabulous enclave, all love and all desire. Desire, yes, but love less often. With rare exceptions the lives of its inhabitants were conducted in a cynically business-like manner, while that of the concubines might, except for the initial circumstances of their being there at all, have been compared to the inmates of a rigidly run boarding-school.

The Palace of Top Kapou was finally abandoned as an Imperial residence in 1853 when Sultan Abdul Medjed transferred his harem and court to other less historic and rather less haunted retreats along the Bosphorus. Since then no Sultan has lived within the Seraglio: but it has remained inviolate, still steeped in mystery, and there, until the rise of the Turkish Republic, a few raddled old eunuchs and some elderly ladies, last remnants of former Imperial harems elsewhere, lingered on among the decaying splendours. Nothing was repaired, rats scuttled, and broken window panes were stuffed with tattered silk against the icy winds which lashed round in winter. There these forgotten derelicts continued, living in the past, in the manner of inmates in some poorly-endowed alms-house, until at last they were removed – 'liberated', in official parlance – and found themselves thrust out into a world they had never known and could not now comprehend. With their departure most of the Seraglio was set in order as a museum, its treasures classified, its principal buildings restored and its history recounted in guide books designed for the visitors who now invaded it in strength.

Only the Harem remained apart, unseen by the majority, a palace within a palace, core of the complex and object of the liveliest curiosity to every frustrated tourist. But as I have had the rare privilege of wandering about it freely over a number of years, I came to know something of its secrets. This intricate and awesome interior has, as might be expected, an obsessive quality. There a strange hush falls – not only the silence of an abandoned building, but some brooding apprehensive stillness reigns. The revenants are at home here, in these halls of yesterday.

Harem – or, more correctly, *haremlik* – signifies the women's quarters, from the Arabic *haram* – forbidden, or sanctuary – the men's quarters being known as the *selamlik* – a place of meeting, from *salam*, a greeting. Thus the Harem of the Seraglio was sacrosanct, inviolate, and, in a sense, remained so until lately, though no curators or directors of the museum should be blamed for having withheld this section from the general public for so long. How could they do otherwise? How hasten the laborious and delicate process of restoration when all was dangerously dilapidated, and every door, cupboard, or attic was a significant part of the whole?

You cannot put a whole rambling warren behind glass. A single careless cigarette stub could kindle the bleached wooden kiosks and frescoed passages of Osman III. One spark could destroy the gilded splendours of the Sultane Validé's apartments, where gilded rococo intricacies (decoration, if you admire them, trimming if you do not) are imposed on the flower of medieval Ottoman faïences. Thus the authorities had no other choice but to set this most marvellous of national treasures apart for so long. And lingering there, within this last bastion of mystery, I used to rejoice selfishly.

When almost all the historic mansions of England, like the châteaux of France, are thrown open, when the great palaces of Vienna or Venice are often turned consulates or government offices, when we can enter the last Tzarina's rather suburban, but ikon-studded bedroom at Tzarskoe Selo, left intact as an awful warning against superstition and autocracy, it was particularly enthralling to know that one fastness remained round which to build every romantic flight of fancy. Although no imaginings could exceed the mysterious atmosphere which is the *haremlik's* own.

The Seraglio has always been surrounded by misconceptions as well as mystery. But besides its sultry reputation there were other aspects of intellectual and mystic austerity which would confound those whose notions were based on whispered Levantine gossip or on a performance of the ballet *Scheherazade*, where eunuchs, slaves and Sultan alike conduct themselves with an impetuosity quite alien to the rigid canons of etiquette which, in fact, prevailed. Moreover, it is often overlooked that within the Seraglio there existed, and still does, one of the most sacred shrines of all Islam. This is the Pavilion of the Mantle, *Khirqa i Sherif* (curiously placed between the Baghdad Kiosk, representing the flesh, and the Kefés, or prison cage, representing the devil). The *Khirqa i Sherif* contains the Prophet's Mantle, three hairs from his beard, his footprint on a stone, and one tooth, lost in the battle of Bedr. Each Sultan was by tradition their guardian, and venerated accordingly throughout the entire Moslem world, and his guardianship was believed to be proof of his divine mission on earth.

The Ottoman court was celebrated not only for its extravagance, but for its culture, the Sultans having a long tradition as patrons of the arts, both within and without their palaces. They endowed mosques, hospitals and public buildings, employing the finest talents of their age. Gentile Bellini was among the painters at one time resident at the court of

Mohammed II. It was this enlightened Sultan who founded the celebrated Seraglio School, designed to educate, with extremely high standards, those boys levied by tribute, seized in wars, or, as some young princes, taken as hostages, but invariably Christian children. They were educated to become Royal pages or to hold high office. The Chief White Eunuch was in charge of all educational questions here, while his sable counterpart, the Chief Black Eunuch, in charge of the women of the Harem, was responsible for such education as they received: though this was generally rather superficial, concentrating more on the finer shades of pleasing.

Besides the institution of the state school, the Seraglio housed numbers of master-craftsmen. By custom every Sultan acquired a trade. Some were carpenters, some goldsmiths, some calligraphers, the Turks being acknowledged masters of this art, who perfected their skill on the parchment firmans or Imperial decrees, on those sweeping arabesques which form themselves into the name of Allah, or on the *tughra*, Imperial Seal or sign of each ruler.

Everything within the Seraglio bears evidence of those standards of perfection which successive rulers enjoined. Here, when a coffee cup is chunked from a single emerald, it is not vulgar, for the quality of its setting, the delicate gold workmanship of the *finjan*, or casing which holds the cup, whether this is of porcelain or a precious metal, makes the whole a work of art. A solid silver cradle, buttoned in rubies, is not ostentatious here: harmony prevails over everything, design, colour, form. . . . Door-locks and bolts – so vital a part of the *haremlik* – are superb examples of the metalsmith's craft, bronze, damascened with gold or silver; bolsters are tasselled with strings of pearls, hangings marvellously worked in gold thread; velvets are blistered with precious stones, while the sumptuous silks from Broussa, like the Iznik tiles and the carpets of Ghiordes, Melés or Bergamo, are the perfect flowering of Turkish artistry.

Every extravagance was controlled, not only by strict canons of taste, but by etiquette and protocol. This applied to the manner in which a person lived, dressed, or was killed. Erring women were sewn into weighted sacks and drowned off Seraglio Point, this operation being ritually performed by the *bostanji* – gardener-boatmen – in the presence of the Black Eunuchs who supervised the women in death as in life. Those dignitaries whom the Padishah had decided to liquidate were also removed in style, their doom being announced to them by the arrival of the deaf-mutes, presenting the ritualistic bow-string for strangulation. In the case of princes, a silken one was decreed. Deaf-mutes were always employed about the Seraglio, carrying messages, running errands; they were a particularly useful lot, for in theory they could neither overhear, nor repeat what went on around them. Though in fact it was otherwise, for they had, over the generations, perfected a sign-language which, combined with some mysterious technique of lip-reading, kept them well informed.

Were a foreign ambassador to be received in audience by the Padishah, Allah's Shadow on Earth, Brother of the Sun, to give him only a few of his titles, etiquette reached its peak. Stumbling on carpets gravelled over with pearls, the visitor was required to don an enveloping garment of gold tissue (much as, today, visitors to maternity clinics are put into sterilized overalls).

Colours, perfumes, fabrics, jewels and furs, too, all had their hieratic significance. The Sultan's turban – and his alone – could be tufted with heron's plumes. Ermine was for one dignitary, fox for another. Certain members of the Imperial family might wear sable, others not. By yellow or red leather boots, a soldier's rank was marked.

Life within the House of Felicity was seldom that luscious world of nineteenth-century romanticism pictured in Miss Pardoe's *Beauties of the Bosphorus*, all sweetmeats and roses. To most inmates of the Seraglio the House of Felicity was also known as the Palace of Tears. Here, in this formalized world, everything revolved round one man – the Sultan, Padishah of the Faithful. From here, he dispensed justice and injustice, gratified his senses and enlarged his domains, which at one time stretched from the Sahara to Vienna. Beyond the Gate of Felicity, Bab-i-Sa'adet, where everyone who entered must first prostrate himself to kiss the threshold, successive rulers lived lives of despotism and indulgence; yet, as has been remarked, sometimes tinctured by extreme cultivation, scholarship and piety too.

The Seraglio reflects this counterpoint at every turn.

In its form, or plan, the Sultan's palace follows those of the Sassanan Persian kings, which must have inspired the first princely Turkish dwellings. The particular model seems to have the palace of Haouch-Kouri, where, archaeologists tell us, three courts succeeded each other in a direct line, as with the Seraglio. The first, or outer court, for guards and commerce; the second, for administrative buildings and personnel; the

third, forbidden to all but a chosen few, containing the monarch's palace
and household. And behind that, inviolate territory – the inner sanctuary
of his harem.

So it is at Top Kapou Serai. After passing through the first, or outer
court, where Janissaries gathered round their legendary tree, sharpening
their scimitars and rattling their kettle-drums in displeasure, a menace
which even the Sultans dared not ignore, one arrives at the Ortakapi,
gateway to the second court. But before reaching its ordered green peace,
with the alleys of cyprus and delicate colonnades leading to the Divan
and the inner Gate of Felicity, a wall fountain 'of the Executioners'
recalls that here they cleansed their swords after spiking their victims'
heads above the gatehouse, or piling the niches beside the fountain with
the ears, hands or noses of others, an inducement to obedience which
few could ignore. On reaching the *haremlik* gardens, beyond the third
court, the lovely terraces, pools and parterres of the tulip gardens which
extend towards Seraglio Point, a promontory lying between the waters
of the Corne d'Or, the Bosphorus and the Marmora, are strewn with
fanciful little kiosks and gazebos, each an exquisite toy set in groves of
myrtle and box. Yet how haunted, still, those ornate empty shells; how
evocative their names. . . .

The House of Desire, the Kiosk of the Sofa, the House of Joy, the
House of Security (a foreboding note, here), the Pearl Kiosk, the Kiosk
of the Turban, or, most celebrated of all, the Baghdad Kiosk. Some were
for informal audience, a meeting between Sultan and Vizier, perhaps,
some contrived solely for the pleasure of contemplating a sunset over
the minarets of the distant city, or for the ecstasy of breathing the fra-
grance of roses. One Sultan devised a domed roof cooled by a constant
flow of water, where he liked to take his siesta. Most were for amorous
play. The Baghdad Kiosk, named after a Sultan's eastern conquests, embodied every voluptuous dream – *le repos du guerrier*. Each of its four
cushioned *alcôves* are framed in a shimmer of pearl and ivory inlay and
the intense blues of intricate tiling. Each *alcôve* seems to invite another
houri, each divan a new embrace . . . .

Amid all these delights of the flesh, of the perpetually replenished
ranks of seductive slaves (the Sultan Ibrahim of abhorred memory at one
time requiring twenty-four virgins in as many hours, until, overcome
by nervous exhaustion, he fell back on powdered ambergris in coffee as
a restorative), both Sultan and concubine must sometimes have been
uncomfortably aware of shadows menacing the *alcôve* where they

sported, for throughout the Seraglio death always lurked. The concubine, her eye falling on a little ornamental boathouse amid the bosky shade of Seraglio Point, far below, was no doubt reminded that it was from here that those of her kind who had failed to please were drowned. This thought must have chilled her blood while no doubt encouraging her ardours.

Let her disappear! was the fatal phrase which the Sultan had only to pronounce for the slave's doom to be sealed. It is recorded that one Padishah, in a fit of ennui, ordered his entire harem of tried favourites to be liquidated overnight, in order to make a fresh start in the morning. We imagine him, Bluebeard in person, idly fingering his amber *tespeyh*, or prayer beads, and issuing the command. 'Let her,' or, in this case, 'Let *them* disappear!'

Small wonder then, that terror took root, and love, in the terms of this book, scarcely at all.

Even maternal affections were corrupted by the lust for power. By custom, the Sultan was always born of a slave, one of foreign blood, never from a Turkish woman, for they were never recruited for his bed. Every inmate of the *haremlik* could possibly become mother of a Sultan, and herself acclaimed Sultane Validé, Queen Mother, Crown of the Veiled Heads, that is, of all women throughout the realms. The Sultane Validé ranked only second to the Sultan himself, and wielded absolute power within the *haremlik*. During the century and a half known as the Kadinlar Sultanate, they so influenced their Imperial sons or husbands that they came to dictate most of the Sublime Porte's affairs of state, and foreign policies too. Every woman dreamed of achieving supremacy, rising through all the hierarchies of pleasing, first as a novice, attached to the court or room, *oda*, of a highly placed inmate (thus *odalisque*, but having originally no erotic connotations, as assumed by the West). Then, proving successful, and perhaps lucky, nominated *güzdeh*, 'one who has caught the Royal eye'. At which she was set apart, groomed and schooled in all the intricacies of pleasing, provided with her own *oda* and slaves. From there, were she to continue pleasing, and now promoted as *ikbal*, an established favourite, she might become one of the four Kadins, equivalent of the four wives sanctioned by the Prophet.

Before that fortunate state was reached, were she to become pregnant, and the Sultan to favour her state, she would be known as *Kassachi Sultane*, of princess's rank. But if the Sultan were to fall under the sway of a rival *ikbal* and lose interest or command the pregnancy to be terminated, the Court Abortionist would be summoned and all her hopes dashed. If the unfortunate creature continued to conceal her condition, and escape his attentions, and a child be born, a girl risked being drowned or stifled forthwith. But even if it were a boy, and the Sultan smile upon it, her troubles were far from over. On the contrary: from now on her own life, and that of her child, would be for ever more threatened by the jealousy of every other mother, each jockeying for power, not only for their child's possible accession to the throne, but their own consequent aggrandizement. As I remarked earlier, love, the tender passions, had little place here; but ambitions raged, bringing with them intrigue, violence and terror.

This uneasy climate prevailed everywhere: in the grandiose state apartments or the sinister quarters of the Black Eunuchs, as in those dormitory-like galleries where the novices languished, awaiting their summons to the Sultan's bed. The contents of these rooms or the more splendid apartments of the favoured ladies were much alike, only varying in their degree of luxury. Eastern living does not require furniture on Western terms. Carpets are of first consequence: then quantities of padded quilts and mattresses, coverlets and cushions. These comprise the typical bedroom, which, by day, when the bedding is stacked or hid in cupboards, changes its character and use, to become the living-room, plenty of space being now free for the *tchibouques*, or water-pipes, the *mangals*, or braziers, and those relays of coffee which punctuate the day.

Painted chests or coffers contained clothes, and smaller caskets, inlaid with silver and tortoise-shell, held the jewels, paints and unguents with which the women enhanced their beauty. Food was served by the negress servants, brought on huge round platters; these *tabla* were sometimes five feet across, and of solid silver. The *mangals* were of brass, beautifully worked, or silver, too; both warmed well enough, save in winter, that dread damp chill of winter in Constantinople, when the more pampered ladies were installed in rooms possessing fine chimney-pieces. Bronze lanterns and candles lit the rooms – the wax candles being brought from Wallachia – while incense, an indispensable adjunct to every Eastern house, like ambergris to perfume the coffee, came from the Yemen. Specially scented soaps and essences were manufactured in the Seraglio, like the *surmah*, or kohl, with which the women darkened their eyes. Mastic, precursor of chewing gum, was used constantly, being said to sweeten the breath and whiten the teeth, though through several centuries teeth were blackened artificially, like kohl-rimmed eyes, and as much admired, while feet and hands were tinted with henna. Looking-glasses were imported from Venice, often ornamented with pearls and enamels. The women passed the long empty hours of their cloistered existence studying how best to enhance their appearance. Their extravagances were indulged, and their bills for finery seldom questioned. Hair was plaited with pearls or threaded with fine gold chains to which diamonds were attached, like dew-drops. Even the lowliest novice was accorded lavish trimmings.

Such hours of embellishment were almost their only occupation. Books were not encouraged, unless a study of the Koran, and many could not read. Embroidery was admitted, musical accomplishments and dancing were favoured. Among themselves they would assume those sidling, writhing poses, undulating their bellies and striking on little tambourines, to perfect themselves against the day when such seductions might help to win the Sultan's love. An occasional promenade into the tulip gardens, or to the menagerie – captives contemplating other captives – or surreptitious consultations with fortune-tellers, smuggled in as purveyors of silks or gee-gaws, or the languorous pleasures of the hammam were, apart from involvements of a lesbian nature, all the distractions upon which the Sultan's women could count. Not all of them reached the Imperial *alcôve*, or, once there, were required to linger, let along exercise their charms, for the Sultans were capricious. Were the rebuffed girl to be returned to the ranks untried, empty years stretched ahead, years of humiliation and taunting.

Every aspect of the Seraglio, its courts and gardens and such of its furnishings and the objects, clothes and possessions of its inmates as are still to be seen, *in situ* or housed in the sections now arranged as museums, reflect not only its history, but the character of its inmates and their daily life. While the Seraglio as a whole housed several thousand persons, the *haremlik*, which the West loosely supposed to be its sole purpose and content, was only one small part: but it was its core. Here the Padishah and his family lived, their quarters, *haremlik* and *selamlik*, were contained within the jumble of dark courts and corridors, pavilions, hammams and guardhouses which had come, over the centuries, to form the whole. Only their immediate suites, and, of course, the Sultans' women, lived here, behind that great doorway comprising four doors, two wooden and two of iron.

The quarters of the women were ruled by the Black Eunuchs under their chief, His Highness the Kizlar Agha, a personage of the greatest consequence, entitled, among other privileges, to three hundred horses for his sole use. The White Eunuchs, a legacy of the Byzantine court, had been the original guardians of the *haremlik*, but were ousted from this internal – could one say domestic? – charge after long years of struggle, and henceforth were about the *selamlik* or Seraglio in general, but no longer in the holy of holies.

After the Kizlar Agha, the first post of importance in the *haremlik* was that of the Lady Stewardess, Comptroller of the Household, then the Treasurer, the Mistress of the Robes, and the Mistress of the Jewels; the Reader of the Koran, the Head Nurse, the Keeper of the Baths, and the Court Abortionist, an overworked person, by all accounts.

In the *selamlik*, the Sultan's immediate suite included pages, scribes, treasurers, grooms, the Keeper of the Royal Turbans, the Chief Turban Winder – *Dulbendtar-agha*, *dulbend* being Turkish for muslin (as used for turbans) and hence the English 'turban'. Then there was the Keeper of the Jewels, Reader of the Koran, and the Imperial Barber, whose position was an onerous one, since the Sultan's beard had an almost sacred significance, every hair being meticulously preserved, as well as his dressers, grooms, bath attendants, apothecaries and many more who revolved around the Imperial presence at close quarters. A host of others, still within the *selamlik*, did not approach closely, innumerable dwarfs and buffoons, the Keeper of Parrot Cages, musicians, astrologers, and the Royal Taster, who must always sample each dish in the presence of the Sultan; and since to err is only human, the Royal Toxologist, who was ever at the ready should dangerous symptoms be manifest. Here organization had been brought to perfection.

Were any men from the outer periphery of the first and second courts of the Seraglio to be admitted – those who stoked the copper boilers for the hammam, gardeners, carpenters or plasterers perhaps, convened on some special task – their approach was signalled well in advance and the Black Eunuchs saw to it that their charges were invisible, under lock and key. Were the Sultan and his Kadines walking in the gardens, the warning cry *Helvet! Helvet!* would ensure that no one lingered there. If by some error, the warning had not been heard, or was neglected, and the petrified intruder be detected by the Black Eunuchs, death was likely to follow such an imprudence. The Tressed Halberdiers, a corps of manual workers, wood cutters and bodyguards, were most often about the place, but even so, subject to the strictest rules. Their name derived from the two long locks of artificial hair that fell each side of their face. These were originally worn, it is said, to prevent their casting any sidelong glances where they should not. Secrecy was everywhere, an inherent instinct of succeeding generations to preserve the sacred mystery surrounding Allah's Shadow on Earth. And when he issued forth from his fastness, to go in state about his capital, he was scarcely visible to its citizens, riding his charger at the heart of the vast cortège hedged by a special guard whose head-dresses of towering fan-like plumes screened him from mortal view.

In spite of the Padishah's seclusion, and the rigid sequestration of his women, the *haremlik* and *selamlik* quarters of his palace were oddly adjacent, hugger-mugger even, separated in some cases only by a door – though all were massively barred. There was no architectural plan or symmetry about the *haremlik*: only a congeries of rooms and courts. Succeeding Sultans had added to the jumble, destroying and rebuilding haphazardly. State apartments adjoined windowless inner bedrooms, libraries abutted on hammams, the Black Eunuchs' quarters were close by the Sultane Validé's splendid suite. But however casual, there was an evident insistence on plumbing. Small marble-walled lavatories, each with their fountains of running water, were attached to every suite, for a most fastidious attention to cleanliness has ever been next to godliness, in Islam. Not far from the grandiose Hall of Audience Within – within the *selamlik*, that is – lay the Kefés or Cage, the prison-dwelling of those wretched princes whose existence might threaten the Sultan or his direct heir. Succession passed to the eldest male relative; thus uncles and brothers were immured there for life, awaiting either a summons to the throne, or the silken bow-string which announced their end.

The Kefés is a small, rather squat stone pavilion with closely barred windows giving on to an inner courtyard. All around, the windows of other suites are also barred or screened by close-carved *mouchrabiyehs*, while inside, lesser windows, or spy-holes, are apertures through which dishes or messages were passed, connecting room to room. This was a feature of most Turkish domestic architecture, which catered for the total sequestration of harem life. But in the Seraglio, especially the Kefés, it implied a sinister system of observation too. A dim twilight pervades these ill-lit rooms. Even the charming tile-work of the princes' schoolroom, with its map of Mecca and its lovely pointed, chequered chimney-piece, cannot overcome the sinistry. In its abandonment, it still envelopes the stranger with a powerful sense of dread, of shadows lurking everywhere . . . the watcher and the watched. . . .

Now a soft scuttle is heard . . . a rat? No, rather, the stealthy approach of the deaf-mutes bringing that message of doom for which some princes listened a whole lifetime. Down the Corridor Where The Djinns Hold Consultation another procession pads past . . . some of the Black Eunuchs are escorting a suitably barren odalisque to distract the imprisoned princes. In the Kefés, while appetites were gratified, the question of progeny must not arise, and the selected concubines, if not already proven sterile, were usually made so. Thus, in an atmosphere of cunningly fostered debauch, the princes were kept apart from all knowledge of the outside world or affairs of state. Their *khodjas*, or tutors, permitted very few books: not for them the educational opportunities of the Seraglio school. Apart from learning a craft, as did every man in Turkey, including those of highest estate, they were left to rot. Small wonder, then, that when, as occasionally happened, one was fetched out of obscurity to rule, he was seldom fit to do so. Some, having been incarcerated for fifty years or so, emerged as vengeful lunatics.

Phantoms everywhere. Brooding shadows, the women, the princes and the abused and humiliated ranks of eunuchs too, for whom no advancements or honours could altogether compensate.

Now, standing in that marvellous alleyway of turquoise and sapphire blue faïence known as the Golden Road, I hear the muffled tread of a ceremonial procession, one headed by the Kizlar Agha no less, for it was down this Golden Road that he, by tradition, must conduct each new, untried favourite-elect, or *güzdeh*, to the Sultan's bed. Yet it is not a joyous procession, for too much apprehension and envy surrounds it. . . . More steps, the capering antics of the dwarfs and buffoons, desperate in their determination to amuse. Now the dragging step of a prisoner led off between guards, but quiet, even in terror. All these phantoms tread softly, on bare jewelled feet, or feet slippered in yellow leather, high patterns or furred overboots, but always quietly, stealthily, in hushed silence, as they did in life.

This hush was always remarked by any outsider invited to enter the Seraglio, ambassadors, clockmakers, or physicians, perhaps. *Horses as well as men know how to tread softe here* records one amazed visitor. It was a stillness as before a storm, an awesome quiet, and it must have hung over the most festive occasions. Even now the state apartments retain this sense of oppression. We read that a fountain played in the Arzodasi, or Hall of Audience, just inside the Gate of Felicity: this was not so much to please the assembly as to ensure any whispered exchanges from the throne were lost to those around. Stealth everywhere. The ceremonies and galas held in the Throne Room Within, where the Sultan fêted religious or family occasions, circumcision festivals and such, and where the women were ceremonially paraded before him, must still have breathed tension and dread. All the refulgence of Turkish rococo and the splendours of the Ottoman court were once centered round this salon, and still much of its magnificence remains. Yet the velvet hangings worked in gold, like the jewelled *tchibouques,* or those solid gold ewers, their handles of crystal or amethyst, like the vessels for amber-scented coffee, in which sherbets made of sugar and violets were served, all remained traps, where dangers lurked. Jewelled daggers, however ornamental, could strike home as ably as scimitars; poison – slow but sure – could lurk in a sip of coffee. Danger was everywhere in this abode of intrigue. Not an *ikbal,* nor even a Kadine, could relax. The sweep of a peacock feather fan, or the flutter of a rival's gauze kerchief could conceal the death-dealing phial; and the excitement of such occasions was a perfect screen for mischief. The elaborate canopied throne, or *lit à baldaquin* (for their form and use was indistinguishable) represented to every lovely creature gathered round her sole chance of advancement, if not survival. Not even the glitter of the countless Bohemian glass chandeliers, shimmering and brilliant, could really lighten the scene. These chandeliers and candelabra (which had to contain a certain mystic number of candles) were imported from Europe during the eighteenth century, replacing the earlier bronze and horn lamps. Such bon-bon colours, ruby, rose, pea-green and sky-blue had a succulent, almost edible quality which appealed especially to sensual Turkish taste, and they continued to be imported in large quantities, not only for the Seraglio, but for every rich house and many mosques about the city too, where they still strike a singularly secular note. But in the *selamlik,* even their sparkle could not produce a truly festive air. And when the Sultan 'cast the handkerchief' to the charmer of his choice, an envenomed hiss must always have sounded behind the applause, the music of an orchestra (strictly blindfolded) or the tinkling merriment of the professional laughter-makers. This body, the reverse of those professional mourners or wailers found throughout the East, were employed much as, today, some hostesses use discreet mechanical music as a relaxing social background. *Plus ça change. . . .*

Yet many women accepted their lot willingly, for the luxury it offered and the possibilities of dazzling advancement it held. And not only the women, for strange as it may seem, the ranks of eunuchs were also largely recruited from willing victims. Oddly enough, those women who were selected for the Seraglio (which always had first pick of the slave market) were, in a sense, far less well placed than those taken into less august households, for they seldom obtained their freedom, later, as the others often did, unless, retired from the *haremlik*, they were presented to some indulged eunuch who retained a morbid interest in women, or were married off to a notable who had earned a mark of Imperial esteem. Still, not every girl recoiled from her fate. Many saw it as an easier way of life then they had known in Europe, or in the rigours of a Caucasian *aôul*. Freedom is, after all, comparative, and the prospect of luxury universally seductive.

Safieh Baffo, the beautiful Italian concubine who was for many years Sultan Murad's only, and adored, Kadine, she who shared with him the loveliest of all rooms for loving, had no need to better herself. Luxury and rank were her birthright. She came of a noble Venetian family, rich and proud in their splendid palazzo. To her, the opulence of the Seraglio must have seemed almost barbaric; and we can imagine the despair of her family when they learned she had been abducted by corsairs and sold into the Seraglio of the Grand Turk. It is not known how she came to be seized, for young girls of her kind were strictly kept: though abduction by corsairs was one of the hazards of earlier centuries. The Barbary pirates operated from Algiers and the ports of North Africa, doing a thriving trade with fair-skinned Europeans, both men and women, whom they sold to the slave merchants. Perhaps those who made off with Safieh Baffo were lying-to beyond the lagoons, and swept down audaciously, within sight of the Doges' Palace, to snatch their prize as she was sailing to Chiogga or some family estates on the Brenta.

I know of no existing portrait, such as that of the Russian Kadine Roxelane, by which we could gauge something of her beauty. But it is certain she enslaved the Sultan to the exclusion of every other woman. It was for love of her, I like to think, and for the purposes of this book maintain, that he built that perfect room known as Sultan Murad's Bed-chamber. Admittedly this Sultan ended up with an enormous harem and left 103 children, though that was at the end of his days, and owing to the machinations of his mother, jealous of Safieh's ascendancy over her son; but for many years Safieh reigned supreme, and it was *her* son, Moham-med III, who succeeded as Sultan, and, in turn, *her* machinations which disposed so ruthlessly of any possible rivals. It was, no doubt, also through her influence that the Italian Domenico Hierosolimitano was appointed a Court Physician – an unimaginable innovation in this closed world.

I imagine the young Safieh in her Venetian girlhood as one of those smooth-faced blonde beauties such as Carpaccio painted, sunning themselves on a roof-top terrace, bleaching their long crimped golden hair in the summer sunshine. Carpaccio's models were the courtesans of Venice, but most noble women also repaired to the roof-tops for the same purpose. Golden hair – that particular reddish gold which Venetian painters and notably Tintoretto immortalized – was especially prized, and said to be maintained not only by regular exposure to sunlight but by assiduous applications of urine.

Daughters of the princely families and courtesans alike shared much the same setting; over several centuries the scene changed little. The frieze of tall, funnel-like chimneys, so characteristic of Venice, was always there. The terraces were embellished with pots of tall carnations, laurel and bay. There were pets to tease: skinny Italian greyhounds or those small, fluffy, muff-like dogs that are everywhere in paintings of the period; and peacocks, strutting and shrieking, or apes, chained by jewelled belts. The women wear stiff brocaded gowns, their sleeves puffed and slashed. Their hair is unbound, or plaited with pearls, or sometimes confined by a little meshed cap. They read poetry to each other, embroider silks, whisper of smuggled love-letters and wonder what the future holds for them . . . girls' talk everywhere. It is a serene and softly flowing life, quiet as the still green canals below. How overwhelming must have seemed that destiny which flung the young Safieh into the Seraglio.

Her beauty and that warm nectarine and gold colouring of the Venetian woman would have attracted immediate attention there, and very soon she was singled out for the Sultan's attention – probably by no less a personage than the Sultane Validé Nur Banu, mother of Sultan Murad, who was herself of Venetian origin. The convenience of placing a fellow countrywoman beside the Sultan, and through her, acquiring even more influence, must have struck Nur Banu Sultane, for she was a woman of implacable ambitions, prototype of those who made the 'Reign of the Women' notorious.

By tradition, it was the Sultane Validé who, on the Night of Power, at Baïram, personally selected the virgin whom she conducted in state to her son's bed, in the expectation that his ardours, agreeably renewed after long abstinence, would ensure a lusty heir. The trembling aspirant was always well coached: she knew that she must approach Allah's Shadow on Earth with proper humility, it is said, by entering the Imperial bed symbolically, from the foot only, inching up by degrees. Etiquette even here, between the sheets.

No doubt Safieh Baffo followed this formalized beginning to her days of love and power.

Let us look now at the setting of her life. This room, an expression of romantic genius, was conceived by Sinan Agha, supreme architect of Ottoman glories, of the greatest mosques and secular buildings of the sixteenth century. He was of Greek origin, but brought up in Turkey. He considered himself wholly Turkish, and his work, breaking from Seldjuk traditions, came to embody the purest Ottoman style. He worked for three successive Sultans; first for Sulieman the Magnificent, then his son, Selim I, and last, his grandson, Murad III. During those reigns he built a large number of mosques, among the loveliest being the Sokölu-mehmet Paçha, the Rustem Paçha, and, greatest of all, those at Edirné. His particular genius was to unite the noblest proportions with a sense of intimacy. This is particularly apparent in the mosque of Rustem Paçha, where colour, the glowing, almost carpet-like intricacies of tile-work and decoration imparts a special richness.

A mosque, it should be remembered, is not a consecrated building in the sense of a Christian church. There is a subtle difference. It is the house of Allah – as sacred, but more personal, more approachable, open by day and night, not only for prayer but for shelter, repose and contemplation; study too, for students are often to be seen there, quite apart from the *medressa*, or theological college, usually attached to the mosque. In the house of Allah, the poorest outcast finds hospitality – a place of refuge – of beauty and luxury too. Here, cool fountains, exquisite faïence, fine lamps and carpets, often beyond price, surround him, as they do the Sultan in his palace. Such is Allah's hospitality.

When Sinan Agha designed Sultan Murad's room he seems to have been inspired by some special grace, as if he were aware that he was building for love rather than majesty. For all its stateliness, this room retains, to an extraordinary degree, a sense of emotion, as opposed to the sensuality of the kiosks. It is a secret enclosure 'in palace chambers far apart'. Sinan Agha probably built this room when he was rebuilding much of the Seraglio after the fire which ravaged the earlier palace in 1574. It lies at the heart of the *haremlik*, as it were embedded in successive layers of mystery, secrecy and silence, and is reached either through the Corridor Where The Djinns Hold Consultation, or by the majestic Vestibule of the Fountain, also by Sinan's hand.

But nothing prepares one for the impact of Sultan Murad's room. Crossing the threshold, it is as if the curtain has risen on some marvellous dramatic scene. 'An Eastern Tale of Enchantment' such as the young Disraeli evoked in his letters from Turkey: yet having nothing of such tinselled pantomime. This is drama, all romance, with some bold, almost barbaric flavour, which gives it force and passion.

Act 1. Scene 1: The Corridor of Consultation with the Djinns
Scene 2: The Vestibule of the Fountain
Scene 3: The bedroom of Sultan Murad

And the cast? Grand Turk, Venetian Kadine, Viziers, Courtiers, Black Eunuchs, dwarfs, djinns, attendant slaves and guards . . . . How well it lends itself to the idiom of the theatre: and since, as has been told, clothing was regulated according to the rank and occupation of the wearer, scarlet for an Admiral, sable for a Vizier, and so on, it has been rightly remarked that the history of Constantinople was in fact a costume drama.

The Corridor Where The Djinns Hold Consultation is as ominous as its name, narrow and stone-flagged; on one side its thickly barred windows give on to an inner court beside the Kefés, and from where, no doubt, a wan face was sometimes to be seen – one of the incarcerated princes peering out for a sight of that world he must never know. On the inside wall of the Corridor, a door, heavily barred and bolted but beautifully worked with inlays of pearl and ivory and a great damascened lock, led to the *haremlik*, the Kadine's quarters and outer cells of the honeycomb. In the sombre beauty of the Vestibule of the Fountain, those few privileged persons summoned to the Sultan's presence in his private apartments were set to wait his pleasure. Although Sultan Murad's bedroom was always known as such, it also served as a living-room, in the turnabout Eastern system already discussed.

Two vast *lits à baldaquin*, the canopied beds which served as such, or as thrones, are the dominant feature, and have given the room its name. They are placed symmetrically flanking a huge chimney-piece, hooded in bronze, one of those tall, pointed, helmet-shaped structures, the *achmak*, found in old Turkish houses and recalling the headgear of Asiatic conquerors. Reminding us, too, that behind all the outward Ottoman luxuries lies a Mongol past, harsh as the wind that howls down from the Asiatic hinterland beyond the Black Sea. The size of this hearth would reduce tree trunks to firewood proportions. In such a gaping maw logs were habitually placed upright, so that the upward draught kept smoke from belching out into the room. The canopied beds are carved and gilded, and must once have been spread with innumerable cushions. Their hangings, or some similar ones used elsewhere in the Seraglio are described as being particularly magnificent, 'of black Velvet, with an Embroydery of great Pearls, whereof some are long and others round, and in the form of Buttons. . . . There is another of white Velvet set out with Rubies and Emeralds . . . a third of a Violet coloured Velvet, embroyder'd with Turquoises and Pearls'. The posts supporting the baldaquins were gilded and painted, and also worked with precious stones, the curtains roped back with swags of pearls, while coverlets of tufted velvet or cloth-of-gold lined with lynx or sable were flung about among the cushions. Even without these furnishings, or the wonderful carpets, Ouchaks, Karabaghs or Konias to make the mouth water, this room is never bleak in its present abandonment. The textures of its lost glories are still sensed, for with all its spacious splendour there is warmth and harmony too. The soaring ceiling is domed, yet it does not seem remote, for the walls rise to meet it without straining, their lofty proportions, which might chill, are rendered intimate, or brought to living level by a deep gilded dado of Koranic inscriptions which circle the entire room and are set above panels of superb faïence. Almond blossom, carnations or tulips bloom here on a background of burning blue, edged with that thread of coral red which is the signature of faïences made at Iznik, the old Nicaea. There are double rows of windows: those placed high – very high, above the dado and almost merging with the dome – do not shed that chilling top-light found in studios, for they have panes of jewel-coloured glass and cast pools of colour on the stone floor, though since this was certainly once criss-crossed with carpets overlaid one on another in that prodigal fashion peculiar to the East, the shafts of light streaming down from the windows must have overlaid colour on colour most sumptuously. The lower lines of windows are deeply embrasured and typify those low-set, door-like apertures, almost at ground level, which are so significant a feature of Eastern architecture, whether domestic or religious.

Such low placed windows, precursors of the modern picture window, always remind me of the raised tent flap in encampments, where the desert's rim is ever visible to those inside. It was from such nomads, roaming the steppes, that the pattern of living and so many tenets of Eastern taste developed. Thus in the Seraglio, as in so many other Oriental palaces, notably those of Moghul splendour, for all its luxury and apparent sophistication, some lavish disorder or wildness lurks. This is the careless, open freedom of a desert or steppe encampment, extravagance beside harshness. The tents of Genghis Khan were of leopard skins lined with ermine.

Throughout the arid East, water is regarded as the ultimate luxury, venerated for its scarcity and man's thirst. The finest gesture of hospitality is to offer a glass of pure water, while fountains and pools obtain almost mystical qualities. Thus, in placing a wide, three-tiered marble fountain stretching the length of one wall in Sultan Murad's room, Sinan Agha set the seal of splendour and pleasure on this room. Curiously, although Constantinople is not a city of great heat and is surrounded by water and green forests where springs abound, the element is apotheosized in the number and beauty of its street-fountains. Some are set exquisitely under gilded eaves, some behind lace-like marble grilles; some gush from porphyry basins in the courtyards of mosques, or beside the entrance to a hammam. Everywhere such hammams, known loosely as Turkish baths, have an element of the temple about them, where the rituals and worship of water prevails. The image of water is found translated into many terms: in the Anatolian cemetery rugs of tradition, which were taken to the cemetery upon which to pray beside the tomb, and to picnic, too, for grave-side feasts with the departed's favourite foods were *de rigueur*. Such rugs are all woven with a blue ribbon of water, a stream, traced round the flowers and cypress trees representing the Gardens of Paradise. Nor do the mourners forget the birds, for Turkish graves often have a little scooped-out hollow where dew collects, and where the birds may drink their fill. . . . Water everywhere, life-giving water, treasured and symbolized in many ways, in mosques or palaces, sacred or profane. . . . Those fabulous diamond sprays that tremble on fine gold wires, a typically Turkish type of jewellery – surely these too were inspired by showers of raindrops, dewdrops, or the jet of a fountain?

Thus in Sultan Murad's room it is the fountain – the marvellous wall-fountain – which is the supreme symbol of luxury. Two tiers of white marble stretch almost the entire length of the wall facing the throne beds, and each tier is set with a row of nine bronze taps, so that cascades of water fall in a shimmering curtain. Moreover, each tap is contrived to sound a different note, thus making a sort of liquid symphony to lull the Sultan's slumbers. Here moonlight, starlight or firelight glittered across the water as it fell, or shafts of sunlight from the jewel-coloured windows above played over it in rainbow arcs. Here is a setting worthy of true love. Here the silences and sighs of passion must have lost themselves in the shadowy dome, or sunk, muffled by the murmuring splash of the fountain. Here the Sultan and his Italian Kadine lived becalmed, shut away from the terrors and tragedies of the Seraglio, indifferent to the extravagance of their setting, perhaps, but figures of unparalleled magnificence themselves. Veronese should have painted them in all their splendour.

I like to imagine the scene and the figures for whom this pleasance was made. They are couched among the tufted velvets and lynx skins. Sultan Murad is a bearded, beetle-browed, long-nosed man, his gigantic turban, heron-plumed, is laid aside, like his jewelled dagger, as he puffs at his turquoise-studded *tchibouque* and fondles the woman at his side. He wears the traditional caftan or surcoat, which changed little through thirty successive Sultanships, only in the nineteenth century giving place to the Western frock-coat, or 'Stambouline', as its local variation was known. Caftans were always monstrously stiff and heavy, in cut velvet and brocades, often lined with sable and fastened by a line of jewelled clasps.

It was the custom to preserve all the garments and state robes of the Ottoman Sultans. They were parcelled, listed, and preserved in the Treasury of the Seraglio, from the fifteenth century onwards. This marvellous record contains blood-stained caftans, telling of violence, as well as the whole art and development of Turkish silk weaving. Upon each Sultan's death, their clothes were packed in numbers of wax cloth wrappers and labelled with both precision and veneration. For example: *The garments of His Majesty the Deceased Sultan Osman the Ghazi Victorious, unto whom all sins are forgiven. In three wrappers.* Many of these Sultan's robes are to be seen in the Seraglio museum – tremendous garments which, topped by towering turbans, gave the impression of having clothed a race of giants. Their stiff, cut velvets and brocades, weighted further by jewelled embroideries, were of Seljuk weaving, and later came from Brusa looms. Against the chill, some were fur-lined, some wadded with raw silk, for the cold of winter in Constantinople was penetrating. To the Greeks, Turkey was 'the land beyond the North wind', and no doubt, compared to Hellenic azures, they saw its pearly skies and vaporous clouds as an overcast grey. Odalisques and Kadines were perhaps sometimes compelled to appear naked beneath their gauzy *chalvari*, those bouffant trousers known as Turkish, but Sultans, Viziers and such are always portrayed in comfortably padded garments.

Thus I see Sultan Murad resplendent in his blue shot-silk under-caftan (now preserved in the Treasury) printed with gold and silver circles, the lining embroidered with crescents. Over this he wears a violet-coloured caftan of *kemha*, velvet brocade, woven with gold thread. Its lining is of sable, and the sleeves of his under-shirt emerald green taffeta. His feet are thrust into yellow leather slippers; his hands are heavily ringed, and while the buttons of his outer caftan are diamonds, the size of gooseberries, those of his under-caftan are gigantic sapphires.

Beside him, Safieh Sultane, as splendidly arrayed. She sits cross-legged, so that her crimson taffeta *chalvari* emerge from beneath a flowing lemon-coloured damask robe, or *entari*, the basic garment of every Turkish woman of quality, worn loose over under-shifts and tunics, its sleeves trailing almost to the floor. It is buttoned with topazes, and belted by a wide, heavy girdle, a mosaic of precious stones, the stomacher-clasp fashioned of enormous diamonds. Her gauze chemise is left open to the waist, revealing her breasts; between them dangle chains of pearls and rubies. The loose sleeves of the *entari* fall back from the gauze sleeves of her chemise, and on each wrist there are bracelets without number. Her feet are bare, and tinted with henna. On her head she wears the traditional *talpock*, a little flat round tasselled cap, studded with pearls and worn rakishly to one side. On the other side, pinned to her hair, a large aigrette of diamonds springs from a brooch which is marvellously contrived to represent a bouquet, a typical Turkish style, with ruby roses, pearl buds, emerald leaves, diamond dew-drops and other such opulent conceits. Her long blonde hair is left unbound, and falls over her shoulders in a molten shower where diamonds glitter, for they are attached to fine gold chains threaded through her locks. She is painted in the bold manner of the Seraglio, her lips crimsoned, her eyes darkened by kohl, and her eyebrows marked emphatically, being joined in one ebony sweep, for this is the fashion from Samarcand to Cairo. We must hope, in the interests of romance, that her teeth were not also blackened in that manner admired and followed for some centuries by ladies of the *haremlik*.

She holds a lute of Venetian workmanship, tulipwood inlaid with ivory, but now she puts it aside and turns towards her lord and master. On a signal from the Sultan a eunuch steps forward and draws the silk curtains round the throne, which, on the instant, becomes their bed. Eunuch, pages and buffoons steal away; it is quite silent in that great room: only the shift of smouldering logs and the faint music of the fountain sounds. Moonlight streams down from the high windows above, and outside, silvers the dark spears of the cypress groves where there nightingales. Firelight, moonlight, bird-song and the sound of a are fountain. . . . Such was the Pavilion Sinan had devised for these lovers.

Conjuring them in their paradise, it does not do to remember the sour finish to such a love: yet it came to pass. After many years, Safieh Sultane's influence became such that Murad would make no decisions of any kind without her approval, and his mother, the redoubtable Sultane Validé Nur Banu, determined to end the idyll. She succeeded, at last, by acquiring numbers of the most lovely slaves imaginable, virgins of such voluptuous promise and variety that even Murad's single-minded devotion wavered, and, at last, vanished. He spent his remaining years in ceaseless debauch, a puppet at his mother's command.

Safieh Sultane, whose character remains obscure, but who, we suspect, was first of all ambitious, accepted her banishment philosophically (which is not the sign of true love) and turned to politics – particularly fostering good relations between Venice and the Sublime Porte. She was in correspondence with the Doges and ambassadors, and also with Catherine de Médicis. She does not appear to have made any effort to obtain her release from the Seraglio or return to Venice, so we must assume the power-game was, at heart, her chosen way of life. Perhaps she had never really loved Murad, or loved better the power she obtained through him. And then, there was her son, the future Mohammed III, whose position, and accession, was forever shadowed by rival brothers and half-brothers: there must be no weakness. Murad's frenetic sensuality had produced over a hundred children, many of them male. Were any one of these to obtain power, she, Safieh Sultane, would never obtain the long-desired position of Sultane Validé. It was evident that she must allow no supine sentiment on Mohammed's part to undermine her plans. When Sultan Murad died and his son was proclaimed successor, there is little doubt that it was Safieh Sultane who steeled him to the frightful holocaust which followed. Nineteen of his brothers were strangled by the ceremonial bow-string, and seven of his father's pregnant concubines (big with possible claimants) were drowned off Seraglio Point, again with due ceremony. Thus the way was clear for Mohammed as Sultan, and for his mother, Safieh Sultane, to become Sultane Validé, Crown of the Veiled Heads, ruler within the *haremlik*, and soon, beyond. Following in the footsteps of her predecessor Nur Banu Sultane, she continued the supply of lovely slaves, thus keeping her son besotted and befuddled, the better to rule as she pleased.

Yet that game of love and power Safieh Baffo knew how to play with such ruthlessness could also be played by others. One day she was found strangled in her bed, that sumptuous bed in the Sultane Validé's quarters which, for many years, she had occupied in triumph, as once she had triumphed in Sultan Murad's bed. I prefer to think of her as she had been then: the Venetian Kadine, forever 'emparadised' in Murad's arms . . . the Grand Signor and his golden favourite, the perfect lovers in the perfect setting, Sinan's own.

Dear dead women, with such hair, too – what's become of all the gold,
Used to hang and brush their bosoms? I feel chilly and grown old.

8

Nohant
France

AURORE DUPIN, Baronne Dudevant, *'la bonne dame de Nohant'*, is first recalled as George Sand, the dashing and romantic creature whose novels, like her love affairs, shook Paris of the 1830s and '40s. Her androgynous silhouette, stove-pipe hat, trousers and cravat, dandy's clothing, with her eternal cigar, comes to mind before the crinolined charmer, jasmine and coral ornamenting her dark ringlets, as she is portrayed by Charpentier and others, gazing out from the canvas with those enormous, sombre 'Andalusian' eyes, 'great sphinx eyes', which wreaked such havoc among her legion of admirers.

The Romantic era, which was that of her youth, was a prodigiously creative one. All over Europe, emotion inspired its music, literature and painting: it was a moment in time quite distinct from that which preceded it, or that which followed: it had nothing of eighteenth-century logic and cynicism, nor the feather-brained gaiety of Offenbach's Paris. Indeed, by its very intensity and the total lack of reserve displayed by its protagonists, it was curiously alien to that formalism which is an essentially French quality. Among the Romantics, high passions were the rage. But while there were gestures of the most flamboyant or heroic nature, all the thunders of Berlioz and Liszt, and that significant first-night battle of *Hernani*, beside all the surge and splendour of Delacroix, there was, too, an elusive strain of melancholy of which Chopin's music is the epitome. Love for love's sake was the creed by which all the pale Romantics wished to live or die, and this was the creed by which the young George Sand (in fact a robust rather than pallid Romantic) lived and worked.

But it was Nohant, her estate in the Berry, which was the centrifugal point of her whole life. It was the house of a country gentlewoman, far removed from the attics or salons of Paris between which the Romantics alternated, according to their degree of fame. Yet this woman who was generally labelled *grande amoureuse*, or blue-stocking (for she was brilliantly educated, an accomplished scholar), was more besides; above all, she was a *force de la nature*, as impetuous, yet as ordered, as nature itself: which is where she differed fundamentally from her contemporaries in the world of the Arts, urban figures all of them, centred on and around the Boulevards.

Although she found fame and adventure and fortune in Paris, she remained, all her life, a countrywoman – a Berrichon. It was from the serene countryside of the Berry that she drew her strength and radiated that marvellous life-force, at once vigorous and calming, which drew so many men of genius to her side. Chopin, Delacroix, de Musset, Balzac, Liszt, Heine, Flaubert, Turgenev, Sainte-Beuve . . . variously, these men and many others were under her spell. Yet however swayed by tempests of emotion (as with de Musset in Venice), she always remained rooted in the abiding countryside that was her heritage. She had been married very young, at the insistence of her grandmother, to the Baron Casimir Dudevant, a Gascon; but she had not liked him any better than life on his estates in Gascony, and soon returned to the Berry, where the marriage was of no more account. Nohant, the charming domain of which she had now become châtelaine, was the magnet by which she drew successive lovers or adoring friends into her domestic and family web. Here she enmeshed Chopin, her little Chop-Chop, as she called him, for eight years of love and bitterness, serenity and torment, and work – above all, of superb creative achievement – until at last, in 1848, this strange relationship was shattered.

Nohant has passed into romantic legend by its association with these two romantic figures, and today we see it as a true Pavilion of the Heart, once inhabited by love and genius. Now preserved as a museum and left almost as it was in their day, it retains an overwhelming sense of intimacy – of the living presence of its châtelaine. It is as if, peering through the gates, we shall glimpse her, tending the flowers she hurried out to greet each morning. . . . Or, entering the dim, stone-flagged hall, find her coming from the busy kitchens, followed by a delicious waft of one of the preserves for which she was famous; or hear a far-away piano touched by a master hand . . . Chopin's celebrated *jeu perlé*. . . . Echoes, shadows, memories . . . Nohant is full of them. . . . It is a house which remains *inhabited*, rather than haunted, by them.

The pattern of life at Nohant was spacious, patriarchal. George Sand had lived there as a child, brought up by her paternal grandmother, Madame Dupin de Francueil, who, being of the *ancien régime*, was uneasy lest the child's exotic ancestry might overcome the strict training she imposed. The little Aurore Dupin was descended from a particularly spectacular and lively stock: her great-grandfather, the Maréchal de Saxe, was the natural son of Aurore de Koenigsmark by August II of Poland; her mother, a camp-follower and dancer, child of a bird fancier by the Seine who captivated a young, aristocratic officer in Bonaparte's army: such stock might well have given her grandmother some anxiety. 'My mother was one of the world's Gypsies,' wrote George Sand, in her *Histoire de ma Vie*. From her, she inherited her craving for nature, and a recurring pattern of vagabondage. It ran counter to the ordered tradition of life at Nohant, but while she always indulged the one, she also upheld the other strictly.

At Nohant, a toy-like village clustered round the big house over which she reigned, and to which so many fine and strange people drove down from Paris to astonish the villagers. The house was beautifully proportioned, soberly elegant, but without splendours: a manor rather than a château, though it came to be known as '*le Château de la Plume*'. It was surrounded by its park, with the tall sequoias and cedars which each generation of the family had planted on the birth of a child, and where the green rides ended in vistas of a placid countryside interspersed by marshes and those deep treacherous lakes which struck an unexpectedly sinister note and were the subject of macabre local legends. Round the house, outbuildings, dairy, laundry, stables and farm were clustered; by

the lodge gates was the cottage that was transformed into a studio for
Delacroix. He was a special family friend, teaching George Sand's son
to paint, as Chopin gave her daughter piano lessons . . . The arts always
inhabited this house; but then genius had become a part of family life –
the life which George Sand valued above all else, and imposed on each
of her successive romantic involvements.

Her strongest emotions were always maternal, and it is this quality
which pervaded Nohant, and which, essentially, qualifies it as a Pavilion
of the Heart. While George Sand adored her children, each lover must
become her child too. *L'amour des entrailles* (love – of the bloodstream –
the guts) she called it, with no mincing sentimentality. Liaisons *must*
have a family flavour. The *alcôve*, that most *dix-huitième* of institutions,
was invariably transformed into a conjugal foyer – though her own
marriage, to a country gentleman from Gascony, was of brief duration.
Thus we see her imposing family life on each successive lover. Jules
Sandeau, from whose literary collaboration her pseudonym derives,
sharing an attic overlooking Notre-Dame, tucking her baby Solange
under his arm as they start out for the opera. Alfred de Musset, the dis-
sipated dandy, crawling on the floor among the toys. Chopin strumming
while her children dance to his tunes and shriek joyously at his antics –
he, usually so aloof and melancholic, knew how to be gay too, though it
was a side the world seldom saw.

George Sand has left a description of how, after an evening surrounded
by adulation, playing divinely and plunging his listeners into profound
sadness by his music, he would turn slyly to a mirror, tweak his hair or
cravat, and suddenly become transformed into the droll caricature of a
phlegmatic Englishman, a squalid Jew or a sentimental woman. She,
watching anxiously over his health and genius, judged that the *mondain*,
yet fundamentally lonely life he led in the Paris salons where he reigned
supreme was undermining his creative powers. She believed that by
cajoling him to join her at Nohant, simpler, more regular ways would
benefit both his health and his work. And he, passionately in love,
followed where she led – even to the depths of the countryside, which
being the most urban of men, he instinctively avoided.

Studying her portraits, we are puzzled to define her extraordinary
attraction: the rather heavy, melancholic face, the somnambulistic
stare, the incipient double chin, or her sallow complexion, 'snuff-
coloured' to her detractors but amber to de Musset, when violently in

love. What exactly was the spell George Sand cast, all her long life, over so many different types of men? In an age when corseted, moss-rose looks were admired, she was swarthy and uncorseted in both her body and her tastes. Even her cigars were exceptional, being composed from Datura leaves, the intoxicatingly scented tropical plant said to madden all who sleep beneath it. But this was no part of her spell. There were simpler causes. Men value a good listener; she knew how to listen with total concentration, to men, or music (even going so far as to crouch *under* the piano when Liszt played, the better to be plunged into the vortex of his more furious inspirations). Chopin always sought her advice on his music. 'Courage, velvet-fingers!' she would exhort him when he faltered.

Then, men, even the most impassioned lovers, are not insensible to their comforts. She was the perfect *maîtresse de maison*, running the house with method, but no rigidity. At Nohant she kept a first-class table and cellar, supervising the kitchens and sometimes cooking some regional speciality herself. There were plenty of devoted servants – twelve was the minimum (while a carpenter and house-painter were employed by the year, keeping up the estate). The wants of her guests were magically supplied. There were two letter-boxes on each floor, one for the mail, the other for guests to place their requests. One, needing a comb, was offered a choice of thirty within the hour.

Above all, men like their health to be a matter of concern to others – especially to the woman they love. George Sand enjoyed best of all to cosset. 'Oh! who will nurse you, and *whom shall I nurse?*' she writes to de Musset after their rupture. It was a cry from her heart, and one, I have often remarked, that was reiterated by nineteenth-century women, who, in general, could only taste power when ruling in the sick-room; though this did not apply to George Sand, the most emancipated of women. Nevertheless, that bossy, motherly pattern predominated during the eight years of her life with Chopin. (For this was a life, rather than a liaison.) 'During eight years I was a mother to him,' she wrote later, and sadly. Passion had soon given place to cups of broth, and solicitude over warm mufflers. 'Chop-Chop' became her third child.

But he, overwhelmingly in love, had not accepted this role easily, as his journals bear witness.

Aurora's eyes are veiled, they only shine when I play: then the world is light and lovely. My fingers glide softly over the keys, her pen flies over the paper. She likes to write to music. Music all around her – Chopin's music, soft but clear, like words of love. For you, Aurore, I will play my sweetest melodies. My darling, with your veiled eyes – you won't be too cruel, will you?

Was she cruel – when she no longer desired him? When she had established her preferred role of mother – or when she feared that the lover's demands would destroy the genius she venerated, and whose precarious health needed, above all, calm?

Before she met Chopin, she had ranged the lists of love vigorously, often choosing men rather as other women choose a bonnet – something they wanted – that suited them for the moment, but was presently discarded without more ado. At that time she *had* to be in love. She believed she could not live or write otherwise, and she went on her chequered way, forever searching, so that her novel *Lélia* is more autobiography than fiction. It is a striking analysis of an unsatisfied, basically frigid woman – one who could love, but still longed to know the transports of a sensualist: which may explain the increasing ascendancy of her maternal side: also, that almost boyish *camaraderie* which she showed to those men with whom she was not emotionally, or rather, sexually involved, for *emotion* she roused in everybody.

Balzac analysed his fellow-writer curiously in his letters to Madame Hanska, his Polish inamorata. He writes of the visits he made to George Sand at Nohant, before Chopin had entered the scene. 'Her *male* [the right man for her] is hard to find,' he wrote. 'She is great, generous, chaste.' Chaste is an unexpected adjective, yet sometimes applied to George Sand by the more discerning observers, who saw below the façade of the *grande amoureuse*. 'She has not a particle of coquetry,' Balzac continued, 'she is *garçon, artiste, camarade . . .* but *not* lovable' (not to be fallen in love with), he hastened to assure Mme Hanska, who had begun to question his frequent visits to Nohant. Such long nights of proximity, both in monk's-robe dressing gowns, both working, sustained by black coffee and cigars, the children tucked away in their beds, upstairs – this was the pattern she pursued with other men of genius, Liszt among them, as he stormed the piano which later Chopin was to use, before importing his own Pleyel. It was a way of life which caused the Countess d'Agoult, Liszt's mistress, as much uneasiness as it did Balzac's faraway lady-love . . . Nohant was not their way, not a way they understood or esteemed, either in the Faubourg, or the Polish estates where, respectively, these ladies had been formed. Both were overloaded with feminine wiles and worldly preoccupations, and both were suspicious of George Sand's *'camaraderie'*.

Chopin and George Sand first met in 1838: she was brought to his apartments in the Rue Chaussée d'Antin by Liszt and Marie d'Agoult. It was not a success, for Chopin thought her altogether too sensational in her masculine clothes, and too overpowering in her Amazonian vitality. 'This Sand! I find her antipathetic. Is she really a woman? I rather doubt it,' was his comment. But she had no hesitations . . . 'A *child*, an angel . . . suffering, exhausted, sad . . .' and 'I *need* to suffer for someone . . .' she added. Some months passed during which time he occupied her thoughts, but it seems that he made no move towards her. Then, suddenly, all Paris knew they were lovers. She was eight years older than he, and by now very experienced in matters of the heart, and the flesh. In her *Histoire de ma Vie*, she notes, 'it was necessary for this angel, strayed down to earth to know something of human love, and its exigencies.' Thus her justification, if such were needed.

In the classic manner of lovers they wished to fly the city to savour their happiness far from the world. They left for Majorca, where the sun was alleged to shine all winter long. Her two children, Maurice and Solange, accompanied them, and so, at once, Chopin was gathered into the family fold. The winter was appalling, and Chopin struggled to survive, composing (among other pieces, some of the best-loved Nocturnes) on a damp-warped piano in the unheated cell of a deserted monastery where they had taken refuge. His hacking cough had alarmed the town dwellers, who, fearful of contagion, had stoned the strangers, so that they fled to the Certosa of Valdemosa, high in the mountains, where beauty abounded but roofs leaked and there was no means of heating. Precipitous miles of goat tracks had to be negotiated before reaching the nearest village, when fetching the limited supplies it offered. The children, reared in their mother's robust ways, enjoyed it all, and to George Sand it seemed a challenging kind of picnic. But for Chopin, who always detested picnic outings, it was a nightmare, only endured because of his consuming passion for this strange, dominant – yet how seductive – creature who had come to obsess and possess him. At this time they were both passionately in love. He surely for the first time; she, doubly rapturous, for here was a man of supreme genius – and fragile too! He was all hers, to love, and to cosset. But she only just got him away from Majorca in time . . . wan and racked with coughing, but all hers!

She installed him at Nohant. Soft, welcoming Nohant closed round him. In the embrasure of her bedroom window she inscribed the date – 19 June 1839. It is still to be seen there, a fatidic date, marking the beginning and the end of a chapter. The beginning of a settled way of life, and the end of adventuring for her. For him, the beginning of those eight years of loving care which fostered his genius and kept at bay his fatal symptoms; the beginning, and the end, too, of his first and only relationship of passionate love and sensual fulfilment.

Nohant was conveniently removed from the tensions and fritter of Paris life: but not too far to be cut off. Across the tree-shaded courtyard, Delacroix, one of Chopin's few intimates, spent much of the year, taking his place in the household and at the table for those delicious meals his hostess knew so well how to organize. Sometimes they were joined by Turgenev and his adored, the incomparable singer Pauline Viardot; or the Bonaparte Prince 'Plon-Plon', Marie Dorval or Arago. Actors, politicians, in particular Republicans, the *blousons bleus*, as they were known, were habitués, for George Sand was strongly Republican in her sympathies. Chopin was not. Liszt described his fellow-musician's prejudices as being a belief that democratic elements were dangerous – an agglomeration of heterogeneous and restless elements wielding too much power. They threatened to destroy art, its monuments and refinements, Chopin thought. Would civilization be safe in the rude and devastating grip of the new barbarians? Thus the arguments raged across the dinner table, in the house that was, in its sober beauty, its unostentatious and selective taste, a perfect example of civilization.

At night feuds and politics were set aside and everyone gathered in the salon round an enormous table built by the estate carpenter to George Sand's design. Here they played nursery games, discussed the most esoteric subjects, made scrap-books, or read aloud chapters of the books they were writing. They drew caricatures of each other (some of those which George Sand made are particularly droll) and laughed uproariously at jolly, and rather bawdy jokes, or together drafted the next act of some play for the puppet theatre that became everyone's passion at Nohant. It was elaborately fitted up, with a little stage, footlights, and rows of seats to house the permanent and visiting audiences. George Sand's son, Maurice, growing up into a clever, spoiled young man, modelled the grotesque puppets marvellously – George Sand dressed them, sewing their uniforms or fantastic garments with equal cunning.

But on the stroke of midnight, she always took leave of her household, vanishing to begin her night's work, writing, smoking, drinking coffee or sugared water till morning. She was entirely disciplined, and known to have finished a book at 1 a.m. and begun another forthwith. 'I don't have a steel spring in my head, that clicks on when I want to write,' complained Jules Sandeau. And de Musset, too, groaned at such precision. Her bedroom was next to that of Chopin, but she had put padded doors everywhere to isolate the household from the sound of his piano. By day, he seldom left his room, admitting only the briefest excursions when dragged out. He, like she, laboured incessantly, and his celebrated *jeu perlé* was less often heard at Nohant than some phrase upon which he was working, reiterated hour by hour, as he strove for perfection. Sometimes, the sound of clapping was heard, and he stood at the head of the graceful curved stone staircase, summoning the whole household round him, to announce that he had triumphed over some particularly tormenting passage.

There were never any servant problems at Nohant. The contented domestics were part of the patriarchal pattern which George Sand believed to be the perfect setting for life and work, friendship *and* love; even so, it had its critics. From afar (though never having known it at first hand) Henry James wrote of it to Edith Wharton. Here is his pinched view.

What a crew! what moeurs, what habits, what conditions and relations every way – and what an altogether mighty and marvellous George! – not diminished by all the greasiness and smelliness in which she made herself – and so many other persons – at home. Poor gentlemanly, crucified Chop! – not naturally at home in grease, but having been originally pulled in, and floundering there at last to extinction.

One wonders what exactly Henry James meant by grease and smelliness. Certainly not the cooking at Nohant: perhaps the rather salty vein of talk that often prevailed there – sometimes too broad for Chopin, the most fastidious of men; but then, was it not all part of that earthy, almost animal warmth, which had first attracted him to George Sand? Henry James' prejudiced, and indeed distorted view is one also sometimes voiced by Chopin's Polish compatriots, who like to blame George Sand for his early death. Yet it is probable that the years at Nohant prolonged his already doomed life, and much of the music he wrote there would never be known to the world but for the house and its châtelaine.

Creative artists, whether well or ill physically, almost all suffer from a certain psychological weakness. Consciously or unconsciously, they crave shelter from the stresses of ordinary life. Their best work is often done when they are lucky enough to become cuckoos in someone else's nest (as was Chopin). They may appear vagabonds, careless Bohemians . . . but what they really need are certain bourgeois stabilities – the ministrations of a devoted wife, or the support of a practical husband. A good servant and a solid bank balance, even if obtained, are not the same thing. At Nohant, in spite of republican politics and being dragged out for the walks and picnics he abhorred, Chopin found there all the rest of the stabilities and cherishing an artist needs.

At Nohant there is nothing bourgeois. The ambience is a mixture of country aristocracy and the intelligentsia, with a leaven of peasant traditions, and below everything, the land, vitalizing in its abiding force. A sense of quiet well-being prevails here: everything is harmonious: the manner in which the house is placed, behind its fine iron gates and beside the little church, snug under its great yews, with the clump of gigantic elms which has sheltered so many generations of birds, as the central point of the village. The long windows of the house open south, on to a terrace, green thickets and lawns: the sequence of rooms are an *enfilade* of quiet elegance, eloquent of a restrained taste but no formal convention. The salon has dark patterned walls lightened by the gilt frames of innumerable family portraits. George Sand's piano stands beside a harp. (Chopin's own piano has since been returned to Warsaw.) Dominating this room is the huge round table which was the centre of family life. George Sand's armchair is beside the chimney-piece and next to a heating grille which she installed there. Another was under her place in the dining-room, for its big white porcelain stove or, indeed, any open fires were never enough for her. The dining-room is spacious yet intimate, panelled and hung with quietly flowered chintzes and lit by a pink and blue Venetian glass chandelier. (Looking up at its intricate curves, one wonders: was this tourist's spoil, some souvenir of that ill-fated tragicomedy of George Sand's Venetian adventure which had begun with the impassioned de Musset and ended with the bewildered Dr Pagello?) In any case, it shines down on the family dinner table, where the original china and glass is still to be seen, laid as if for one of those lively meals which were the signature of Nohant's hospitality. Circling this table, the visitor hangs over the place-cards which a proud curator has arranged with authenticity . . . Turgenev beside Chopin, Prince Napoleon on the hostess's right, Delacroix across from Flaubert or la Malibran . . . so that were it not for the knowledge that all these and many more such legendary figures did gather round this table, it might seem one of those unconvincing pageants or waxwork peep shows where famous persons are all lumped together in an excess of historic zeal.

Beyond the dining-room, panelled doors lead to the beautiful formal bedroom once inhabited by George Sand's grandmother, but rarely by herself, except when first married. Later, she used a small adjoining dressing-room which was her study, when, in 1832, she wrote *Indiana* and opened her shutters (the midnight's kind admittance) to one of her first loves. She liked best to sleep in a hammock: the hooks are still to be seen, spearing the *toile de jouey* of the walls. It was a defiant vagabond's gesture against formality, which, at that time, she still suspected might engulf her, so that as often as not she slept out in the fields.

Upon her return to Nohant from Paris, to settle there permanently, she moved her bedroom upstairs; her Empire bed, like the walls, were hung with a gay blue and white percale. The furniture was rustic in its simplicity: but one particularly fine *demi-lune* commode was a present from Chopin. Of his room next door there is now no trace, for when he left Nohant, in the bitterness of their parting, she had the room entirely changed, partitioned into two, and lined with shelves and cabinets to house her collection of minerals and shells.

It had been such an unworthy quarrel: it flared up after years of minor irritations which had been fostered by the attitude of the children, now grown up and reacting, each in their own way, to the presence of their mother's lover – for so the world still saw him, though he always referred to her with meticulous discretion as 'my hostess'. Or was it his form of irony, since, in essence, she had become just that and no more? Intricacies of jealousy developed: Solange, malicious and greedy, set out to filch Chopin away from the still too fascinating mother of whom she was always jealous. Maurice came to open warfare. There were ridiculous scenes as to who should have the best cut of chicken; George Sand's maternal instincts favoured her real child, and Chopin sulked. But perhaps, since he had long been denied a lover's feast, lesser appetites began to matter. Nursery squabbles, they seemed, to those who saw them from the outside, but there were subtle undertones. And all the while, George Sand wrote on, tirelessly. Now her fame was assured, but she was goaded by economic necessities, for the way of life and the various demands on her purse were heavy, and the generosity of *la bonne dame de Nohant* was legendary.

For some years they had been in the habit of keeping a set of rooms in Paris, in the Square d'Orléans, where she and Chopin could receive more easily. This was in the nature of an elaborate *pied-à-terre* (rather than a Pavilion). They visited it spasmodically: it adjoined the apartments of several friends, with whom they shared a dining-room; it had a club-like quality, and it was here that everyone of note in Paris life came. The rooms being designed principally as salons, or reception rooms, were *mondain* rather than family in essence. Chopin's had *café au lait* walls lit by numbers of girandoles. The upholstery was dark velvet: there were Chinoiseries and ormolu, and the Pleyel upon which he gave lessons to favoured pupils was the centre-piece. Elegance was very much to Chopin's taste; but George Sand made a gesture of defiance, emphasizing her nomadic leanings by eschewing a bed. She replaced this by a pile of cushions and a mattress on the floor, covered with Oriental rugs: its effect was exotic, wildly exotic by contemporary standards, and it served to remind *'le tout Paris'* of those gypsy origins of which she boasted. Here she would hold court, stretched out voluptuously, perhaps wearing those scarlet embroidered trousers and gold slippers which fascinated Balzac, as did her beautiful hands. 'Anti-Republican hands' the Goncourt brothers called them, praise wrung from them unwillingly, for they were never sympathetic to George Sand. All the same, they described her hands as 'graceful, lost in lace ruffles like a flutter of white butterflies as she lit, and re-lit her eternal cigars'.

In spite of this romantic aura she could be coldly practical, showing a cynical awareness of the world and its ways. When Solange (now married to the equally dislikable Clésinger, a sculptor, and forever pressing her mother for more money) threatened to set up with some rich protector, her mother lashed out. She did not waste time on moral strictures, for she was no hypocrite: but then, her own relationships, however free, had never been for anything but love. 'Remember,' she wrote, 'men with money to spend want women who know how to earn it. *Do you know?'*

Yet all George Sand's knowledge of the world and men did not prepare her, or protect her, when the break with Chopin came. She had not envisaged their rupture could be final. When, after a particularly acrimonious dispute with Maurice, who put an ultimatum to his mother – either Chopin or he must go – George Sand thought it best for Chopin to absent himself – for a while. And so, in 1847, Chopin left Nohant – never to return. George Sand sent back the piano he had wished her to keep. 'He can't pay me off with a piano,' was her bitter reply; but she continued to fret over his health from afar, often reminding his friends to care for him as she had done: but who could do that?

Less than three years later, he was dead. Nothing was left but echoes. . . . How often she must have listened for those divine nightingale songs he sang for her. . . . How often echoes of his plaintive harmonies must have sounded, below the busy hum of the household, the laughter and talk which continued unheeding round the big table. How often she must have listened for the sound of his step on the stair, or heard again, in the night, that fretful cough in the room beside her own. No one ever slept there again: the partition and the shelves of minerals took care of that. But she kept a scrap of the blue and red wallpaper, putting it under glass. It always stood on her work table. 'I was very fond of that paper,' was all she would say: all that she ever told of the emptiness that remained.

Yet Nohant could never be truly empty: she had lived too many wonderful hours there, and continued, in a quieter key, to live them till her death there in 1876. Long after Chopin's music there were the five-finger exercises of her little grand-daughters: and all about her, friends and adorers still, while the gardens and countryside, nature itself, was forever renewing the greenness she loved.

And there were her memories. It is only those who have never known the fires of love who have no hearth of memory at which to warm themselves. At Nohant, the fires had blazed; but they never turned to ashes, sinking rather to a golden glow.

9

Blagodatsk
Siberia

THE ROMANTIC undertones of the gigantic and sombre fresco of the Dekabrist Rising of 1825, 'the Revolution that stood and waited', have remained untarnished by every succeeding mood of Russian historians.

Whatever the viewpoint on the insurgents – the Dekabristi, so called from the fact that their abortive rising took place in December – who have been variously described as saviours, traitors, muddle-headed idealists, princely hypocrites or the noblest forerunners of the Russian Revolution, the devotion of those women who abandoned everything, freedom, luxury, rank – even their children – to follow their condemned husbands to Siberia, is unquestioned. The tumbledown *izba*, or hut-dwelling, in which Princess Wolkonsky and Princess Troubetsköe were first quartered, remains an object of veneration, while in Chita, the street known as Damskaya Ulitza – the Ladies' Street – honours them to this day. As to the cell where Princess Wolkonsky at last rejoined her husband, although now no trace remains, of all my Pavilions it can most truly be described as such.

To understand something of the events which brought about the Prince's sentence to the convict mines of Siberia, and his young wife's voluntary exile there, it is necessary to know something of the Dekabrist tragedy. The principal characters of this abortive stand for freedom, and its whole tragic aftermath, have obsessed many of the greatest Russian writers, Pushkin, Tolstoy, Herzen, Nekrasov . . . Pushkin, but for a twist of fate, would have been among the insurgents, and one of his most celebrated poems is addressed to them, while Nekrasov's lovely verses *Russian Women* were inspired by the Dekabrist wives. Tolstoy was at one time obsessed by the Dekabrist drama, and it was his original inspiration for the vast historical novel which, after a number of fragments and false starts, came to be situated a generation earlier and emerge as *War and Peace*, with Pierre Bezoukhov as an ideological forerunner of the Dekabristi. Thus we shall never know how he would have evoked this doomed band, with their conflicting characters united by their absolute belief in liberty. Strangely, Tolstoy came to condemn them as setting Russian against Russian: but then, as one of the aged survivors told him, 'You cannot hope to write about us – to understand us, you would have had to be one of us – then.'

Yet in the character of those women who joined and sustained the prisoners – in particular, the Princess Maria Wolkonsky – Tolstoy would have found a heroine, and a love, worthy of his genius.

She was young, charmingly pretty, and cultivated, the daughter of General Raievsky, a hero of 1812. Her family divided their time between St Petersburg, where they belonged by birth to the inner circle around the Court, and the patriarchal way of life on their country estates. They were rich, aristocratic and privileged. The young Princess had always lived in the careless, unquestioning luxury of her kind. At eighteen she had been married off to Prince Sergei Wolkonsky, whose mother was Mistress of the Robes to the dowager Empress. The marriage was favoured by both families, though for Princess Maria it was not a love match. Her husband was nearly twenty years older, often absent serving with his regiment, and preoccupied, along with so many other Guards officers, with long-cherished, vague dreams and, alas! extremely ill-organized plans for a military coup which would obtain for the country certain desperately needed reforms – above all, a Constitution.

But when the ailing, disabused Tzar Alexander I died unexpectedly, in mysterious circumstances, far away in Taganrog, it was found that his heir and brother, the Grand Duke Constantine, had abdicated in favour of the youngest brother, Nicholas, an implacable autocrat – 'despotism made man'. With his accession, all hopes of reform perished. Thus before the Dekabristi could strike a blow for freedom they were already doomed, while their own confusion, delays, mystical doubts and sudden scruples finished them off. They were mostly of the high military caste – blazing with an idealism first sparked by the political institutions and liberal climate they had found around them when, as very young officers in the Napoleonic wars, they had been part of the victorious Allied armies occupying Paris in 1814. Their enthusiasm had, in the ensuing years, led them to become increasingly critical of their own country, its backward conditions, the absolute autocracy which prevailed there, and the continuation of such abuses as the military colonies and, above all, serfdom. They founded a number of secret societies spread about the country, where, at the frequent meetings, they spent their time talking – talking, far into the night, demagogic discussions, politico-idealistic dreams of unrealizable projects and reforms; but never any really concrete plans.

The death of the Emperor Alexander I caught them by surprise. It was the crucial moment of Nicholas I's accession, when the army were being sworn in, taking the oath of allegiance to their new Tzar, that seemed a propitious moment to make a stand, influencing the army to withhold its allegiance until a Constitution was granted. Unfortunately, many members of the Northern Society were then absent from the capital. Nevertheless, the nucleus marched on the Senate Square, there to put their demands. This vast classical expanse lies at the heart of St Petersburg, and is as icy, grandiose and inhuman as was the new Tzar, who was to fix the rebels with what Herzen has described as his 'pewter stare'. In this gigantic setting of granite and marble and bronze, man seems reduced to pigmy proportions; in the sketches and prints which recall the fatal confrontation, even the massed troops and the huge crowds of onlookers appear ant-like, lost in the immensity. Especially lost, the forlorn little band of insurgents.

'There is very little chance of our succeeding, but the attempt must be made. It will be an example, and perhaps, bear fruit later,' said Ryliev, the brains behind the movement. But the fruits it bore did not fully ripen until a century later with the Revolution of 1917, and by then they were of another flavour.

On that 14 December 1825, of the sixteen Guards' regiments then quartered in the capital (which has been described as an armed camp), only one battalion and a few companies were beside the insurgents. Other troops who might have marched to their support were stationed too far away. With this handful the rebels faced the Tzar's infantry, three thousand cavalry and twelve hundred artillery. So grave had their menace seemed to the new Tzar, at first. So pitiful did it become.

When Nicholas I rode out from the Winter Palace he meant to make short work of them, but seeing them, standing there irresolute, he too hesitated, so that both sides 'stood and waited'. The silent, watching mob now began to side with the rebels, stoning the Emperors troops when at last they charged. The rebels reformed their ranks, and still no *pour-parler* had been achieved. As the short winter's day darkened, the insurgents were wildly discussing a plan to cross the Neva, seize the fortress of Peter and Paul, and from this vantage point train its guns on the Winter Palace, directly *en face*, thus compelling the Tzar to accept their ultimatum. But before this stand could be made, the Tzar ordered his artillery forward. However, confusion was not only among the rebel ranks. It was now discovered that no ammunition had been brought with the guns – a situation worthy of Gogol's pen. When at last this was rectified, there were more delays, for the gunners held back, openly defying their officers' commands in a manner which threatened mutiny. For a moment it seemed that they might go over to the rebels. At last, their officers forced them to open fire, and panic spread across the Senate Square as the terrified onlookers were mown down and the insurgent troops, ignoring their commanders, fled across the frozen Neva, where the ice broke under them, so that many were drowned. Among the Chevalier Guards lined up behind the Tzar, watching the carnage, splendid creatures in their flashing helmets and breastplates, their big bay horses stamping and fretting in the freezing air, there were fourteen who were also members of the various secret societies, and who had shared the insurgents' liberal aspirations. What were their emotions as the guns opened fire? 'Sombre destinies, Russian destinies;' in the words of the Russian historian Constantin de Grunwald.

All those whom the Dekabrist Rising touched, or who were involved in its tragic aftermath, shared the same sombre destiny. Those who were not shot down on the Senate Square were rounded up during the night and brought, fettered, to the Winter Palace, there to be interrogated by the Tzar himself. For the most part they were both straightforward and naïve: he was neither. And here, as in subsequent Russian trials, we see that curious national characteristic which appears to almost wallow in self-recrimination or 'spontaneous confession', something not always brought about by inhuman pressures, but perhaps more by an inherent, or atavistic craving to submit.

The Dekabristi believed that once they confessed, or disclosed their patriotic aspirations, it would open the young Tzar's eyes to Russia's need for reforms. On the contrary, it hardened his resolve to suppress the slightest moves towards liberalism.

The sentences he passed, in the name of God and justice, were merciless. Death, exile, life imprisonment . . . day after day he signed away the lives of his prisoners. Five of the Dekabristi were hung. They had not been warned, but were led out, very early one morning, and in sight of their comrades, watching it all from the windows of their cells, were strung up. The effect of these hangings on the country was one of disbelief, and horror. The death penalty had been in abeyance in Russia for a century or more. Neither the public, the prisoners, or their families believed it would be revived. But it was, and hideously mismanaged, too. No hangman could be found until one was fetched from Sweden. The scaffold was badly constructed and the ropes broke, the condemned men crashing into the pit below, breaking their bones, lying there bound and helpless while fresh ropes were sought. It was early morning and a search had to be made for a shop that was open and sold rope. Some of the prison authorities argued that no man could be executed twice – it was God's will they should now be freed.

'Hang them! Hang them!' shrieked the prison Governor, and the whole gruesome business began all over again. 'Unhappy Russia, where they can't even hang one properly,' said Ryliev, awaiting death with composure.

The executions were followed at once by the departure of convoys of prisoners for Siberia, and it is with one of the first groups that the name of Wolkonsky remains forever linked. Prince Sergei and seven others were marched from their cells to set off, on the instant, eastwards, to the mines of Nertchinsk, a penal colony that even the most hardened criminals seldom survived. On that same July night there was a ball at the house of Prince Kotchubey, Minister of the Interior. It was a sumptuous affair, part of the festivities by which the Coronation was celebrated. The Tzar himself was present, and dancing with Princess Sophie Wolkonsky, Sergei's mother, when the convoy was seen passing below the brilliantly lit windows of the Kotchubey palace. A shudder of despair ran through the ballroom. Many of the guests were related to the Dekabristi – but they knew they must always hide their feelings, smile, continue dancing. On the Tzar's commands life and the Court was to go on as if the Dekabrist Rising had never been. Thus Princess Sophie Wolkonsky continued to partner the Tzar while among the convicts passing outside was her son, haggard, emaciated, and in irons. She was never to see him again. No prayers, no intercessions moved the Tzar. He was adamant. These wicked men had dared to question the divine rights of an absolute monarchy. He had punished them, and soon they, and all that for which they had stood, would be forgotten.

But he had not reckoned with their wives.

For some while Maria Wolkonsky's family had succeeded in keeping news of the executions from her, as they had hidden the departure of her husband for Siberia. She was at the Raievsky's country house, where she had just given birth to her first child, and they believed she would, in time, forget the past and build a new life round Sergei's son. But when at last she learned her husband was dispatched to Nertchinsk, she announced her intention of following him. Her frantic family appealed to her reason, to her love for her baby, they dwelt on the appalling hardships and the vast distances that would separate her from all she had known; but her mind was made up. Nothing would stop her. When they found she had already applied to the Tzar for permission to rejoin her husband, they pulled every string to prevent her request reaching the Autocrat. Princess Troubetsköe had already confronted the Emperor with the same request, and gradually, more were to follow. At first the Emperor refused them all, but they persisted; and since he, the stern moralist, always upheld the sanctity of marriage, he found himself cornered. Grudgingly, he gave in. But the conditions he imposed were characteristically harsh. They must give up their rights, fortunes and titles, being known as 'the Criminal so and so'. Their children must be listed as serfs, as was customary with convicts. Each stage of their journey, like all their correspondence, must be under the supervision and will of the local governors and police. Once there, they might never return; when their husbands' sentence expired, both must remain to be posted wherever the authorities chose, as 'free' settlers. Nor, were they to be widowed during their exile, could they ever return – they had accepted the convicts' lot, and for them Siberia was to be their life and death. Such were the terms Princess Maria signed.

She made her preparations for departure in a state of exaltation, amid the grief and despair of her family. On the eve of setting out, she was in Moscow, among a group of friends. There was music, but the guests were overcome with melancholy, knowing this to be their last sight of her, as she too had known when leaving her baby with her family that this would be her last sight of him. Instinct – prescience? He was to die within the year. Nevertheless, she believed with her whole heart and mind that her place was with her husband. She had not been in love with him – she had not the impetus of that passionate love which existed between Princess Troubetsköe and her husband – but she believed with an equal passion in the cause he had supported. Had she been a man, she would certainly have stood beside him on the Senate Square. As it was, she could at least stand beside him in Siberia, proving both to him, and to the world, the strength of her convictions and the love she now felt for him.

As the candles burnt low and her friends began their leave-taking, blessing her, through their tears, with the triple kiss of Russian ritual, she asked for yet another song. Leaning hungrily over the piano, she is recorded as having listened with tragic intensity.

'Again – again! Remember, I shall never hear music again,' they heard her say.

Pushkin, who was among the guests, was profoundly moved. (There is a belief that she was the unspoken love of his life.) He had known her first when exiled to the Caucasus, and she was a pretty, playful little creature of fourteen. As a grown woman she appeared full of light, careless gaiety, but in fact she possessed a force of character, a courage and integrity which was to sustain her, her husband, and his fellow prisoners through the long years to come. These were qualities which Pushkin was never to find again, in any of the many other women he loved.

Princess Maria's journey from St Petersburg to Irkutsk was four thousand miles by relays of bone-breaking tarantass and troikas. She had left Moscow on 27 December, a year and thirteen days after 'the Revolution that stood and waited' had been crushed. She reached her goal – the convict settlement beyond Irkutsk – at the end of the following February. All the way she had forced the pace, scarcely stopping to eat or sleep at the wretched *korchmas* (village inns), or the posting stations. Sometimes she was forcibly detained, under the cold, unsympathetic eye of the gendarmerie, while an officer questioned her papers, or some reactionary provincial Governor, bored by his isolation, amused himself by tormenting her with needless red-tape restrictions, or attempted to dissuade her from proceeding further, so that she might, perhaps, mitigate his ennui by accepting his hospitality.

Her route lay across the Urals by way of Tobolsk and Krasnoiarsk to Irkutsk, last outpost of civilization, where the town – a conglomeration of small, low-roofed houses and peasant *izbas* – crouched round the few fine new buildings, the Governor-General's mansion, in the classic St Petersburg idiom, some gold-domed churches and monasteries, and the ornate, turreted, robber-baron style dwellings popular with the rich merchants. They traded chiefly in furs and precious stones. Much business was done with the Chinese, at the nearby frontier post of Kiakhta, where, as token of gratitude for thriving enterprise, the merchants had endowed the little Orthodox church with solid silver doors studded with jewels, emeralds, rubies and the local, freshwater pearls, a tribute of barbaric largesse which was in keeping with the prodigious nature of Siberia itself.

At Irkutsk everything was on an excessive scale: riches, or a lack of them, heat, cold, empty horizons. The unpaved streets soon petered out into snow, slush or mud, knee high; in the brief and torrid summers there was blinding dust and plagues of mosquitoes. All around, the vast nothingness of Asiatic wastes marked only by rare tracks, north to the fathomless immensity of Lake Baïkal, an inland sea, or east to the Mongol and Chinese hinterland. Everywhere, seeming to press close like some dark menacing tide or vegetal force, surged the *taïga*, impenetrable forest regions where no man lived. The rare convicts who escaped to hide there soon died, or returned to give themselves up, facing the prison knout rather than the *taïga*.

This, then, was Princess Maria's last contact with the outside world before leaving on the final stage of her journey to Nertchinsk.

The mines there were known, ironically, as Blagodatsk, or Bliss. There were a few Buriat-Mongol encampments nearby, a strong guard surrounding the prison stockade, and nothing else. There was no possibility of escape – except by death. Conditions at Blagodatsk were appalling: the prisoners worked long hours, every day, all the year round, in fetid darkness, often up to their waists in water, mining iron ore. Their overseer admitted to hoping he could drive them to death. Their food was often putrid, scurvy ravaged them, and already one of them had gone mad. They slept, as they worked, chained, the heavy leg-irons biting into their flesh. They were ragged and verminous. No news reached them from the outside world; a hopeless silence enclosed them. They were still mostly young men – and it seemed, forgotten men, as the Tzar had ordained. But these princes, these brilliant men of the world, Guards officers, poets, intellectuals and idealists, were not forgotten.

They, like the Tzar, had not reckoned with their wives.

The conditions of living, or dying, by slow degrees, in which the Dekabristi found themselves at Blagodatsk were in almost inconceivable contrast to their former lives. For most of them, their birthright had been great wealth, cultivation and ease. It was just this which had begun to play on their conscience. In the Memoirs of Prince Kropotkin and Baron Wrangel, both a succeeding generation to the Dekabristi but brought up in a similar style, we read of the arrogance and privilege their caste enjoyed. Wrangel's aunt, a survivor from the Court of Emperor Paul I, spoke the French of Versailles but could not tell the time. 'For that sort of thing I have my women,' she would say, ringing for her serf-maid. Batches of serfs were gambled away at the card table, or were married off or separated from their families on the owner's whim: *le droit du Seigneur* went unquestioned. Such was the way of many landowners: but not all. An enlightened pattern also existed, and from such a background came the aristocratic Dekabrist ringleaders.

The old country houses of the Troubetsköes, Wolkonskys, Davidovs and Raievskys maintained a tranquil pattern; vast wealth and culture was combined with an aristocratic sense of responsibility verging on the democratic. Such families were of, but ideologically apart from, the Court. Their country houses were elegant, though unpretentious in terms of St Petersburg splendours. Often built of wood, they had colonnaded porches and wide verandahs. All around, smaller dwellings, stables, outhouses and farm buildings gathered in intimate proximity. In the gardens classical statues were sometimes placed rather casually, tangled with lilac or ivy; alleys of pleached lime or acacia usually led to a lake, or the willow-fringed river. Beyond, woods, forests, fields of wheat and the dependent villages stretched into that far, quiet distance which is ever the signature of Russia's countryside. This was the setting of Princess Maria's childhood, and, she had supposed, would be that of her married life.

Servants abounded in this feudal ambience. For a family of eight, fifty servitors about the house did not seem excessive. There were generally some useful resident extras, such as a piano tuner, a pastrycook, a tailor and an orchestra of twelve or more, all excellently trained musicians, all of them serfs. The estate carpenter made much of the furniture, often of exotic West Indian woods: but there were fine imported Empire and Directoire pieces, eighteenth-century French stuff, Dresden dinner services and Bohemian glass; and the larger houses usually contained, besides libraries and boudoirs, a pillared ballroom to which the neighbouring nobility came, driving enormous distances to dance, in a manner and a setting that Pushkin's *Eugene Onegin* and Tchaikovsky's opera of that name have immortalized.

In the Ukraine, on the Davidov estate at Kamenka, where the Dekabristi used to meet in secret and where Pushkin liked to loll on the billiard table when writing, the summers were fiercely hot and flies abounded, so that mirrors and pictures were generally tied up in muslin bags to prevent them becoming fly-blown, a homely touch beside much elegance. In such houses, the library shelves were stocked with classics and the latest volumes of French, German or Italian literature in their original. Poetry, philosophy and political treatises, and the latest reviews were found there – all of them absorbed and dissected ardently in endless coils of talk, forever renewing themselves, self-generating, timeless, prolonged all through the night. With no exigencies of wage-earning to be considered, and not the least physical effort to be made with so many serfs to hand, all energy could be concentrated on the intellect, and, of course, being Russians, full rein was given to the emotions too. In the case of the Dekabristi, Utopian reforms were also envisaged. But behind all their mystic mazes of idealism, their theoretic, rather than positive plans, the planners were sustained by a background of traditional ease and luxury.

Imagine, then, the horror which now engulfed the prisoners at Blagodatsk. Imagine, too, the violent impact of that moment when the Princesses Wolkonsky and Troubetsköe first came face to face with the truth of Siberian prison life. Until then they had imagined their husbands' imprisonment in vaguely dramatic terms – an abstraction of persecution. But when, for the first time, Princess Troubetsköe caught sight of the Prince through a chink in the prison stockade, and saw this skeletal figure in a ragged convict's smock, stumbling in chains and spitting blood, she fainted.

Blagodatsk

When at last the guards led Princess Maria to her husband's cell, she found herself in a filthy, dark, kennel-like enclosure, four by six, and too low for her to stand upright. Confronting her, a ragged, chained creature – the man she had come to love and venerate as a symbol of man's fight for liberty. In a sublime – and extremely Slav – gesture of love and abnegation, she knelt down and kissed his chains.

Although nothing could lessen the sublimity of this gesture, nor her subsequent years of courage and devotion, it must be said, anti-climax or no, that as the years went by conditions of life for the Dekabristi did improve. Probably this was due, first, to the presence and ceaseless efforts of the wives, and the vigilance of the wealthier families, who contrived to send them money (with which they set up a fund of pooled resources, to the benefit of the less fortunate prisoners, who received nothing). They even received medicines, sewing materials, books, and the latest periodicals – among them, by some Slavic confusion or perversity, those which were banned in St Petersburg as politically inadmissible!

The prison Commandant, old General Leparsky, proved a benevolent despot, but he was also a stickler for regulations. Princess Maria, like the other wives who followed her, was at first only allowed to visit her husband once a week for one hour. For that one hour they were alone together in the cell, with its pallet bed, or bench, and verminous coverings: or he would be led to her hut-dwelling like a leashed animal. During these snatched moments together, as on any other occasions, such as exchanges through the stockade (where the wives used to station themselves on the chance of glimpsing their husbands through the cracks) it was forbidden to speak in French, lest the guards might miss something of political significance. Thus even their softest murmurs were monitored by sentries stationed at the door, just as their closest embrace was chilled by the chains that clanked about them.

When by their burgeoning silhouette some of the wives began to proclaim their approaching maternity, the old bachelor Leparsky was indignant: 'But, ladies, you had no *right* to become pregnant!' he said: though he set about demanding better living conditions. Even so, St Petersburg refused permission for any considerable ameliorations. Children were not accounted for in the Dekabrist conditions of imprisonment, and were referred to by the bureaucracy as 'the innocent victims of unbridled passion'.

It was at Leparsky's instigation that in 1827 the Dekabristi were moved from the mines of Blagodatsk to an abandoned Cossack fort near Chita – again the Buriat-Mongol frontier regions. Here they felt almost snug; work was reduced to a token level, mostly of an agricultural order, and their chains were at last removed, so that they came, later, to recall this period with nostalgia. At Chita they were still lit by a glow of illusion and hope: they believed their reprieve *must* come soon . . . But it did not. Presently they were moved – on Government or Winter Palace orders – to a less casual administration at Petrovsky Zavod, an insalubrious area edged by marshes: what of it, if they fell ill or perished? But there, at last, the presence of their wives had to be acknowledged officially and married quarters provided, though to begin with the rooms had no windows. (The Tzar had personally approved this as a security measure.) The guards made their rounds each evening at nine o'clock, removing all candles and locking the doors until morning.

In these conditions the once pampered Princesses continued to cook and sew and mend, making a sad mess of it, at first. After some years they were able to acquire domestics – the untrained but willing local peasants – and in time, too, they obtained a piano and formed a musical group, so that Princess Maria did, at last, hear music again. Life went by. More children were born; some of the original band died of their hardships. The lovely fragile wife of Nikita Mouraviev died, and was buried beside the prison stockade where she had so often taken up her place, consoling her husband and his companions by her presence. Still the Dekabristi held to their courage, adapting themselves as best they could. They refused to be defeated by Siberia. They formed a debating society. (One wonders, was this really necessary, considering the Russian appetite for discussion, at all times?) They set up classes for their children, conducted various agricultural experiments, and were the first to introduce tomatoes to Siberian soil. But they were growing older, and, at last, disillusioned: nothing could dispel their basic melancholy now they realized the tragic ineffectuality of their stand. As the years passed and all hopes of a reprieve vanished, they became almost reconciled to their lot, valuing the brotherhood which their common suffering and ideals had welded, as they all loved and revered the women who had joined them.

'O sombre Russian destinies!' After thirteen years, an even more tragic destiny confronted them, and they were to look back on all their earlier trials as something endurable, ennobled by unity. They were to describe it as 'the poetry of our youth'. But the poetry lay in the plural. They had been *together*. In middle age they were suddenly, ruthlessly, torn apart – ostensibly pardoned – to be dispersed as 'free' settlers, thrown out to fend for themselves, while yet under irksome restrictions, in some remote area where, in some cases, only Buriat tribes were living. Never again were they to know the comfort and close companionship of their brotherhood. Some obtained leave to join the army, in the ranks, of course, and so, fought and died in the Caucasian wars. Some went mad, took to drink or committed suicide; some married local peasant women; a few found employment teaching in the newly opened schools. There, they formed a cadre of outstandingly brilliant students, renowned later throughout Russia for their attainments. All of the Dekabristi tried to keep in touch, to keep up each other's morale, but they had lived and suffered *together*, and now were dying off – apart.

The Wolkonskys were more fortunate than most. They spent the remaining years of their sentence in Irkutsk, in positively affluent circumstances, with a spacious house and twenty-five servants. The Troubetsköes were also in Irkutsk, both families becoming a source of pride to the inhabitants. 'Our Princes' they were called fondly. When Princess Wolkonsky entered the new opera house with her little daughter, who had been born in prison, her ovation was so overwhelming that the Governor-General, fearing political demonstrations, was obliged to forbid her appearing in public.

Although there is nothing left of the old Dekabrist prison quarters, there are a number of relics preserved in the Museum at Irkutsk, pathetic trifles to recall so heroic a band. . . . Most poignant, their chains and some pieces of jewellery which were fashioned from their iron fetters, like the legendary Dekabrist wedding rings. The women had been compelled to forfeit even their wedding rings before entering Siberia as convicts, something which had caused them particular anguish, until they were replaced by those fashioned from their husbands' chains.

The house in which the Wolkonskys lived their last years of exile – until, in 1856, they were reprieved by order of the newly crowned and idealistic Tzar Alexander II (he who was to liberate the serfs) – still stands in a quiet backwater of Irkutsk. There are now plans to transform it into a museum of Dekabrist history, something which I hope will come about. When I visited it a few years ago, I found a dilapidated yet charming old wooden building, with ornate but crumbling shutters and tottering stairways leading to different floors then let off in sections, the whole being far too near a fish pickling plant. But the legend, the aura of drama, still seemed to envelop the place, overcoming fishy blasts. True their lives had at last become comfortable (with twenty-five domestics to awake echoes of ancestral ease), but Siberia still held them prisoner, still stifled them.

Sitting beside the high wooden gates of the old house, I imagined the Prince, sixty or more, become a bearded patriarchal figure, entirely involved in his market garden and agricultural projects. I saw him talking with the peasants and farmers who were now his only companions, and who loved 'Our Prince' for his simplicity' and greatness. Looking up at the blank windows, where a thin curtain hung awry, I thought I caught a glimpse of a woman's face within. The Princess Maria herself? But now I did not see the lion-hearted young wife of Blagodatsk, but a sad-faced woman, marked by resignation, careworn by the life of love and abnegation she had chosen, a woman for whom the reprieve was to come too late, for she died soon after returning to Russia, a woman who never saw herself as embodying a heroic or romantic legend, yet who did so, from that moment when she first entered her husband's cell and in so doing made it the Pavilion of their most unhappy hearts.

10

Triebschen

Switzerland

N O DISCUSSION of Pavilions or the settings of true love could deny a special place to Triebschen, that snug house in Switzerland inhabited, during the first years of their perfervid love, by Cosima von Bülow and Richard Wagner. From that union, in that house, stems some of the music which exalts and most perfectly expresses love. When the lovers first came together there, Cosima (Liszt's daughter) was married to von Bülow, the conductor, Wagner's devoted friend. For some while Cosima's conscience kept her from joining Wagner; but, presently, she gave up the struggle and a child was born, though accepted as von Bülow's. Triebschen was a retreat where Wagner sought peace from the infatuation of his patron King Ludwig II of Bavaria, while yet encouraging him by the most fulsome letters of admiration. From Triebschen the lovers faced an international scandal. Among those who most loudly condemned them was Liszt; his admiration for Wagner as a musician was unbounded, and he had been very generous, promoting Wagner's earlier operas at Weimar. But the liaison with Cosima, his daughter, von Bülow's wife, outraged Liszt, who by now appears to have forgotten the scandals of his own youth.

Von Bülow behaved with noble restraint, his belief in Wagner's genius overcoming the bitterness of the injured husband. He continued to conduct the operas and further Wagner's glory. The King reeled from the shock of discovering his adored one, 'My saviour! My God! My Only One!' was not wholly his. But Cosima's tact and everyone's realization of Wagner's stature overcame this difficult passage, and the royal patronage remained unshaken. The lonely monarch continued between the exaltation of operatic performances and wandering phantom-like about his various palaces. At Triebschen, not all the plush *portières*, potted palms, pictures on easels and heavy, German Renaissance-style suites massed there could smother the steamingly sensuous atmosphere these two created around them. It was a far cry from those other German Romantics we associate with Schumann's music and the paintings of Begas, Schwind or Kersting, where lovers sit placid in the lamplight beside their families, and someone plays the flute. *Der Stille Garten. . . .*

On the face of it, Cosima and Wagner are not a prepossessing pair, not the figures we associate with high passions; long-nosed, humourless Cosima (though one would have to be humourless to live with Wagner) with her rather masculine features, a caricature of her father's, and Wagner, a stumpy figure, prone to skin diseases of nervous origin, wearing that frightful Rembrandt beret and fiercely convinced the world owed him every luxury and indulgence. 'I am *different*,' he writes, 'the world owes me what I need! I can't live on a miserable organist's salary like your Master Bach! Is it unheard-of presumption if I think I am entitled to a bit of luxury I like? *I* who give pleasure to the world – to thousands!'

And there is the truth: for that divine music we admit and forgive his tiresomeness and monstrous behaviour alike. King Ludwig poured out more money from the state coffers of Munich for Wagner, the worshipped. Wagner, while composing his masterpieces, was apt to come down from the clouds, at times, and plunge into earthly luxuries (on the King's money), ordering more and more lilac satin négligés – feminine outfits also soothed his nerves and sensitive skin – while more and more swathes of lilac satin decorated his walls, and more and more velvet cushions surrounded him. But that was before he reached the haven of Triebschen, and Cosima's love.

Triebschen was a square, shuttered, typically bourgeois Swiss house overlooking the lake of Lucerne and surrounded by a grassy orchard garden. It was very comfortable, and the King's largesse kept it that way, with a staff of servants to oil the wheels, leaving the lovers free to concentrate on music, and each other. Across the lake the great mountains loomed up, or vanished in the mists; when the *Föhn* blew with nerve-wracking insistence, it drowned the customary sound of bells which drifted across the water from the far shore, and so the lovers' isolation from the world seemed complete. They wished it so. 'We have joys quite unlike those of others,' wrote Cosima, vibrating with the overpowering emotion of loving and being loved by Wagner. 'Few have a life like ours,' she continues, with the complacency of mutual love. How they loved to love! The Wagnerian tempo was maintained at fever pitch. 'He says he knows only one thing . . . since the world began, no man of his age has ever loved a woman as he loves me.' Cosima regarded him as a demi-god. 'I stay with him while he writes the words' (of *Siegfried*). Her cup overflowed with rapture, as well it might. To have been part of this man's working life, his inspiration, as he said she was, must have compensated her for all those sad years of childhood, when she was kept cruelly at arm's length by Liszt, relegated to governesses.

At Triebschen in 1869, at 4 a.m. on a June morning, their son Siegfried was born. Wagner rushed upstairs, 'an incredible orange glow as of fire lit the wallpaper, and was reflected on the blue casket with my portrait on it, so that the picture was transfigured with an unearthly beauty.' That morning the sun had risen in splendour over the Rigi; but to Wagner, it was first of all some supernatural, divine ray, illuminating *his* likeness. In August 1870, the divorce obtained, they married; on the following Christmas day, Cosima's thirty-third birthday, Wagner arranged for a small orchestra from Lucerne to gather on the stairs outside her room, to awaken her with the *Siegfried* (or Triebschen) *Idyll*. Indeed, she knew joys few others know.

One really endearing aspect of Wagner's nature was his affection for animals. Dogs and parrots were part of the household. Dear little Peps, or the large dog Russ, who accompanied Wagner (who wore sensible, but gaudy red waterproof boots) on his daily ritualistic walks at Triebschen. Later, at their last home, Wahnfried, 'the house of happiness' (still very much a Pavilion, for their love, however ecstatic, was of enduring stuff), Wagner was able to realize a cherished dream to have his adored animals beside him after death. A series of little graves multiplied under the trees, each marked by a fond inscription. 'Here lies and watches Wagner's Russ', 'Here lies Wahnfried's faithful guardian and friend, the good and beautiful Marke', 'Our good little Faf and Frischi' – all were there.

There too was *The grave*, the last resting place designed for Cosima and Richard, and which might be regarded as a future Pavilion, since they saw it as such. 'It is wonderfully comforting for us to know the exact spot, and to tend it daily, the spot where we shall one day find heavenly rest, together, in the ground and soil for which we have the generosity of your love to thank,' wrote Cosima to King Ludwig, who had given them a land-grant for Wahnfried. (The King, pursuing the morbid strain in which all three wallowed, was to order every piano in his palaces to be hung with black after Wagner's death.)

Ah Wagner! Ah Wagnerian loves, funeral pyres and magic philtres! They lived every minute of it all, sobbing aloud at rehearsals at Bayreuth, where the Valkyrie were lodged at a neighbouring *Gasthof*, and the Giants and Gods were on demi-pension elsewhere. . . . Wagner was a superb actor, miming the various roles for each singer and trying, above all, to infuse the force of emotion which he knew into others, trying to galvanize a rather tepid tenor with such force that the singer crumpled under him. 'Have you *no* idea of the volcanic force that consumes?' he goaded Siegmund. All this uproar vibrated through the theatre, keeping pace with the frenzies of emotion that were centred round the Master's bedroom.

In a rather quieter vein, those emotios *The grave* aroused. Before going to bed, they often stood on the terrace overlooking it . . . a last glimpse of that last bed awaiting them. Cosima notes, 'Moonlight, I walk out on the balcony with Richard. We see *The grave* . . . .'

It was a fittingly Wagnerian note on which to end their day.

11
Balçic
Rumania

ONE OF the most perfect expressions of my title is that little folly in the Dobrudja at Balçic, on the Black Sea, where Queen Marie of Rumania built herself a romantic retreat. Here she could indulge all her fantasies and desires. Unlike her son, the wayward King Carol, she always managed things with great style, never allowing her station to be overshadowed by her temperament. Her appetite for the picturesque was without limit. The trappings of Royal Ruritanian romance, which in her manner of living and dressing she came to personify, as did her palaces or houses – especially Balçic – make her a particularly intriguing subject. She was a beautiful, generous, emotional, daring and remarkable creature, quite outside the accepted pattern of Royal ladies. Above all, she was a woman – a queenly women, or perhaps, a womanly queen – following that Oriental formula of discretion *Great lady by day, woman by night*.

While seeming in some aspects to derive straight from the pages of an Elinor Glyn novelette, she was in fact of other, sterner clay. Reading her autobiography, *The Story of my Life*, one is brought up short by its particular quality, its simplicity and at times brutal force, qualities seldom found in Royal biographies (but then few queens, of late years, have had such a life to tell, as they tread the tight-rope of popularity, struggling, diligently and successfully, to appear blandly negative). As Queen Marie's life progresses, she is at the summit of the terrible and tragic times she shared with the country that had become her own, and we see her frivolities and turbulence disciplined to selfless patriotism. It is the character of the woman, or the circumstances of her life and ancestry, which make Balçic a cumulative expression of all three: which is why I dwell at some length on this remarkable women – Queen *hors série*, at least in the world of today.

'Missy', as she was to her family, was born in 1875, English by her father, the Duke of Edinburgh, Queen Victoria's second son, and Russian by her mother, the Grand Duchess Marie, only daughter of the Tzar Alexander II. It was an indigestible mixture. Flashes of Romanov excess sometimes disturbed the restraint of her English heritage, which was something she treasured above all else: that is, until at last she knew herself heart and soul absorbed into the country of her adoption, and was one with it.

Only one who has lived in the Balkans – and I have known that perfect happiness – can truly comprehend its peculiar flavour, at once pastoral and Ruritanian, or so it was in her heyday, and the flavour still lingered when I first knew it, at the end of World War II. Here Europe ends, and the Balkans – neither East nor West – begin. Yugoslavia, Bulgaria, Rumania – these are the Balkans proper. Turkey and Greece, though neighbouring, are apart: so is Hungary, which, bordering on the Transylvanian and Carpathian provinces of Rumania, is sometimes confused with it. The Balkan flavour is at once voluptuously Oriental and dramatically Slav, like the minarets and cupolas of its two faiths. The country is by turns savage and soft, meltingly beautiful, or harsh, like its music and its races. All this the young Crown Princess assimilated slowly, painfully, but at last was won. When after long years of apprenticeship, she became the Queen in 1914, she was wholly Balkanized. Indeed her critics said she saw herself as a new Byzantine Empress, her domain stretching from Transylvania to the Bosphorus.

Though her Memoirs contain no rancour, one senses that, in the beginning, she considered herself as unjustly fobbed off on an inconspicuous German prince, heir to the newly formed Kingdom of Rumania, over which his uncle, of Hohenzollern blood, had been invited to rule as King Carol I. At a time when genealogical trees counted for so much, hers was a superb pedigree and should have placed her better on the Royal marriage chessboard. Perhaps spite played a part. Her overbearing mother frankly detested life at the English Court. She thought it stuffy, dowdy and dull, after the Winter Palace, and she writhed at Queen Victoria's unmarried daughters taking precedence over herself, a Grand Duchess of Russia. No daughter of hers was to be allowed to make an English marriage, nor was the English Royal family to dictate the husbands she chose for her daughters. Neither would she consider any of the Russian Grand Dukes as suitors cousins or no, they were 'fast'.

At one moment a boyish prince then serving with the Fleet stationed at Malta, who was to become King George V, showed a most determined interest in Missy who was also at Malta, where her father, the Duke of Edinburgh, was Commander-in-Chief of the Mediterranean Fleet. The young prince had to be hurried away, since this budding romance was also considered unsuitable.

One wonders how the history of the British monarchy might have shaped, had King George's Queen been Marie instead of Mary. Idle speculation; yet the King never quite forgot Missy's fatal charms. All her life Missy treasured a crystal watch Prince George had given her, inscribed *From George, to darling Missy*, while Queen Mary was said to display a certain reserve towards her, to the end. If, rarely, she permitted herself to comment on some irregular, or highly coloured incident, she would remark that by such goings-on one might almost imagine oneself to be in Rumania.

Missy's mother had said princesses must marry young, before they began to think for themselves, a most dangerous state of affairs . . . and so Missy suddenly found herself, at sixteen, married and dispatched to Rumania. It was at the other end of Europe – the Eastern end: most people knew nothing about it at that time, except that even Bucharest, the capital, was said to be very primitive. Queen Marie's accounts of her early years there are poignant in their evocation of desperate loneliness.

It took many years of heartbreak, high endeavour and enterprise before she could emerge from the smothering blankets of Germanic protocol by which the almost gaoler-like uncle, 'Der Onkel', King Carol I, ruled his country and family. He was a stern man, living only for duty, who ordered the young couple's life, even their nursery, their friends and the whole pattern of their existence with unwavering severity. To the timid Crown Prince, 'Der Onkel's ' word was law, and he remained cowed, of no support to the rebellious young woman he had married and loved to distraction. Only very gradually did she dare to break away from 'Der Onkel's' traditions, to follow a more liberal way, as she discovered both herself and the fascinating country where her destiny lay.

Perhaps, in the end, no other country would have suited her so well. In her pursuit of the exotic, the sumptuous, she was, consciously or unconsciously, reviving something of the splendours of the *hospodars* and *boyars* of an earlier Rumania. In their brocaded caftans stiff with gold thread, lined with velvets or furs, the nobles of the Moldavian and Wallachian provinces also recalled an earlier ancestry – that of Byzantium. We see them in the frescoes at Hurezi and other monasteries of the country, family groups, rigid figures of splendour, their rather foxy, Oriental faces topped by huge fur *kalpaks* stabbed by a jewelled aigrette. The women – the Domnitza – are as extravagantly adorned as any princess in an Indian miniature, sprays of diamonds pinned to their veiled heads, with waterfalls of jewels dangling from their ears, their mantles of sable or fox open over brocaded robes studded with precious stones. This opulence, this Asiatic display of jewels, was very close to the extravagant Russian Court – one half of Queen Marie's ancestry.

Thus, both by her appearance and her way of life, she came to personify her people's conception of a Queen. Those dramatic, romantic draperies which were her signature were understood by them. This style might be described as basic Balkan Royal, a style she bequeathed to her daughters, respectively Queens of Greece and Yugoslavia, something quite apart from the more rigid pattern which used to be associated with her Royal relatives in England. As she matured, she never conceded an inch to contemporary fashions in an attempt to look realistic – the very fact of queenship set her apart; she stressed this, never attempting the ordinary touch. 'I, the Queen,' she would sometimes say, but without pomposity. Gradually those draperies in which she moved with such grace seemed part robes of state, part widow's veils, part négligés. . . . They were the trappings of an emotional woman who knew how to dramatize herself. There were layers of chiffon, swags of pearls and avalanches of ermine. She wore her jewels like her orders and decorations with a sure sense of display: many of her most magnificent were of Imperial Russian origin, being inherited from her mother. Huge ecclesiastical-looking jewelled crosses reefed bouquets of full blown roses to a sumptuous corsage. Tiaras and crowns were in the *kokoshnik* or Russian style. And then there were the veils, half nun-like, half Salomé's own, which wound and framed, and came to set off so perfectly, a sunset of great beauty.

Although she is seen chiefly as an almost mythological image of queen-ship, crowned and adorned, or else in those clinging draperies reserved for more intimate moments, and lit either by that fierce light that beats upon a throne (basking in it, even) or else glimpsed in some candle-lit retreat such as Balçic, she was, also, very much of the sunlight. Her English heritage was apparent in her love of outdoor life, of gardens, flowers and animals, picnicking in all weathers, in all sorts of wild places, something which, like her sharp sense of humour, at times tried her entourage, either muffled and shivering as they munched, or suffering agonies of suppressed laughter at some solemn ceremony. Above all, riding was her passion, for she was a superb horsewoman, as tireless as fearless, choosing the most challenging mounts, outriding her cavaliers, whole regiments of cavalry streaming after her across country. At such times she was transformed, becoming an Amazonian figure, riding astride, wearing a dashing Cossack uniform, dark blue and scarlet, belted and barred with the regular silver cartridge cases, top boots and a fur cap to complete the image. Once again, she is presented in her own, supremely personal terms of romance and drama.

With the years this highly individual expression of her nature and tastes was also applied to her palaces or houses. These ranged from wooden tree-top hide-outs in the forest to Carpathian baronial castles such as Bran, or the princely Ruritanian style of Sinaia or Pelez, or the Bucharest Palace of Cotroceni. All these were a frame for the Queen, but Balçic, which came late in her life, was the frame for a *woman*; she had designed it knowing what best suited the life she meant to have there. When she rearranged the existing Royal palaces, she emphasized local traditions, yet merged all manner of objects and styles to a triumphant Balkan whole. Existing turrets outside might reveal imposed Byzantine pillars within; often the interiors she devised recalled those medieval Russian palaces such as the Terem (or the Royal Women's quarters) deep in the oldest part of the Kremlin. These she must have remembered from the time when, as a young Crown Princess, she had been present at the Coronation of her cousin, the last Tzar, Nicholas II. She softened the dramatic and rather gloomy severity of her palaces with prodigal masses of flowers, and the glow of innumerable candles glittering over the rich darkness of the ikons she had collected many years before they were sought as decorative objects. In some of her rooms she had added pillars of burnished gold or silvered walls, and floors of sea-green glazed tiles. There were the lovely Oltenian rugs of Rumanian tradition, while bearskins were piled on divans. For curtains, pieces of old local embroideries, both ecclesiastical and peasant, hung straight, rather than being looped and draped in the manner of the satins and laces then *de rigueur*. This was the setting she devised, seeking sources and inspiration from around her, renouncing the ponderous Germanic Royal, which prevailed when she first arrived, or that international Louis xv décor then generally favoured, particularly in palaces. The finicky Edwardian interiors of her English contemporaries, knick-knacks, wishy-washy chintzes, frilled lamp-shades and cut-glass vases holding sweet peas and asparagus fern were not her style. Her sense of theatre recognized and capitalized on the barbaric splendour of the wild land in which she now had her being.

Just as she came to love and appreciate her adopted country, so that country loved and appreciated her. It has been said that she formed a whole generation – every man was in love with her, every artist inspired by her, every woman wished to look like her, and blessed her for throwing open the closed windows behind which they had lived in Oriental stagnation. Rumanians are a gay people; they shared her fundamental *joie de vivre*, some of which she attributed to her marvellous or 'Russian' digestion. They laughed with her, and the Court laughed at her, on occasions when her unconventionality seemed too strange to them, painting a tea service, for example, when she could perfectly well have bought one in Dresden; wearing peasant clothes in the country, sharing some greasy dish of *mamaliga* with an old shepherd, when the Royal chefs could have packed a proper luncheon hamper; refurbishing her palaces with disintegrating naïve and brilliant embroideries or worm-eaten carvings; but mostly they loved her.

It had always intrigued them that she was said to maintain a lively private life (although matters of the heart were never something to suppress, or deny among Rumanians). It did not matter that two of her children were said to have been fathered by others than the King. They were certainly fathered by Rumanians. Above all, they were *hers* – as if the force of her personality, her love of life itself, had, in some kind of self-generating exuberance, engendered this handsome brood, made so unmistakably in her image, hers alone – the Queens' children, *tout court*.

It was during the First World War that Queen Marie emerged as a heroic figure – Mama Regina suffering, struggling, fighting, retreating, advancing beside the army in the battles which decimated the country. The Germans, whom she loathed, with satellite Bulgarian and Austrian troops, were overwhelming Rumania. Russia's promised aid proved disastrous, for soon, with the Revolution gaining ground, there were only uneasy units more ready to join with the Red Armies in Southern Russia than to support the Rumanian troops. Next, there was famine and fearsome epidemics, but Mama Regina remained a rallying point. By her example she galvanized the women of all classes to work with her in the Red Cross units she organized so efficiently. Her war work was not of that pictorial order where we see some severe Madonna-like figure in suitable uniform at the soldier's bedside, or winding bandages among volunteers. She chose to work at the front lines, meeting the ambulances, helping to sort out the dead from the dying, working in the primitive field hospitals or at bases where exanthematic typhus raged and the floors, in the words of a lady-in-waiting, literally heaved with lice. But the Queen continued, often stumbling with fatigue at the end of an eighteen-hour day, there beside the wounded and the dying, taking down their last messages, giving them her hand to hold. Although the doctors begged her to wear gloves as a precaution against typhus and other infections raging round, she refused. 'They all want to kiss my hand – they cannot kiss a rubber glove', she said with finality. A dying man whose face is half shot away asks her to wash open his eyes, so that he can once more see . . . she does so, unflinching, and is rewarded by the gratitude she reads in his eyes . . . terrible, terrible times. . . . There are few drugs, not enough supplies of bandages or anaesthetics, food, fuel, space or transport for an army fighting on three fronts. Losses of battles, losses of men, why is there never good news, she wonders sadly. Gone now the diadems and clinging chiffons she loved: gone all her luxuries and *voluptés*, her indulgences and pleasures, the hedonistic joys she had known in her beautiful houses, her admirers and her own beauty. No more time, now, to ride the horses she loved so passionately; most were taken into the army, dragging guns, shot down, slaughtered for food perhaps – their fate unknown.

It was at this time that the Queen lost her youngest child, the baby Prince Mircea; but anguished as she was, she rushed back from his burial to resume the ghastly round, while knowing that the grave she left would soon be part of enemy-occupied territory, where she could never be again. She adored all her children with a fiercely maternal love; but it was Mircea who mattered most to her, and his lingering death, which she describes with heartbreaking pathos, was something to which she could never become reconciled.

While she herself was plunged into the horrors of war, unvarnished, she did not try to shield her children from reality. If war must be part of the country's destiny, then it must be theirs too. Princess Mignon learns how to hold steady a limb for amputation. Prince Nicholas performs any gruesome hospital orderly's task allotted him. Elisabetta seems less able to be useful, less able to stomach some of the sights and sounds of the hospitals, breaks down and is sent away, tried and found wanting. Carol, the Crown Prince, is on one or other of the fronts with the King, but presently elects to cross the frontier into Russia, there to contract a morganatic marriage with a commoner, Zizi Lambrino. The Queen is stunned with horror, but this is no time for recriminations or anything which distracts her from her single-minded determination to sustain the Rumanians until victory is theirs.

The agonies which Mama Regina shared with her people at that time brought them even closer, and they turned to her, instinctively, as their leader. At the end of the war, furiously resentful at her country's neglected place among the Allies, she overruled her husband and stormed up to the Paris Peace Conference, unexpected and unannounced – 'to give my country a place in Europe,' she said – and won her way magnificently. Through her, Rumania obtained all of Transylvania, the Bukhovina to the boundary line of the Dniester, as well as the Black Sea province of the Dobrudja, wrested now from Bulgaria, which had not taken arms against Germany or sided with the Allies, as she, after long and bitter struggles, had persuaded her German-born husband and his ministers to do.

It had been in the early days of her reign, during a state visit to Constanza, the Rumanian port on the Black Sea, that she had first caught sight of the minarets and blinding white cliffs of Balçic. It was a *coup de foudre*. From that day she dreamed of building a house there, something in the local style, simple but exotic, where she could be far away from the Court and protocol. But Balçic then lay over the frontier, in Bulgarian territory, so her dream remained unrealizable until, with the terms of the Peace Conference, the Dobrudja was ceded to Rumania, and so her dream became reality.

At Balçic, if I may quote myself, she found 'The Wilder Shores of

Love'. There climate and population were as exotic as the tropical luxuriance of nature. There she was steeped in exoticism and quite free of Court sycophancy. Beyond, above the little fishing town, Gypsies lounged about their *mahallah*, or camps, tawny savages who returned her love, swarming round her boldly, hailing her as one of themselves. They sensed, as she knew, that she was often closer to their ways than to those of the capital. At Balcic, she could have her fill of their wild, sensuous music, which she had always craved. In her giddy heyday they had always been as much part of the scene at her more informal Palace parties as the legion of her enslaved beaux. The heady atmosphere this combination had created was not eyed sympathetically by the older Court, and a band playing Viennese waltzes and extracts from Messager-type operettas were imposed as a calming influence. Not that it worked; the Gypsies, like the young Russian Grand Dukes, her cousins, and their suites, numberless foreign diplomats, Russian statesmen, soldiers, musicians and men of letters, all fell under her spell, creating an atmosphere charged with emotion.

But there and then she was not free to follow her inclinations. At Balçic it was otherwise, and she plunged into the intoxicating Turkish-Balkan atmosphere, which was in part fostered by the presence of such minorities as the Gagaoutes and Tartars and other offshoots of Islam, besides the Gypsies. Although to many Europeans the Rumanian flavour of her northern palaces, with their undercurrents of Byzantine and Slav, might seem exotic enough, by the heritage of her Russian blood it was, to Queen Marie, already part of herself, of her childhood. Her mother, obstinately continuing the habits of her Russian background, was always accompanied by an Orthodox priest and two chanters, as essential a part of her household as her maids or the chef. Thus to her daughter, whose earliest memories were of Clarence House, alongside St James's Palace, the drifts of incense, the deep smoky voices and the glitter of many ikons were everyday stuff. But in the Dobrudja, exoticism could be pushed further, to a purely Eastern idiom such as Balçic was to provide so satisfyingly.

The little house that was her joy and folly, Tenta Hova, the 'Quiet Nest', was built entirely in the local Turkish style, clotted white walls, arcaded and chunkily pillared, very simple. There are very few rooms. Downstairs, a dining-room salon, rather Graustark hunting lodge in its conception; rough white walls, dark oak coffers, some heavily carved medieval chairs, bearskin rugs, massive candlesticks, a huge fireplace. Above, reached by a narrow stairway, an octagonal room, its windows jutting out towards the sea in the overhanging Turkish style. The bed, the celebrated alcove bed, principal and indeed primary object of the room, was raised on a daïs. When I came to know it, there were no more silken covers and piled cushions, so that the room seemed almost austere in its basic simplicity. A cavernous chimney-piece filled one wall, but can seldom have been needed, for the climate of Balçic is languorously hot. But then firelight is the best of all lights . . . A low carved doorway led to a dressing-room with a miniature hammam, or Turkish steam bath, with its marble slabs and the customary domed ceiling, letting in dim shafts of light round which the vapours must have hung, pearly and opaque. Another even narrower stairway led up to the minaret which the Queen had fancifully placed beside the house, imparting a further note of exoticism. Latterly, I believe she came to adopt the Orthodox faith of her subjects, of the majority, that is, but of this I am not certain. The Moslem minorities, ever dear to her heart, however, were thus included at Balçic, embraced, as it were, within her domain. I do not think she carried her sense of theatre so far as to obtain a *mollah* to sound his haunting call to prayer from its little gallery. But from there, in lieu of the muezzin, a wind-harp tinkled with a sort of childish charm. Sometimes, I was told, the Queen spent long hours there, absorbed in the beauty which lay all around, sometimes in some romantic *tête-à-tête*: hours which would precede, or follow, those violent cavalcades, those furius *gallopades* for which she, the superb horsewoman, was celebrated, and which favoured guests were invited to watch, in the manner of a star turn, the Queen being, at moments, it must be admitted, something of a show-off.

With her son's accession to the throne as King Carol, in 1930, came the realization that he was not proving all she had hoped, and she began to spend more time at Balçic, withdrawn from the Court, although politics, statecraft, remained a passion she found it difficult to renounce, and at various times of stress she had always returned, to assume Regent's powers or to further agrarian reforms and other legislative measures for which she had fought and been originally responsible.

Gradually Balçic became the true expression of herself – the woman superseding the Queen. There, unchanged, was the beautiful countryside, her gardens, and the obsessive Gypsy music she loved, with all its passion and colour to revive the tempo of earlier days. Balcic seemed steeped in such rhythms, or those almost equally obsessive, of the Rumanian peasants, all fire or languor. But now, instead of the Court chamberlains and the presence of spoil-sport official personages of earlier days, there were only those with whom she chose to share her paradise.

Nothing that a romantic could desire had been omitted from Balçic: Turkish baths and Arab steeds, fountained courts, minarets and lily ponds . . . it was the quintessential frame for love. But by the time she had achieved this, through the experience of a lifetime, perhaps she found herself betrayed by time. Perhaps the person she would have wished to her side was no longer alive. Tragedy and romance are generally interwoven, and nostalgia, which is a blend of both, a longing for the unattainable or the lost, makes of every romantic an exile.

At Balçic, nostalgia casts a particularly potent spell: one is aware that this Pavilion was the realization of a lifetime's longing – perhaps realized too late.

Today, the Queen's Folly has become a tourist outing, and sometimes the Government lent it to specially favoured visitors, or members of the Diplomatic Corps, which is how I first came to know it. As the hordes tramp about and snap each other standing in the lily garden, backed by the minarets and picturesque huddle of the old town further along the cliffs, I wonder if they sense the amorous implications of this retreat a queen devised?

Once a chosen few of the Royal staff were discreetly dispersed about the grounds. The resident masseur, couturière and dresser were also lodged close at hand, the chimneys of their little dwellings pricked up like rabbits' ears among the foliage. With such involved costumes as the Queen's, the services of expert hands must have amounted to a necessity rather than a luxury. The young Princes and Princesses, by then mostly grown up and living agitated lives of their own, were always welcome there, and their adoring mother had apportioned equally discreetly dispersed Pavilions for their own use. Though I doubt her eldest son's affections, when fixed on Madame Lupescu, were encouraged at Balçic. The Queen had always put the dynasty and interests of State first when she reigned.

On my last visit, I remember leaving the house at sunset to wander about the deserted, but still romantic gardens where everything grew with such extravagance: one long parterre was entirely massed with mauve and white flowers, planted, I learned, in memory of Queen Marie's favourite sister, the Grand Duchess Kyril of Russia. Beside a terrace planted with lilies, bordering the cliffs overhanging the Black Sea, a huge tree – a Turkish chenar, its leopard-dappled girth of gigantic proportion – shaded a group of stone seats. A throne-like marble chair and a truncated Greek column footstool still struck an Imperial note. This was the Queen's lair.

'Here Her Majesty liked to take coffee,' said the caretaker, a handsome man, once one of the Royal boatmen, as he reverently brushed some fallen leaves off these relics. The westering sun slanted through the heavy foliage, sinking slowly towards those faraway Turkish horizons the Queen had longed to incorporate into some vast neo-Byzantium, herself, perhaps, some neo-Theodora. I imagined the beautiful profile once glimpsed here, through all those flowing draperies, so misleading in their nun-like folds, so alluringly lit by the afterglow. . . .

The afterglow. That was the melancholy which pervaded the whole place when I came to know it. It was a gentle melancholy, but omni-present, for the place had become a last monument to Ruritanian queens and high adventure.

She had wished to die there, and had been carried there on a stretcher for a last farewell to all its beauties and memories. Her doctors had com-pelled her to return to the more bracing mountain climate of her earlier, northern palaces. She died at Sinaia, in 1938, leaving instructions that her heart should be buried at Balçic, and this was done: it lay in a jewelled casket in the little Byzantine chapel she had built in the gardens where she had lived and loved.

In death as in life, she knew how to dramatize, how to create an atmosphere of intense romance. For her funeral, she decreed that the streets of Bucharest should be hung, not with the customary black, but with *violet* draperies. And this too was done. She had been born in the purple, and in this she died. An eyewitness told me the effect was extra-ordinarily impressive, at once majestic and magical, as if the violets, lilac, petunias, heliotrope and all the other mauve flowers she had loved had drifted down, colouring the whole city, and recalling once more the Imperial splendours which she, grand-daughter of a Tzar and an Empress, had instinctively coveted for her country and herself.

Later, stern authority removed her heart from its resting place at Balçic and buried it elsewhere – more suitably, was no doubt the official expression. But then, officialdom has never been susceptible to romance, in any guise, and now there is no place, either in municipal planning or life itself, for Pavilions such as Balçic, or for those who devised them.

12

Bibi Hanum's Medressa

Samarcand

ALL OVER the East, historical sagas, tales of magic or folklore have always been an integral part of daily life, like the itinerant story-teller who wandered – and still does – from bazaar to café and street corner, spinning his marvellous tales. Although now on the decline, his livelihood threatened by the rise of literacy, the story-teller continues; especially across the wastes of Central Asia. While few nomads' tents are now without their transistor radio, and in the towns, television sets perform eccentrically, the story-teller can still count on his audience. In remote towns such as Tash Kurghan (much as it was when Marco Polo described it on his way to Cathay) I have watched them in the *tchai-khanas*, or tea-houses, and market-places, surrounded by a circle of rapt listeners, crouching figures, their dark, hawk faces intent, as the age-old tales unfold: tales of mighty Caliphs and mythical warriors, Saladin beside Rustem, bawdy harem intrigues interwoven with death-less loves, Nasreddin of Bokhara beside Leila and Majnoun. . . . This is the many-coloured world of the Arabian Nights Entertainment, Eastern

Pavilions of the Heart

world without end, a world not yet wholly given over to oil derricks and housing developments. Here there are still narrow alleyways smelling of spices, musk and dung, where *mouchrabiyehs* screen each window, and women go veiled, and some scent of mystery remains. Here everyone is not yet infected with too much schooling, Romantic and supernatural themes still rank as entertainment along with the jugglers, snake charmers, and sometimes, as in the regions between Balkh and Bokhara, those troupes of dancing boys, the Batchas, whose undulating, sipping steps and provocative postures were esteemed above the charms of women. (*A woman for breeding, a boy for pleasure* as the local saying goes.)

Here the story-tellers still recount tales of magic, and the turbaned lorry drivers climb down from their naïvely frescoed lorries, which are hung with pious or mystic symbols and talismans, to refresh themselves with tea and (along with radio news bulletins) tales of djinns and peris. But then to people hereabout, both the machinery of the lorry or the wireless, like the jet plane, are seen as clear proof of magic – the abracadabras of necromancy rather than man-made achievements of engineering. And after all, is a jet plane any less magic than Simurg, the giant bird of Arabian legend, or Borak, Mohammed's winged horse?

Thus the story of Bibi Hanum and her vanishing lover is accepted as truth. Indeed fact and fable are curiously interwoven here, for Bibi Hanum is known to have existed, the favourite wife of Tamerlane, or Timur-i-leng, as he is known in Samarcand, once his capital and seat of all his glories. Moreover, the beautiful *medressa*, or college, which goes by Bibi Hanum's name, still stands there in crumbling majesty, admired by archaeologists and historians alike. And then – fact merging with fable giddily – the Uzbegs and Tadjiks of this region will always point out the soaring minaret above the *medressa* and tell you it was from there that Bibi Hanum's love 'took wing'.

'Took wing': a curious phrase, yet the same words were used when I first heard the story from a rug dealer in Aleppo; and again, years later, when a Turcoman exile in Shiraz recounted it to me. He was originally from Samarcand, where he had traded in karakul skins, like his father and grandfather before him. Everyone knew the story was true, he said: only strangers like myself ever questioned it, he added, and launched into a dissertation on the power of djinns. But Asiatics, like Hamlet, know there are more things in heaven and earth than are dreamed of, and no explications are ever necessary where lovers or djinns are concerned.

Bibi Hanum's Medressa

When later I reached Samarcand, it seemed natural to go along with such views, for plainly they were shared by those around me, the Uzbeg, Tadjik and Turcoman peoples. Samarcand itself possesses an extraordinary quality of magic, shimmering in the turquoise haze cast by its peacock-bright buildings, its mosques and mausoleums and minarets, all glittering blue, rising from the legendary wastes of Afrosaïb. So I wandered from one marvel to another, from the *medressa* of Uleg Beg or the mausoleum of Tourkan Akha to the lion-fronted façade which dominates the Registan, where, beneath each arch or dome, the merchants stack their cannon-ball mounds of green melons, and the citizens sit drinking tea beneath the dappled plane trees. On a breathless summer evening, when I sat in such a *tchai-khana* beside Tamerlane's tomb, the Gur i Mir, I watched a story-teller recounting some fabulous legend to a circle of enthralled listeners. They sat cross-legged on wooden bedsteads spread with rugs, drinking green tea out of little china bowls as blue as the dome of the Gur i Mir. I suppose my yearning glances spoke for me, for presently I was invited to join the circle, and by the good offices of a young science student from the University of Tashkent, who offered to interpret for me, I persuaded the story-teller to give me his version of Bibi Hanum's tale. Although the science student seemed disapproving of my romantic choice – shrugging it off as a non-progressive programme – he was indefatigable in relaying the story-teller's words, flowery phrase by flowery phrase.

This is what he told.

Bibi Hanum was a Chinese princess of unparalleled beauty: 'hers was the loveliness of the full moon; her lips like the ripe pomegranate, her eyes like the darkest jade, her waist slender as a rattan frond. . . .' All the Oriental similes were lavished on this paragon, who was so full of learning and virtue beyond all telling. She was Timur-i-leng's favourite wife, loved above all the rest of the women in his *anderoun* or harem. 'There she lived, behind forty silk-hung walls, and the Great Khan sought her company by day and night, taking his joy in her beauty and wisdom,' said the story-teller, at which the circle of turbaned men around him swayed backwards and forwards, clicking their tongues in approval, and shaking their heads in assent, for this is the East, where all is otherwise and a nod stands for no.

Now when the astrologers came to Timur-i-leng and told him the hour was propitious for his setting out on new conquests, he bade farewell to Bibi Hanum and turned eastwards, towards India. He rode out from Samarcand at the head of a mighty army, accompanied by his generals and scribes, his astrologers, musicians, physicians, his cooks, and the Master of his Horse, his hunting leopards and falcons, two hundred Afghan hounds, horses without number, and a thousand she-camels to provide milk for them on the barren desert crossings. There were, besides, a train of sixty elephants to carry silken carpets from Persia, and ceremonial tents, with their silver poles adorned with yak tails and hangings of gold brocade lined with sable against the cold, for splendour surrounded this mighty Khan wherever he went.

When Bibi Hanum parted from her lord and master, 'tears of pearl fell on her alabaster cheeks,' and she withdrew to a painted pavilion on the roof-top of the *anderoun*, from where she kept watch, 'by sunlight and by starlight,' for that far distant cloud of dust which would tell of Timur-i-leng's messengers bringing assurances of his love . . . 'But after thirteen moons and thirteen days had passed,' Bibi Hanum dried her tears, and raising her veils, planned to build the most wondrous monument in the world to honour her overlord. It should be a *medressa*, to house a thousand students, each of whom should have his fees paid from Bibi Hanum's own purse, as well as twenty silver *tengas* each month to buy food. The *medressa* must be built without delay, so that it should await the mighty conqueror when he returned in triumph. But there were difficulties in finding an architect worthy of the project, for, as was his custom, Tamerlane had taken the finest with him in his suite, so that they might study the noblest buildings of other kingdoms, and returning do likewise in Samarcand, thus making it Queen of Cities, and all man's delight – as it is to this day, added the story-teller, and no one contradicted him.

It is known that Tamerlane's suite did indeed include such experts. The melon-domes of Samarcand are said to derive from his admiration for one of the largest mosques in Damascus; when he laid siege to the city he ordered that particular mosque to be spared in the ensuing sack. But the fires ravaged the city and reduced it to ashes, so that Tamerlane rounded up all the local builders who knew the secrets of such beauty, and taking them back to Samarcand with him set them to work there, to build those ribbed, melon-domes which are a derivation of the Damascus original and which became typical of Central Asian architecture. More-over, Tamerlane's descendants are said to have imposed them in India, where they are found in some of the mosques of Delhi, and elsewhere. Further afield, northwards, the same lovely swelling curves and bulbous, onion-domed variations took root in Russia, and are also held to derive from a Central Asian inspiration.

But these are architectural digressions. Let us return to the story-teller's tale and Bibi Hanum's dilemma. This was solved by her learning of one remaining architect within the city, young and as yet untried, but of excellent promise. He was commanded to appear before Bibi Hanum, and when she descended from her roof-top pavilion to confer with him, he found favour in her eyes, for the plans he submitted expressed all that she had wished for the *medressa*. He was, besides, handsome as a young falcon, said the story-teller. The foundations were laid forthwith, and every mason and carpenter and tile worker between Merv and Bokhara was pressed into service. Each day Bibi Hanum came to watch the *medressa* grow, carried there in 'a camel litter hung with silver bells and scarlet tassels, and escorted by a guard of archers, and accompanied by twelve virgins of rare loveliness and noble blood,' said the story-teller, now well into his stride, my interpreter panting after him.

'Before the almond flowers had fallen,' he went on, 'Bibi Hanum's beauty and wisdom had inflamed the heart of the young architect so that the twelve high-born virgins of rare loveliness appeared as toads. For twenty more moons the building of the *medressa* continued, growing in all the magnificence that Bibi Hanum had desired.' At last the loftiest minaret was completed, and the tile workers were covering the colossal dome with arabesques of turquoise and sapphire blue faïence, and below, in the shadowed vaulting, calligraphers worked on the gilded inscriptions which adorned the walls, while the wood-carvers inlaid panels of cedar wood with ivory and ebony, and the metalsmiths plated the entrance doors with sheets of bronze embossed with silver and gold, so that the sound of hammering rang across the city. But now that the *medressa* was almost finished, the young architect knew that his days of happiness were numbered, for soon Bibi Hanum would make no more visits to confer with him and marvel at the beauty he had created. . . . His task would be done, and all hope of seeing Bibi Hanum would wither. Therefore he devised a plan by which the last, finishing touches were delayed . . . a panel of tiling still wanting from the main *ivar*, or façade . . . one door still not set aright on its hinges, an inscription unfinished . . . ever and again some small imperfection remained. At last Bibi Hanum grew uneasy, for rumours had reached Samarcand that Tamerlane had sacked Delhi and was on his homeward journey, a train of princely hostages and captives in his train. Therefore she urged that the work should be hastened. While the *medressa* remained an unfinished masterpiece it would not find favour with Tamerlane, and her proud offering would appear unworthy of him whom she sought to honour. But all her arguments, persuasions or commands failed to move the young architect, who had so marvellously interpreted all her other desires. He inclined before her, promising all she asked, but still there were strange delays, and still Bĩbi Hanum went to the *medressa* every day, in her scarlet tasselled, bell-hung litter, to urge on the workmen – to confer with her architect – which was, of course, precisely what he, her adorer, had planned.

He was clearly a most romantic creature, and at this point, I interrupted the story to ask his name and to be given some account of his appearance. All earlier versions of this story had dwelt entirely on Bibi Hanum's charms. He was, the story-teller repeated, handsome as a young falcon, and he was, too, strong as a lion and tall as a young cyprus: all the Oriental similes again. I imagined him one of those towering Uzbegs, slit-eyed and high cheek-boned, their eyebrows joined in a dark sweep, men who ride like centaurs and tread delicately in their high, soft leather boots, wearing the striped *tchapan*, a padded surcoat sashed in rainbow silks from Bokhara, and lined with flowered chintzes, a little round embroidered cap crowning that dense dark hair which, among Asiatics, resembles the plumage of some sleek bird. There are many such men in these territories.

'And his name?' I pressed, but for once the story-teller seemed at a loss. While he hesitated, his listeners prompted him, less from knowledge, I fancied, than from a civil wish to satisfy the curiosity of the stranger in their midst. 'Tangrikouli,' said one. 'Moukhouddin,' said another. 'Assadjan Kaloum,' said a third, by which I realized the young architect had passed into legend as Architect, or Lover, *tout court*. Let us call him Kaloum, for it is less taxing on the memory than other names from these parts.

For all Bibi Hanum's commands, for all her urgings, summer had passed into autumn, the roses bloomed and fallen, and the figs ripened, and still the building was not done, till at last Bibi Hanum grew desperate and threatened to have Kaloum impaled on one of the unfinished gateways. Yet if Kaloum were no more, who could finish the *medressa*? She was about to take counsel with a celebrated necromancer who lived in an ill-famed quarter behind the Registan when a messenger rode up out of the east, telling that Tamerlane was on the march and would reach his

170

capital before the waning of the next moon. On hearing that which once would have rejoiced her heart, Bibi Hanum tore her veils and wept, and when Kaloum saw tears falling like dew on the alabaster of her cheeks he swore that would she but pay his price, all should be as she wished, and the *medressa* stand ready for the Great Khan's return.

The price which Kaloum asked of Bibi Hanum was one kiss. When Bibi Hanum heard this, she paled, trembling like a leaf on the peepul tree, for she was the most virtuous of wives. But she was also the most wilful among women – and a wilful woman cannot be denied, said the story-teller, looking round the circle for agreement, and all the turbaned heads shook vigorously in assent – *shook*, for as I remarked earlier, a shaken head for yes, a nodded one for no.

'What then?' I asked, eager for the dénouement of this romantic situation.

'Then,' said the story-teller, savouring the whole attention of his public, 'then, Bibi Hanum reflected that one kiss was not so terrible a price to pay, were she to obtain her way – and besides, she had observed that the Architect was a comely youth.' So she lifted her veils and Kaloum kissed her.

'Alas! with that one kiss, all this noble lady's virtue and wisdom melted before the fire of Kaloum's desire. Throwing her arms round his neck, like a collar of pearls, she gave him back his kiss a hundred times, and he returned them a thousandfold, and their kisses melted together like honey on their lips. . . .'

Thus it fell that while, by day, the wood-carvers and tile workers and metalsmiths busied themselves completing the *medressa*, by night, when the first stars pricked the darkening sky, Bibi Hanum stole out from the *anderoun*, concealed beneath the *bourka* of a bribed serving girl, and reached a side door in the *medressa* where Kaloum awaited her. There, as the moon swam high, moving to its waning, they lay together in one of the cells where soon some student would begin his studies among the parchments of learning. But now it was a bower of loving, for Kaloum had spread it with carpets from Bokhara and silken cushions, and there the lovers clipped and kissed and sported, and Kaloum 'ceased not to play the porter at her door nor the preacher at her prayer niche,' in the words of the Arabian Nights story-teller, and although these were not the exact words used by mine, what he said, according to the science student, amounted to much the same thing.

When Tamerlane's advance guard reached the city, Kaloum knew his hours of delight were done, and Bibi Hanum rose up from the cushions of delight, and hiding herself in the servant-maid's *bourka*, crept back to the palace by by-ways where none challenged her. There she arrayed herself in her robes of honour. 'Her hair was plaited in many strands and tasselled with jewels. Her girdle was coral and turquoise, her necklace of beaten gold and pearls from Mosul, and the veils that fell over her robes of Samut velvet were transparent as the mists of morning, and coloured like the sunrise. She painted her cheeks and lips with vermilion, and darkened her eyes with kohl, so that they resembled twin lakes beneath the archer's bow of her eyebrows.' Thus her lord and master would not find her beauty less than that of the women of India, those Ranees and dancing girls whose praises, said the story-teller, returning travellers had always sung.

When Tamerlane entered Samarcand in all his might he saw, rising before him, more splendid and lofty than all the other mosques and palaces of his capital, the *medressa* that Bibi Hanum had raised in his honour, and he marvelled at its perfect loveliness. Bibi Hanum was awaiting her lord before the bronze and silver studded doors, surrounded by her women, while his other wives and concubines, finding less favour in his eyes, stood to the rear. As Tamerlane approached, they all knelt, kissing the ground between their outstretched hands. Signifying his pleasure, Tamerlane raised Bibi Hanum, desiring her to name the architect who had conceived so splendid a building. At which Kaloum knelt at the Khan's feet, and Tamerlane swore he should be honoured above all other architects in his city. Then, taking Bibi Hanum's hand, he led her within, saying that she and the architect should conduct him about the *medressa* even before he shook off the dust of his desert travels. Standing under the soaring blue dome he marvelled at all the many wonders. 'Here shall wisdom flourish,' he proclaimed, and striking on the door of one of the cells, commanded it to be unlocked that he might know in what manner future students would be housed.

Now by some fearful mischance, or the sport of some malevolent afrits perhaps, it happened that this was the very same cell where Bibi Hanum and Kaloum had spent the noon of every night in lovers' bliss. Moreover, in their haste to be gone and to make ready for Tamerlane's return, Kaloum had turned the key on their paradise, and not thought to remove the Persian carpets and the silken cushions, nor the ewer of rose water, the dishes of pomegranates, the drinking cups of jade and the roses, now faded in their golden goblet. . . .

Therefore, when the door was opened, it disclosed, not the parchments and quill pens of learning, but a frame for loving, a nest from which the love-birds had clearly not long flown, and laughter burst from the astonished multitude, so that Tamerlane was greatly angered. What jokester had dared to trick great Tamerlane and make mock of Bibi Hanum's *medressa*? Tamerlane vowed the culprits should be brought to justice forthwith. While Kaloum stood as if turned to stone, staring disaster in the face, Bibi Hanum fell to the ground swooning, and her women laid her down beside the fountain that graced the centre of the inner court. 'When Tamerlane saw her lying there, like a broken pillar, he was unmindful of all else, and lifted her veils, that he might know if she still breathed.'

There on the ashy pallor of Bibi Hanum's lovely face a burning mark appeared – the imprint of a kiss, that fatal kiss that had undone all her vaunted wisdom and virtue. Tamerlane let drop the veils, and as he rose to his feet, his eyes met those of Kaloum, and all was made clear to him. Uttering a terrible cry which reverberated round the great dome and made every man's blood run cold, Tamerlane drew his sword and sprang at Kaloum.

'Shall the dog lie in the lion's lair?' he cried, as his sword flashed above Kaloum's head. But Kaloum leapt aside and made for the narrow, winding stairway that climbed the minaret, Tamerlane hot in pursuit, while below every eye strained to follow them, knowing that once the topmost gallery was reached, 'the crying place from where muezzin calls the Faithful to prayer', Kaloum would be slain, like the very dog to which Tamerlane had likened him. There was no way of escape left, nor was he armed.

Here the story-teller paused dramatically, as we hung on his words, and as if to prolong the suspense, he called for another bowl of tea, sipping languidly before resuming his tale. Then, it seems, the multitude below saw the two figures emerge on to the gallery, silhouetted dark, like puppets in a shadow play, against the blue of the sky. They saw Tamerlane's sword glitter as he raised it – and they saw, or swore they saw, Kaloum leap into the blue and vanish!

'Vanish? – you mean he fell to his death?'

The story-teller nodded maddeningly, meaning 'No', in the confusing manner already described. 'Not so,' he said. '*He took wing*. He did not fall to his death, nor did he perish by Timur-i-leng's sword. Nobody saw him fall to earth. His body was never found – no one ever saw him again.

Pavilions of the Heart

This was the work of the afrits, or the djinns, the *good* djinns, for there are many such; they took pity on him, and letting him take wing among them, he vanished from man's sight, to become one of their own. The good djinns have always loved lovers, you must know,' he added, turning his small sly eyes on me intently; and I believed him, then and there, as I do, here and now, writing it all down as he told it.

Next day I returned to the café, but he had gone, nor was he to be found. Find me another story-teller, I begged, but this the Intourist Bureau seemed unable to supply. I told them I wanted to know more about Bibi Hanum; how she had lived. Was there nothing left of Tamerlane's palaces or possessions, or furnishings? Where were the silken hangings that once adorned the forty walls behind which his *anderoun* was hid? Would they open for me one of the cells in the *medressa*? They had almost crumbled away, but perhaps I should come on some shred of a silken cushion, some fragment of a drinking cup, that would speak to me of the lovers. I thought it more prudent not to tell them I was in fact searching for a Pavilion of the Heart. Even so, the Intourist staff looked blank, and suggested the Museum (where, surprisingly, there is a Goya) or a visit to the tombs of the Shah Zindeh, or to the huge block of grey-blue marble, the Kok-Tash, said to have been Tamerlane's throne; though neither thrones nor tombs were the sort of furnishings I had in mind.

It seemed that all the rest had vanished into thin air, that dry, crystalline air of Central Asia, spirited away, like Kaloum. But then time itself is the djinn of djinns, causing, at last, all things and all men to vanish.

> The samovars of Samarcand
> Stand smoking in the sun
> While melons, tiger-striped and cool
> Are stacked beneath the shattered dome
> Where Bibi Hanum's love took wing,
> And she and Tamerlane, and all the Khans
> Lie sleeping in their turquoise tombs.

13

Rue
Chantereine

France

T HE LIFE and love of Napoleon and the Empress Josephine crystallized at Malmaison, backed by Imperial splendours, but it is the
little house in the Rue Chantereine (later Rue de la Victoire,
honouring Napoleon) which best qualifies as their Pavilion. It was the
beginning of both love and glory for the young General Bonaparte. For
Josephine, six years his senior, an infinitely seductive thirty-two, no
more than an affair, one of so many, until that opportunist streak which
both her carefree nature and hard times had fostered, led her to take her
young and ardent suitor seriously. Malmaison remains intact, a monument to that perfection of taste and elegance which was ever Josephine's
signature, from the furnishing of her houses or palaces, to the shawls she
draped about her person with such incomparable grace, but also to that
sure and sober taste which marked all Napoleon's possessions and surroundings. The house which harboured their first fevered meetings, and
where they spent their thirty-six-hour honeymoon has vanished. We
know something of it by hearsay, however. Josephine had leased it, as

she furnished it, on credit, in 1795 when she was living her high-styled chancy life, queening it at Barras's salon in the raffish society of the Directoire. The idle, good-natured, careless, creole had learned how to please men – all kinds of men. Her *hôtel particulier* in the Rue Chantereine was the parlour or honey-pot for many a fly, both before and after the eagle took possession, for he bought it in 1796. It was a deliciously pretty, stylish doll's-house of a dwelling, standing low on the slopes of the Butte Montmartre, surrounded by a small garden with an entrance path shaded by pleached limes. There were outhouses and good stabling, for a smart turn-out and blood horses were essential to a woman of fashion. With supreme confidence in her charms, Josephine hung the walls of the house with mirrors: on the doors, on the panelling, in the corridors, especially in the small rotunda she had transformed into her boudoir – mirrors everywhere, reflecting candlelight, firelight and embracings, as from mirror to mirror the lovers were reflected back and forth, eroticism without end. It was a charming, frivolous ambience, to match the châtelaine. There were flowers in profusion, pale coloured silk hangings and *toiles de jouey*, Montgolfier's balloons, the temples and rustic shepherds of tradition, and newer designs too, already depicting the young General's military prowess, tents, bivouacs, drums and sabres wreathed in laurel leaves. One room, next to Josephine's bedroom, was painted from floor to ceiling with flowers and birds in tropic profusion. There were delicate pieces of satinwood and inlaid woods which had been the style of the *ancien régime*, but they were rather shabby and needed re-upholstering. The showier pieces – new stuff, and an Aubusson or two – were all on credit, while the saucepans and such were borrowed from better equipped friends. Josephine did not bother over much about stocking a kitchen, then. She had more important matters on her mind.

To this little bandbox of bliss the young General came constantly, falling each day more fatally in love, spellbound by the creole's voluptuous ways, strangely allied to her high-bred manners. He accepted all her capricious humours in the intoxication of her kisses. When Mérimée was officially commanded by Napoleon III to edit the great Emperor's papers, he reported that Bonaparte's early letters, dating from the time of the Rue Chantereine, were made up entirely of kisses. 'He can talk of nothing but kisses – kisses everywhere – and upon portions of the anatomy not to be found in any Dictionary of the Académie Française.' After some months of such ardent wooing Josephine began consolidating the comforts and elegances of her house. Credit again, but Bonaparte was rising fast in the hierarchy; she plunged, reckless as ever. Upholsterers and painters swarmed round: she engaged a chef and a small staff. On the evening of 9 March 1796 they were married, and returned to the Rue Chantereine to spend there their brief honeymoon in the little bandbox. *Femme de chambre*, chef, gardener and coachman awaited their new master and were joined by Bonaparte's valet-orderly, all of them crammed into the inadequate servants' quarters. But Bonaparte, due to leave within hours for his Italian campaigns, swept his bride straight upstairs to the bedroom, and cared little, at that moment, if life below stairs was chaos.

According to an old print, their bedroom looks singularly austere with its walls hung in striped *toile*, which covers the ceiling, tent-wise, while the rather heavy furniture is entirely masculine. But the two beds, we learn, could by some ingenious device be joined to make one, while the bedside tables were contrived from military drums – a complimentary gesture from Venus to Mars.

When Bonaparte had been Josephine's lover, Fortuné, the pampered pug, had been tactfully banished from her bed, for he was snappy to intruders. But now, as husband, Bonaparte found he must share the bed with Fortuné. Secure in her wifely position, Josephine insisted Fortuné was not to be disturbed. Here is Bonaparte writing to Arnault:

My rival! He was in possession of Madame's bed: I tried to put him out – vain attempt. I was told I had the choice of sleeping in another bed or sharing that one with Fortuné . . . the situation annoyed me – but it was a question of take it or leave it. I resigned myself. The canine favourite was far less accommodating than I – of which my leg bears proof.

Fortuné must have passed many restless hours at the Rue Chantereine before it was abandoned for the grandiose Italian palaces of the young General's first years of victory.

In 1806 Bonaparte, now Emperor, made over the bandbox of love to a young cousin as part of her dot. It does not seem to have held any further romantic associations and was demolished around 1860. Better so, than to be left standing forlorn, coming at last to dilapidation or housing offices, and its mirrored perspectives, which had once given back myriads of Josephines and Bonapartes enlaced, now giving back endless, visions of typewriters and filing cabinets.

14

The Winter Palace

Russia

T HE NAME alone casts an icy spell: impossible to imagine happiness taking root there, nor love, either its softer undertones or its fevers. The Winter Palace! In a livid flash of northern lights we see it, gigantic and sombre, glittering with a frosting of ice and snow, like the classic perspectives of marble and granite which surround it and are the signature of that superb city which Peter the Great first forced from a Finnish swamp. We see its stupendous façade (nearly three-quarters of a mile long) emerge fitfully from the chill miasmas which engulf it for so much of the year. Its sombre crimson walls are the colour of dried blood, once a colour reserved for all Imperial buildings, and in view of history, a singularly appropriate choice. Now we see its crimson muted by the milky twilight of those White Nights which Dostoievsky has immortalized; now, in the moonlight, crimson has turned to purple. . . . We stand, pygmy-like, beneath one of the colossal porticos, before the great bronze doors, imagining the lavish almost Oriental splendours within, and which once surrounded those mighty princes who knew pomp and power and luxury there – but seldom joy.

Only Alexander II – 'the Tzar Liberator' who abolished serfdom in 1866 was to find supreme happiness within its oppressive walls. There, in defiance of every canon of domestic conduct or Court etiquette, he installed the young Princess Catherine Dolgoruky, in rooms, unhappily placed above those of his dying wife. But nothing ever clouded the overwhelming love they shared there.

When Alexander II first saw the Princess Catherine she was a child of twelve and he a discouraged, exhausted man of forty-two. He was on manoeuvres in the district of Poltava and visited her father's estate, Teplovka. Riding through the park, he came on the young Princess who was vainly trying to set her pony at a jump. The Tzar chaffed her, and she, humiliated before the stranger, answered back sharply, at which he laughed and rode on. Only later, when fetched to the salon to make her *reverence*, did she realize the rider was the Tzar in person. Neither of them ever forgot their first meeting.

The Dolgorukys were one of the most ancient and noble families of Russia, but their association with the Crown was unfortunate. Ivan the Terrible's first wife, Maria Dolgoruky, did not give satisfaction, and was drowned, on his orders. The Tzar Michael Romanov also married a Dolgoruky Princess, who died, poisoned, a few months later; while Tzar Peter II betrothed to yet another Dolgoruky Princess, died on the eve of the wedding.

Over the centuries, the family fortunes had declined, so that when Prince Michael, father of the young Princess Catherine, died, his widow and children were left almost penniless, the estates mortgaged and most of their possessions sold up for debts. Catherine and her younger sister Marie were packed off to St Petersburg to be made wards of the Crown, a common practice among the impoverished nobility. They were placed as pensionnaires at Smolny, the celebrated Institute for the Education of Demoiselles Nobles, which had been founded by the Empress Elizabeth. Rastrelli had designed its luscious sky-blue, cream and gold refulgence; but within, the Demoiselles Nobles lived austerely, their uniform dresses of serge meekly aproned. The curriculum was conducted on lines likely to fit them for either a position at Court, as one of the Maids of Honour, or for a suitable marriage. Languages, history and deportment were essential, and their curtseys were miracles of style. Herzen's caustic pen describes one of these demoiselles he remembered from his youth – many years before Catherine's time. 'She spoke French with revolting correctness,' he writes, 'raised her eyes to heaven every time she spoke of the Empress, and was, of course, in love with the Emperor' – Alexander I, in this case.

Smolny was under Imperial patronage and the Royal family made regular visits, taking an especial interest in those pupils whose names or families were known to them. Catherine had been there for several years when, in April 1865, the Emperor visited the Institute in place of the Empress Marie Alexandrovna, an invalid who was gradually retreating from public life. He remarked Catherine's promise of beauty, and recalled his visit to Teplovka, and the little girl who had answered back with such spirit. Learning of the Dolgorukys' straitened circumstances, he decided to watch over their interests in person. Perhaps, too, his paternal solicitude was already influenced by Catherine's charms. She was an ingenue of sixteen . . . he was a lonely, disillusioned and sensual man of forty-six. But his continued visits to Smolny were not attributed to his growing interest in her, and even when he decided that she should leave before graduating and live in her brother's house, the sooner to make her debut, nothing was remarked. Catherine was launched with some style, for the Tzar had seen to it that part of the family property had been, like their jewels, redeemed. Thus Catherine could face the cruel and snobbish Court as her birth entitled her, rather than as a penniless provincial miss.

We do not know how her changed fortunes, or the Tzar's marked interest appeared to this inexperienced, unsophisticated girl. At first, it is unlikely she could imagine anything so wildly improbable as the Tzar's interest being that of a *man*. To her, as to most of his subjects, the Tzar was an object of mystical veneration – far above mere mortals, an Olympian figure beyond criticism – beyond *love* in human terms. Autocrat of all the Russias, of Moscow, Kiev, Vladimir and Novgorod, Tsar of Kazan, Astrakhan, Siberia, Poland, Georgia, and more besides. . . .

At Court, Catherine's beauty was remarked at once. So was the Tzar's growing infatuation. The courtiers shrugged. *Le démon du midi*, they said; an ageing man's weakness for a young girl. The Tzarina's chronic invalidism excused such peccadilloes. There had been other mistresses, though considering the Tzar's opportunities, he had been very restrained. Was *la petite* already his mistress? Anyhow, a chit of a girl, of no real consequence, they said.

For a year the Tzar courted Catherine, falling ever deeper in love. For a year she held him off, frightened, flattered, and above all, bewildered by the situation in which she found herself. They met as often as he could snatch time from the cares of State. Often, his carriage would 'happen to be passing' her brother's house (not in a particularly elegant quarter) and there, the Tzar would throw the whole household into agitation, bounding up the stairs, lover-like, with bon-bons or flowers, begging Catherine's sister-in-law to be allowed to share a few moments of family life around the samovar. But it was Catherine's life he wanted to share. Sometimes, they met on the Islands, a favourite promenade, or in the Summer Gardens, walking there in snow, or sun: but chaperoned at a distance by her companion and his bodyguard. As yet, they had never been alone together. Side by side they would follow the statue-lined paths, the towering figure of the Emperor in his long grey military over-coat passing unrecognized among the nursemaids with their little charges, or the prim governesses with theirs – some scarcely younger than Catherine, then barely eighteen.

There are no photographs which convince us of her beauty, yet contemporary accounts agree she was the most charming-looking creature imaginable, slim, with a lovely skin, large dark eyes, a mass of bright chestnut hair and the animation which goes with perfect health. In short, the antithesis of that wasted, wraith-like woman whom, once, the Tzar had loved, the Tzarina, lying resignedly in her darkened rooms, removed from the formalities and glittering ornamentation of the state apartments.

As the Tzar's passion grew, it awakened that of Catherine – Katyia, or Catiche, as he called her. The schoolgirl was becoming a woman in love. At last, nothing else counted for either of them. They forgot the existence of the Tzarina, the scandal that was beginning to flame round them, the inevitable opposition of their families and the hostility of the world at large. He forgot she was a vulnerable young girl – ward of the Crown, thirty years younger than himself. She forgot the man she loved was Tzar of all the Russias.

13 July 1866, the anniversary of which they kept religiously ever after, when the park of Peterhof was *en fête*, and fireworks blazed across the sky, Catherine joined the Tzar at one of the several Imperial pavilions dotted about the park. The Belvédère of their rendezvous was at Babigon, a rather remote part of the grounds. Who was there to observe

its lighted windows and a waiting carriage? There at last, ceding to his pleadings and the dictates of her own heart, Catherine became his mistress – from that moment on, in the words of her enraptured lover, his 'wife before God' – the woman he vowed to marry the day he would be free.

Ostrich-like, they imagined no one was the wiser. But although they were not subjected to the audacious reporters, telescopic lenses and vulgarities of a latter-day Press, servants, guards, the secret police, their families, and soon, the Court and the Corps Diplomatique too were well aware of the liaison. From now on, their lives were to swing between extremes of longing and fulfilment – loneliness and unity. The Tzar's life was almost entirely absorbed by his official duties. His daughter (who was to marry Queen Victoria's second son, the Duke of Edinburgh) and his four sons, the Grand Dukes, two of whom were older than Catherine, rallied furiously round their mother, and showed little understanding of their father, nor any appreciation of the lovers' efforts to keep their relationship private. Every day the Tzar endeavoured to spend an hour or two with Catherine; sometimes, this could only be a snatched meeting in a carriage, or an hour at the house of a discreet A.D.C. Gradually, with growing audacity they would contrive their meetings in his study at the Winter Palace, or, it is said, in that bleak room where no one ever ventured, for it was there Nicholas I had died – his iron camp-bed, military overcoat and other souvenirs remaining untouched, in the morbid manner enjoyed by so many nineteenth-century bereaved. (Queen Victoria's preservation of the Prince Consort's bedroom is one example. However, there is, I believe, no mention anywhere of his son, Edward, either when Prince of Wales or as King Edward, ever selecting this room for one of his frequent assignations.) When we consider that the Winter Palace contained one thousand seven hundred rooms, the Tzar's choice of either his study, which by the picture we see to be crammed with portraits and souvenirs of his family, or his father's death-chamber seems lacking in romantic imagination. But then this lusty pair had no need of more inviting surroundings. Wherever they were together became their Pavilion. Secrecy was their only necessity. They remained in a state of frenzied excitement over each other, 'clenching like hungry cats' are the words often used by the Tzar in his letters to her, recalling their transports.

Some years ago, this correspondence was allowed to fall under a French auctioneer's hammer, knocked down for a trifle. It passed from one private collector to another, extracts of certain letters being occasionally seen, or printed. Those which I have seen were mostly in French – a curious mixture, pedestrian domestic details and affairs of state follow revealing evocations of their most intimate moments, which they refer to, in their own private language, as *bingerles*. Always the Tzar is her slave, her adorer, hers forever . . . she is his life, his idol, his adored little wife. They swim in bliss, overflow with emotion, ache with longing to be together forever. She calls him Mounka, worries over his asthma, prays that God will continue to bless their 'union', complains of the unbearable loneliness and recalls their 'delicious *bingerles*'. The Tzar, who may have inherited some of his great-grandmother Catherine's ardent nature, is in a perpetual erotic fever; they 'plunge each other into ecstasy to the verge of madness'; the frowning walls of the Winter Palace must have positively vibrated with their emotions.

They cannot endure the separation his official duties impose. Whenever possible, she follows him – on journeys about the realm, for the cure at Ems, or in the Crimea. There, when he leaves the marble palace of Livadia to be with her in a small house, there is only one servant, an old Tartar woman who cooks them local dishes; but they are in heaven, and the chefs and marble terraces await him in vain.

In Paris, when the Tzar made an official visit there in 1867, being received in great state by the Emperor Napoleon III and lodged in the Elysée Palace, Catherine was nearby in a small hotel under an assumed name, and contrived to join her lover at the Elysée each night, entering by a little garden gate on the Avenue Marigny. The Tzar's host, Napoleon III, was just the person to sympathize with such goings-on, and then, the whole ambiance of Paris was traditionally conducive to *l'amour*. Even an attempt on the Tzar's life by terrorists could not persuade the Tzar to curtail his visit as his suite had hoped. Perhaps they were unaware of the garden gate and the unaccustomed long hours together which it allowed the lovers.

Apart from his liaison, the eighteen-sixties were momentous years for the Tzar in relation to his country. Besides his liberation of the serfs, he brought about many agrarian and domestic reforms. However vacillating he sometimes became, overruled by reactionary advisers, he was at heart profoundly liberal. There was a soft melancholy about him which his enemies dubbed flabby. 'Looks liverish,' was Lord Melbourne's comment, observing the young Queen Victoria's tender feelings for Alexander, then Tzarievitch, and on a state visit to London. But his grandmother, on first seeing him in the cradle noted, 'he has a pathetic little look'. That look remained: his was a compassionate, sentimental, generous and trusting character, his idealism too often betrayed by his own weakness and reactionary advisers. It has been said that Catherine influenced him towards many reforms, particularly the plan to grant a Constitution, and that at the house where he set her up apart from her family, he was able to meet left-wing and progressive elements. Perhaps: though by the general estimate of her character, jealousy apart, she appears to have been a rather silly, uncultivated, childish creature, quite unaware of the larger political issues. But then the Tzar did not seek a political salon in her house. He needed, and found, an *alcôve*; and presently, a nursery.

Their first child was born in 1872. Catherine, struggling with labour pains, set out for the Winter Palace, which the Tzar had decided would be the only sure place for the birth to pass in secrecy. (It seems that her figure had remained almost unchanged, and none of her family were aware of her condition.) She entered the Palace by a small side door to which, according to some of her biographers, she had the key. In any case, suffering atrociously, dragging herself along the labyrinth of dark, inner corridors and back stairs, she reached the Tzar's study unperceived. With that inexplicable inefficiency and disregard for comfort which so often appears characteristic of grandiose establishments, no preparations had been made, and Catherine lay writhing on a stiff sofa, with no one to attend her but the distracted Tzar. The midwife, fetched by an old soldier guarding the private apartments, only arrived just in time to deliver the baby – a boy, George, or 'Gogo', as he was known.

Three more children were born in the following years, the Tzar going between his two families until, with the increasing threat of terrorist bombs, it was decided that Catherine and the children should move into the Winter Palace. That way the Tzar could visit them safely without running the risk, as he had done for so long, of being assassinated going to and from her house, a route and a house now well known to the terrorists. 'The Black ones', or Nihilists, believed only in violence as a means to their ends, and were stalking the Tzar like a hunted animal. 'Why do they want to kill me?' he asked plaintively, after yet another attempt on his life had been miraculously foiled. He had made so many reforms – he meant to make more. He could not understand that the Crown stood for centuries of oppression and injustice, and that there was no more patience left.

By installing Catherine in a suite directly above that of his wife, he showed an almost indecent insensitivity – a long way from those earlier years of discretion. Below, the Tzarina was coughing her lungs out, and could hear the children of her rival romping overhead. 'I forget the insult to the Empress, but I cannot forget the torment inflicted on the wife' is said to have been her only comment.

The Court bristled with hostility, but as Catherine seldom went beyond her rooms (although created a lady-in-waiting, to ensure her official presence at Court) she escaped much disagreeableness. Her life with the Tzar satisfied both her physical and material appetites: she had become sensual and greedy. She wanted jewels, money and advancement for all her family. The Tzar could deny her nothing. Although now living under the same roof, whole days passed when he was too occupied to be with her, but letters still flowed between them, hourly bulletins frantically reiterating their love and longing.

I know of no description of the Princess's rooms in the Winter Palace. They were probably of that stuffy, plushy bourgeois order then fashionable; massive carved woods, ousting the delicate elegance of earlier pieces, knick-knacks, and bric-a-brac and pom-pom fringes edging everything. No doubt the Tzar gave her a free hand, but *fashionable* was likely to have been her only criterion: she was, after all, an inexperienced and uncultivated girl. Not for her the eclectic taste of the Empress (something of a blue-stocking), who chose from among the limitless treasure-house of the Palace to transform her sick-room into an ambiance of rare beauty. Paintings by Flemish and Italian masters, Persian rugs and tapestries and the fine pieces of French furniture Catherine the Great had commanded, together with flowering plants and songbirds, surrounded the Empress to the end. Even her private train, in which she travelled searching for health was lined with pleated blue silk hangings, *objets d'art* in profusion, here too.

But that was a purely personal expression of one woman's taste, a lonely woman who had learned to find consolation in *things* rather than people. Generally, the endless *enfilades* of the Palace glittered with mirrors and exuberant gilding, the shimmering expanses of parquet punctuated by mammoth urns of malachite or lapis lazuli. The private apartments of the Imperial family too, were on such grandiose, rather than comfortable lines. An earlier Empress, wife of Nicholas I had begged her husband to build her a cottage 'in the English style', where in her own words she could rest her eyes from the glare of all that gold.

Beyond the ingrown idyll lived by Alexander and his mistress, currents of hatred and jealousy deepened. It was said she was venal, accepting money for advancements and concessions she obtained from the Tzar. He was said to follow her dictates blindly, recklessly. She had lived in the shadows for fourteen years: she was still young and beautiful. How long would she be content with such seclusion? To what ruin would she lead the Tzar? Dolgorukys had always brought disaster to the Crown . . . so the whispers, circling the Palace like birds of ill-omen.

On 3 June 1880 the unhappy Tzarina died, and was buried with suitable pomp. What were Catherine's feelings as she watched the lugubrious splendours of the funeral cortège pass below her windows and heard the bells tolling mournfully across the hushed city? Did she doubt that the Tzar would redeem that fourteen-year-old promise to make her his wife? Did she see the crown of a Romanov Empress, as well as a wedding ring? Her enemies believed so.

Alexander made no hypocritical show of grief. At last he was free. Forty days later, after the ritual Orthodox service of remembrance for the dead, and against the appalled protests of the few persons in his confidence, he married Catherine, Catiche the adored, his wife before God – and now, before· the whole world. The ceremony of 6 July, almost a furtive one, was held at Tzarskoe Selo, only two witnesses being present. Catherine had, in her excitement, lost the wedding ring she was exchanging with the Tzar – an ill-omen, said her maid – but nothing clouded the bride and groom. As his morganatic wife, Catherine was created Her Serene Highness the Princess Yurievsky. The children, until then nameless, were also made Serene Highnesses, taking the Yurievsky name.

Their half-brothers, the Grand Dukes Vladimir and Alexander, were now married men; the eldest, heir to the throne. Fuming, they believed their besotted father might go so far as to crown Catherine Tzarina, even putting her children before themselves or their own children in dynastic succession. Although this was a wild supposition, the Tzar's passion for Catherine now appeared unbridled. He had smothered her in jewels, settled a huge fortune on her, given her property in Russia and abroad, and acknowledged her children as Serene Highnesses. Where would it all end?

They did not have long to wonder. It ended on Sunday, 13 March 1881, just eight months after the wedding. The Tzar was returning to the Winter Palace after reviewing his troops at the weekly Razvod, or parade, when his carriage was shattered by terrorists' bombs. 'To the

Palace – to die,' he was heard to mutter, as his escort placed his mangled body on a sledge. They carried what was left of him up to his study, the carpeting of the stairway darkened by a trail of blood. Both legs were almost severed, his head covered with wounds, his hands mutilated. Doctors and the high clergy were called. The Tzarievitch and his wife, the Grand Dukes and their children, statesmen, courtiers, servants, all stood petrified round the dying man who lay on that sofa where he had so often clasped Catherine. The doctors could do nothing more. Only then did someone remember to fetch the Princess Catherine from her apartments. She had been quite unaware of the tragedy, and suddenly appeared, wrapped in a pink négligé, her hair falling round her. Uttering heart-rending screams she fell across the body of her husband. The Tzar's remaining eye was open, but he could not see her. 'Sasha! Sasha!' she kept screaming, but he could not hear her. She lay there, his blood soaking her ribbons and laces. In less than an hour he was dead.

The new Tzar was cool enough, there and then, to take possession of certain papers in his father's desk, papers which were, the very next day, to have granted the country its long awaited Constitution and which the Tzar had signed only a few hours before. There were no more hopes of liberal reforms. Alexander III proved a rigid reactionary.

At the funeral, Imperial protocol once more overcame humanity. Catherine, the Tzar's morganatic wife, had no official place in either the cortège or the cathedral. She waited, in a special little tent, put up for her outside. When all the sombre panoply of the Orthodox rites were over, the gold-coped clergy and the black-robed mourners departed, and each member of the Imperial family in turn mounted the daïs, to bestow the last farewell kiss on the body in the open coffin – that body the embalmers had found almost impossible to render suitable to view, one side of the shattered face being shrouded in scarlet tulle – a side door opened and a woman, darkly veiled, was supported to the daïs, where she fell on her knees sobbing.

It was the Princess Yurievsky, permitted, at last, to bid her husband farewell. As she turned to leave, she was seen to place something in the coffin – it was a long swathe of that beautiful chestnut hair the Tzar had loved. She had cut it off, to go with him into the grave. Even the most rigid protocol could not forbid that last gesture of love.

And afterwards – what of the emptiness which closed round? The Tzar's will had stipulated she was to remain in the Winter Palace as long as she liked, and there she stayed until, a year later, she moved to the Pink Marble Palace, a sumptuous little building bought for her by her step-son-in-law, the new Tzar. It was faced with pink Olonetz marble, had floors of ebony and pearl inlay, and was the epitome of luxury. There she continued her retired life, for her spirit was as shattered as the Tzar's body. Later she removed to France, settling in Nice, in magnificence, with a suite and staff befitting the widow of an Emperor. Her blazoned carriages and her liveries, like her manner, all recalled those Imperial glories that had been snatched from her. In a glass case beside her bed she kept one of the Tzar's fingers, which had been found near the scene of the ex-plosion, while a portrait of him on his death bed, with every ghastly injury meticulously rendered, was almost more than callers could stomach. Besides such gruesome reminders, certain pieces of furniture moved with her wherever she went. I have been told by some of the old Russians who knew her, that chairs from the Tzar's study in the Winter Palace were cordonned off and marked by plaques proclaiming their origin, her salon turned *chapelle ardente*.

The Princess lived entirely in the past. Her children were dispersed and her fortune dwindling. With the Revolution of 1917, both her pension and Imperial protection ceased: but she continued her ex-travagant *train de vie*. She was quite incapable of understanding money or daily life, let alone economy. She had gone straight from the schoolroom to the Tzar's protection. Her family had always preyed on her for sup-port. Her son Gogo was a good for nothing spendthrift. When she died, in 1922, there was nothing left but debts and the dogs she had doted on, who had kept her company through the long years of widowhood. Like so many Russian émigrés she is buried in Nice. Her relics of the Tzar, including his finger, are in the Russian Cathedral there.

While statues of various Tzars still adorn Russian cities, there are, oddly, none of the Tzar Liberator, who, of all of them after Peter the Great, should most merit remembrance. But the Church on the Blood – an elaborate and tasteless edifice, built to mark the spot where he was assassinated, and now disaffected as a church – always has flowers placed about it, little bunches, a single flower, some green leaves, rather than wreaths or bouquets. No one knows exactly why they are there – no one ever sees who places them there, or knows what they commemorate. I like to think that in spite of the bleak conditions and stern struggles of daily life, the Russian people still recall a Tzar who was not only 'The Liberator', but a great romantic.

Index

Index

Index

Levsky, Vassili, 42
Lewis, F. J., 22
Lichnowsky, Felix, 35
Ligne, Princesse de, 53
Lisbon, 94
Liszt, Franz, 25–36, 123,
 126, 127–8, 129, 149–50,
 151; *Les Glandes de
 Woronince*, 31; *Poèmes
 Symphoniques*, 36
London, 15
Louis xiv, 94
Lucerne, 150
Ludwig ii, King of Bavaria,
 18, 149–50, 152
Lyautey, Maréchal, 76
Lyons, Amy, 59; *see* Lady
 Hamilton

Majorca, 128
Malibran, Maria, 131
Malmaison, 175
Malta, blockade of, 63
Marabouts, 73–4, 92; *see
 also* Tedjani people
Maria Carolina, Queen of
 Naples, 57, 60, 63–4
Marie, Grand Duchess, 154
Marie, Queen of Rumania,
 153–64; *The Story of my
 Life*, 154
Marie Alexandrovna,
 Tzarina, 180, 181, 182,
 185, 186
Marie Antoinette, 57
Marie de Médicis, 53
Marmora, sea of, 104
Marseilles, 75
Marvell, Andrew, 22
Mary, Queen, 155
Mediterranean, 57, 58, 64
Melbourne, Lord, 183
Mérimée, Prosper, 176
Merton Place, 56–7, 66–9
Merv, 169
Mexico, 14
Michael Romanov, Tzar,
 179
Mignon, Princess, 160
Minerva, 64

Mirabeau, Octave, 55
Mircea, Prince, 159–60
Moazabites, 83
Mohammed ii, Sultan, 102
Mohammed iii, Sultan, 112,
 120–1
Moika Canal, 13
Mongols, 116
Montgolfier, Joseph, 176
Montigny-le-Roi, 71
Moscow, 141
Mouraviev, Nikita, 146
Munich, 150
Murad iii, Sultan, 15, 99,
 112–21; room of, 99,
 112, 114–18
Musset, Alfred de, 28, 123,
 125, 126, 130, 131
M'zab, 83

Naples, 57–8, 61, 69
Napoleon, *see* Bonaparte
Napoleon iii, 176, 183
Napoleon, Prince, 129, 131
Napoleonic wars, 137
Nekrasov, Nikolai, *Russian
 `Women*, 136
Nelson, Horatio, 57, 65–6,
 68, 69
Nelson, Lady, 61, 65
Nelson, Lord, 56–8, 61–9
Nertchinsk, mines of, 139,
 140, 142
Neuchâtel, 52
Neva, river, 138
Nice, 188
Nicholas, Prince, first
 husband of Princess
 Caroline of Sayn-
 Wittgenstein, 29, 35
Nicholas, Prince, son of
 Queen Marie of
 Rumania, 160
Nicholas i, Tzar, 29, 35,
 137–40, 143, 146, 182
 185
Nicholas ii, Tzar, 157
Nihilists, 184
Nile, Battle of the, 61, 63
Nisbet, Frances, 61; *see also*

Lady Nelson
Nohant, 123–34
Northern Society, 137
Nur Banu, Sultane Validé,
 113, 120, 121

Ortakapi, 104
Osman iii, 101
Ottoman court, 101, 111,
 114, 116
Ouargla, 84

Paganini, Niccolo, 25, 26
Pagello, Dr, 131
Palermo, 63, 65
Pardoe, *Beauties of the
 Bosphorus*, 103
Paris, 25, 27, 94, 96, 122–5,
 128–9, 132–3, 137, 183;
 Peace Conference, 160
Paul i, Tzar, 65, 143
Pavilion of the Mantle, 101
Pearl, Cora, 15
Pelez, castle of, 157
Péres Blancs, 76, 85
Peter ii, Tzar, 179
Peter the Great, 178, 188
Petrovsky Zavod, 146
Piccard, Aurélie, 71–92
Pink Marble Palace, 188
Pocahontas, 15
Podolia, 29
Polo, Marco, 165
Poltava, 179
Port Royal, reforms of, 95
Portugal, 94–5, 97
Potocka, Marie, 98–9
Princesse des Sables, 71,
 84–5, 90; *see also* Aurélie
 Piccard
Pushkin, Alexander, 13,
 136, 141; *Eugene Onegin*,
 144; *Fountain of
 Baktchiserai*, 99

Raievsky, General, 136,
 140, 143
Rastrelli, 179
Rhodope mountains, 38
Rilla, 39, 42
Rose Valley, 38, 48

Index